UNDER THE WIRE

UNDER THE WIRE

Marie Colvin's Last Assignment

Paul Conroy

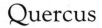

First published in Great Britain in 2013 by
Quercus
55 Baker Street
Seventh Floor, South Block
London
W1U 8EW

Every ... rial
reprodu ... d, the
publishe ... unity.

A CIP catalogue record for this book is available
from the British Library

HB ISBN 978 1 78206 525 8
TPB ISBN 978 1 78206 526 5
EBOOK ISBN 978 1 78206 527 2

10 9 8 7 6 5 4 3 2 1

Text and plates designed and typeset by Ellipsis Digital Ltd

Printed and bound in Great Britain by Clays Ltd, St Ives plc

In memory of
Marie Colvin, Remi Ochlik, Neil Conroy and the 72,305 Syrians
reported dead at the time of writing.

Thank you in as near to alphabetical order as possible.

My parents Joan and Les Conroy; Jenny and Alan Conroy; Kate, Max, Kim and Otto Conroy; Abu Hanin and the media crew in Baba Amr; Abu Lailah; Dr Ali in Baba Amr; Annabelle Whitestone; Arwa; Assif; Bonnie Hardy; Bryan Denton; Dolores and all the staff at London Bridge Hospital; Edith Bouvier; Ella Flaye; Dr Hakim; Javier Espinosa; John Witherow; Joss Stone; Maher; Miles; Dr Mohamed Al-Mohamed; Parri; Razan; Ray Wells; Richard Flaye; Rola; Salah; Sean Ryan; Tom Fletcher and family; The unknown smugglers; The Vet; Wa'el; William Daniels; Zara; The Farouk brigade of the FSA; Neil and Tim of CNN; Annabel, Laura and Tim at Peters Fraser and Dunlop; Richard Milner and Josh Ireland at Quercus; *The Sunday Times*, News International and all of my colleagues who rallied to my support during my recovery; all of my twitter friends.

The people of Syria.

PROLOGUE

'They're drugging the fucking journalists'

18 March 2003, Qamishli, Syria

The boat seemed ridiculously out of place in the tiny hotel room. I looked at the four large lorry inner tubes lying on the floor, lashed together with bits of rope and wood. I'd even added luggage straps for my camera kit. Now, after days spent slaving over it, my home-made raft was finally ready to be deflated and transported to its launch site – the west bank of Syria's Tigris river. The boat's mission: a one-way voyage from Syria to northern Iraq. I stared out of the window of the shabby hotel room and absorbed the empty vista – desert, miles of unbroken desert. I looked back at the boat. It seemed more incongruous than ever.

It was a boat born of desperation. As America and its allies prepared to invade Iraq, the world's press corps, sensing a televisual bonanza, began to gather at strategic crossing points along the Iraqi border. I had chosen to cross into Saddam Hussein's doomed state via northern Syria. Once inside, I planned to link up with a battle-hardened bunch of Kurdish rebels known as the Peshmerga and then follow them as they advanced south towards Baghdad from their mountainous stronghold in the north. There was, however, a

1

slight hitch: I needed permission from the Syrian regime's ruthless intelligence service to cross the river border into Iraq. As the drum roll of the Iraq war intensified, Syria's secret police dug their heels in. Three weeks passed and still the Mukhabarat refused to give us permission to cross.

The wait would have been bearable if only the Syrian border town of Qamishli – the desert outpost that lies on the crossroads between Iraq, Turkey and Syria – hadn't been one of the least salubrious places in which to be stuck. There were no bars, no restaurants and, by now, there was virtually no hope of receiving the fabled piece of paper that would permit a crossing into the Kurdish-held parts of northern Iraq.

To add to the boredom, everything had begun to grow depressingly familiar. Every day for weeks on end between twenty and thirty lethargic journalists would drag themselves out of bed and traipse over to the intelligence service headquarters five hundred metres down the road from the hotel. We would be ushered into an office, told to sit down and given glasses of hot tea. After an hour or so an expressionless officer would enter the room. He'd shake his head and announce with a hint of hostility that, once again, we'd been denied permission to enter Iraq. The group of increasingly crestfallen journalists would slowly shuffle back to the delightfully named Petroleum Hotel, where the facilities, rather sadly, lived up to the hotel's name.

And so it was that we had become trapped, tantalisingly out of reach of the battle that we'd come to cover and stuck in what appeared to be an unfinished, downmarket version of a British Travelodge, built in the desert.

The intelligence headquarters had once been a family home, but all signs of cosiness and domesticity had long since been removed. In place of family portraits were the badly printed photographs of men wanted by the Syrian authorities. It now looked more like a committee room from Stalinist Russia. The boredom and nervous frustration of the past few weeks were visible on the faces of my fellow journalists, who sat and drank tea listlessly, waiting for something, anything to happen.

I remember one particularly tedious day when the small room was near full to bursting. Journalists who were unable to find a seat on the sofa or the armchairs sat on cushions on the floor, while others dribbled down their chins and struggled with wobbly-neck syndrome to stay conscious. Suddenly the door crashed open on this scene of total lassitude. A lone female appeared, wearing a battered brown suede jacket and with a black eyepatch covering her left eye. She stood stock still in the doorway and surveyed the room with a smooth, feline movement of her head. She paused as she absorbed the motley bunch of comatose journalists in front of her.

'My God, they're drugging the fucking journalists. They must be drugging the tea,' she exclaimed in absolute disgust. And that was it. She never said anything else. She just turned on her heel and left the room.

Some of the journalists couldn't even muster the energy to look up at her, so deep was their stupor. A few managed to turn their heads but only to blink in her general direction. That was my first sighting of the legendary Marie Colvin.

As the ritual disappointment of the Mukhabarat office began to take its toll, all my plans to cross into Iraq and link up with rebel fighters seemed doomed to fail. It was time to act. And so it was, as I watched the lifeblood begin to drain from the journalists gathered in the Petroleum Hotel, that the idea of the boat was born.

My partners in crime for the boat project were Norwegian filmmaker Paul Refsdal, a young *New York Times* stringer called Liz and a Kurdish cab driver called Ali. I put Ali in charge of procuring the necessary boat-building materials. He would also act as chief smuggler to get us through the Syrian military positions strung out along the river. We needed the inner tubes of lorry tyres, rope, wood, netting and handpumps, all of which Ali acquired with amazing speed from the backstreet workshops of Qamishli.

Ali was a superstar. Clad at all times in a bright mustard-coloured tracksuit – made from synthetic fibres visible from the moon – his eyes lit up and sparkled like a little boy's when I told him about the boat plan. Kurds like Ali in the Qamishli region had suffered heavily at the hands of the Syrian regime. I guess Ali saw the smuggling operation as a small way of hitting back, of getting one over on Syrian intelligence.

The plan was to waterproof all our kit in plastic bags and then paddle across the roughly mile-wide stretch of river into Iraq, steering with our feet. We constructed life jackets from plastic Coca-Cola bottles, complete with safety ropes to connect us to the raft. The construction was pretty straightforward. I simply inflated the tyres in the room and lashed them together with rope before attaching the floor, which was made up of planks of wood tied together with baling twine and then lashed to the inner tubes. It was designed so we could deflate it, carry it outside the hotel to a waiting car and then reinflate it once on the banks of the river.

We tried to keep our plans secret. Among the stranded journalists lurked their security advisors – ex-military personnel who, if you believed what they said, were all ex-SAS troopers. Now call me cynical but, after nearly twenty years in war zones, I seem to have met more ex-SAS personnel than the SAS could possibly have trained in that time. There were exceptions (the BBC's security team are fantastic), Kevin Sisson and Kevin Sweeny being prime examples of guys I would trust my life to, but many I'm sure promoted themselves from the logistics or catering corps to the role of special forces commando or Royal Marine elite in a frenzy of Tippex blotting and document scanning. They were there to provide security advice for the broadcast media – the likes of Sky News. Their real job, however, was to stop journalists being naughty – by building boats, for example. But they had no control over the freelance element of the Qamishli press corps. And so, when they did finally get a whiff of what we were planning to do, we were told in no uncertain terms that we would spoil it for everyone if we went rogue and attempted an illegal crossing.

On the day of departure we disposed of everything other than the bare necessities. Liz got rid of her body armour, helmet and a surprising amount of silk underwear and Paul abandoned a whole suitcase of clothes. I had no excess baggage or body armour, so I added a few cartons of Marlborough cigarettes to my kit. We double-wrapped everything in bin bags to keep electrical kit safe and to ensure that we had dry clothes on the other side.

I had sent Ali out earlier with $500 to make sure the Syrian army looked the other way when we passed through the checkpoints. He arrived back from his mission on time at eight o'clock.

We'd spent long hours discussing how to smuggle the boat through the hotel without being too conspicuous but in the end we'd decided that this couldn't be done. So instead we ended up lowering it out of the hotel window on a towrope to Ali's cab, which was parked below. We then trooped nonchalantly through the hotel under the suspicious gaze of the security teams in the lobby.

We drove in silence to the border. The invasion of Iraq had already begun and we knew we were taking a serious risk by travelling illegally into a fully-fledged war zone on a home-made boat. It was a preposterously silly plan, but we were now fully committed. The desert night was clear and star filled, punctuated only at times by a bright flash on the horizon as a coalition bomb exploded somewhere inside Iraq.

Luckily, Ali, who was still clad in his discreet mustard tracksuit, had done a good job: we cruised past army checkpoints as the soldiers waved us through without even a second glance. It was $500 well spent. The journey to the river was tense but uneventful. We told Ali to stop at a prearranged position on the road. We said our goodbyes. Ali shuffled back to his car, laughing and tapping his head with his forefinger – the universal sign for 'they're crackers'.

Prior to becoming a journalist, I had spent six years in the British army. Although I never reached the dizzy heights of Field Marshal Montgomery and can lay no claim to a role in Britain's special forces (mainly because I really hate running), I was still a pretty competent soldier. I spent four years in Germany as a forward observer in the Royal Artillery so I knew a little about the importance of reconnaissance work. And I could have sworn that I had properly reconnoitred the river we were about to cross. In fact, I had even done so in the company of one of the 'ex-Royal Marines'. But the gently meandering river that we had observed only days before bore no similarity to the torrent that now raged in front of us.

For all my military experience, I had failed to factor in the warm weather preceding our D-Day-style invasion of Iraq. The snows had melted from the surrounding mountains, turning the once peaceful river into the black and churning stretch of pure misery that now lay before us.

'By the time we paddle across that we'll be floating through Baghdad,' I announced to Paul and Liz, only half joking. The silence that followed indicated that they both fully believed we could indeed be in Baghdad by morning.

We began to assemble the raft in anxious silence. First, we had to inflate the inner tubes. Almost immediately the hand pump failed on us. Huddled in a small wadi next to the river, we froze in disbelief as the sound of voices drifted down from the hilltop above. Syrian army, I thought. Although Ali had spent our $500 wisely, we knew it didn't apply to random border patrols like the one now rapidly approaching our position.

We huffed and puffed with renewed urgency to inflate the boat. More voices drifted down from the hill. This time they were louder. We quickly tethered the raft to a small tree and slipped it into the turbulent water. Suddenly a volley of automatic gunfire cracked over our heads. The bullets were close: not life-threateningly so, but our position had clearly been compromised.

We abandoned the boat and moved swiftly along the river's edge towards a small town where we thought we might be able to steal a more traditional boat. We moved silently. Eventually we came across a narrow path that hugged the edge of the meandering river. To our left was a small cluster of dark, apparently unoccupied buildings. Best to go around them, I told the others. But, as we started to skirt the buildings, a unit of soldiers screamed at us in Arabic and I heard the awful sound of rifles being cocked, stopping us dead in our tracks.

A soldier rushed out from the doorway of one of the abandoned homes. He was shouting frantically and pointing a Kalashnikov in our direction. More soldiers loomed out of the other doorways, sprinting through the darkness towards us. For a minute it looked like we were going to be shot.

The proper response when confronted by ten soldiers all cocking their weapons and screaming at you is to pop your hands up, assume the air of a lost tourist and say, 'Good evening,' as politely as possible in the local language, if known. But this standard response failed to have the desired effect. The soldier who'd originally spotted us must have been in shock. He continued to shout and scream and seemed rather intent on killing us on the spot.

In situations like this it's often nice to find someone in control. On this occasion, however, the soldiers appeared to be a group of conscripts who were young and trigger-happy – a bad combination.

They hustled us into a small room illuminated by a single 10-watt light bulb. A few office chairs and an upturned ammunition crate that served as a table were the only items of furniture inside the room. We were promptly tied to the chairs and left in the company of two young and nervous guards, their Kalashnikovs cocked and at the ready.

For the next hour or two someone would enter the room, shout at us in Arabic, get more frustrated, shout louder and leave. I guess it's the same with the English abroad: if at first someone doesn't understand, then simply increase the volume and shout a little louder, because they're obviously deaf. And so it was with our Arabic captors: they just kept getting louder. It was a relief when a soldier finally entered the room, smiled at us and said in perfect English, 'So, where are you from?'

'Liverpool,' I replied.

He beamed back at me. 'Steven Gerrard, Michael Owen. Liverpool – such a great team. I love Steven Gerrard!'

Perfect, I thought. A kindred spirit. 'Manchester United are shite,' I said, smiling as ingratiatingly as I could.

The solider agreed with this analysis and a long discussion about the pros and cons of two of England's fiercest football rivals followed. He untied my hands, made me coffee and handed me a cigarette.

At this point a voice from the corner of the room said rather churlishly, 'I don't suppose you could get your new friend to untie us too.' It was Paul the film-maker. I had completely forgotten about them during my conversation with the soldier. My new best friend obliged and untied Liz and Paul. I got the feeling we were safe so I ventured a question.

'I don't suppose you could call us a cab to get back to Qamishli, could you? We appear to have got a little lost tonight,' I said tentatively.

His smile disappeared. 'I'm sorry, my friend: you must first speak to some other people before you can go home.'

What followed over the next forty-eight hours was a bizarre and confusing journey through the unfathomable, labyrinthine command structure of Syria's intelligence service. First, we were taken under armed guard to buildings in the middle of the mountains where we were searched and then interrogated. Then they moved us to another building where the same process took place all over again. This happened over and over for two days.

The three of us had already agreed on a cover story: we were journalists who had got lost looking for war refugees near the border. Admittedly, it was a weak and flimsy excuse but we stuck to the story like a mantra, repeating it so often that we almost began to believe it ourselves. But I couldn't shake the fear that the intelligence agents might discover a video cassette of me actually building the boat, which I'd concealed earlier in my jacket. So, on one of the car journeys between buildings, I pulled the tape out and threw it from the moving vehicle.

Our guards woke us up at dawn on the second day. They were polite and friendly: they had come to accept that we posed no obvious threat to them and that we appeared not to be the American invasion as they'd initially imagined or feared. They remained sombre though.

'You must see General Omar today,' one of the guards said, almost apologetically.

'Not good?' I asked, shaking my head.

'Not good,' the guard replied ominously.

We drove down from the mountains for an hour, stopping at what appeared to be a solid concrete wall in the middle of the desert. Bristling with barbed wire, the walls formed a huge, impenetrable and menacing military base. Its location in the middle of the desert and fortifications gave me the impression that many people entered this place – but few left. The guards fell silent. To my surprise, what seemed like an immovable slab of reinforced concrete in the wall opened, and we drove through the gap.

Once inside the grounds of the military base, the driver stopped the car by a set of heavy steel, reinforced, doors which seemed to lead to nowhere, no building was visible. We stepped out of the 4×4 vehicle and followed a soldier down into what appeared to be a secret bunker. It had Bond villain written all over it.

I told Paul that I wouldn't be able to contain my laughter if we found General Omar inside stroking a fluffy white cat.

'Don't you dare fucking laugh,' muttered Paul, as we descended deeper into the bunker.

We stopped outside two massive steel doors with guards flanking us on either side and waited for the signal to enter. I stood there desperately fighting back the images of Bond villains and white cats. When the signal finally came to enter, I had to bite my lip, just in case.

'Jesus Christ,' I muttered as we entered.

What greeted us may not have been the white cat that I had imagined but it wasn't far off. On the wall opposite hung a huge poster of the Syrian president, Bashar al-Assad. A large mahogany desk – out of place in this spartan bunker but worthy of any self-respecting Bond villain – stood beneath the portrait.

I was suffering horribly. Behind the mahogany desk General Omar sat in a high-backed leather chair facing the wall with the picture of Assad on it, his back turned to us. I was trembling with the urge to laugh. He played it perfectly. In a slow and practised motion, the general swivelled effortlessly in his chair to face us. He stopped, appraised the three shabby journalists in front of him and smiled.

Oh no, I thought. He had a gold tooth, he was dressed in an immaculately tailored suit and he had slick, oiled-back hair. I was on the edge of cracking. I could feel the other two willing me not to laugh. General Omar continued to smile as he spoke.

'So, you want to go to Iraq?' he asked.

We all smiled obsequiously back at him and explained how we had become lost looking for refugees at night near the river.

'But we found your boat,' he said, without breaking his gold-toothed smile.

Silence. The word 'boat' hung in the air like a solid object. I tried to form a sentence. The only word that popped out was a very quiet 'boat'. The general smiled again.

'Yes, we found your boat,' he repeated, clearly relishing this sentence.

I was beginning to smile again. 'Oh, that boat. You mean the boat,' I said involuntarily.

'Yes, the boat,' he said, mimicking my emphasis.

The game was up and to make matters worse I was now smirking at General Omar.

'Oh, yes. Sorry about that. We were a little bit desperate,' I said.

'You try to go to Iraq?'

We nodded sheepishly like naughty kids in front of the headmaster.

'Well, you are journalists and have to do your job. Here in Syria we believe in free speech and so I am going to let you go,' the general announced.

I was stunned. Here we were, in the lion's den, caught red-handed by the Syrian regime's most dreaded security service and all General Omar, who appeared to be head of the north-eastern secret police, was going to do was let us go.

'You must, however, leave Syria. Immediately,' he said, still smiling.

All three of us nodded sincerely. 'Of course, of course.'

He gave us back our confiscated kit and equipment and his men drove us back to the Petroleum Hotel, where we were greeted by a rather nervous-looking Ali. Paul and Liz left the same day for the Syrian capital Damascus. Paul eventually got into Iraq on a human-shield visa. Liz was mugged in Damascus and I haven't heard from her since.

I laid low in the Petroleum Hotel to wait for the fuss to die down and to work out a Plan B. As expected, the rest of the press pack shunned me for 'ruining things for the rest of us'. I skulked in my room, smoked and read the instruction manuals for my camera because I had no books with me and all the television stations were in Arabic. After two nights I made a rare foray into the restaurant in search of anyone willing to talk to a pariah journalist. No luck. My presence was met with icy stares of hostility. I was studiously avoided as if simply associating with me would render a crossing into Iraq impossible.

Suddenly, the restaurant door burst open and there stood Marie Colvin. She cast her head around the room and shouted to the gathered journalists, 'Who and where is the boatbuilder?'

Silence ensued as everyone in the room turned to stare at me.

'I am,' I replied meekly.

Marie strode over to my table and stuck out her hand. 'Marie Colvin,' she said in her inimitable American accent. 'Good to finally meet someone with some balls round here. You like boats then, eh?'

That night, over a bottle of whisky, a friendship was born. Marie's reputation as a hard-arsed war reporter – one of the toughest, best and bravest of our time – preceded her. The terrifying courage she had displayed after losing her eye in a rocket-propelled-grenade attack in Sri Lanka was the stuff of legend.

I had heard other stories: her stubborn refusal in East Timor to abandon refugees who were being hunted by the Indonesian army, a decision that ultimately saved hundreds of lives; her eight-day march across a mountain pass in Chechnya, braving hunger, exposure and altitude sickness to escape Russian forces; how she smuggled herself in disguise into the closed-off Iraqi city of Basra during the Iran–Iraq war; how she refused to leave Baghdad during the allied bombing of the city in 1991. These were the tales that explained why Marie had gained a reputation for being one of the last journalists to leave the world's most dangerous places at their most dangerous times.

As the whisky flowed between us and the layers of her personality were peeled back, the legend became human. Her rebellious nature was immediately apparent: she clearly admired my attempt to cross into Iraq illegally on a home-made raft and she thought the other journalists ridiculous for shunning me. But she also revealed a gentler, calmer side as we drank our way through the bottle of Glen Diesel, the cheapest Scotch available. She spoke at length about sailing, a shared passion that offered both of us an antidote to the mayhem of war. And despite her reputation as one of the world's greatest war correspondents, she found it easy to laugh at herself. She had a superb sense of the absurd.

Eight years passed before I saw Marie again, this time in a hotel in Egypt. We were en route to Libya, where we'd been sent by our newspaper to cover the final months of Colonel Muammar Gaddafi's rule together. Over the following year, as the Libyan conflict intensified around us, we formed a bond unique to people who repeatedly share the horrors of the front line. We witnessed the brutal killing of innocent civilians, the fierce gun battles between rebel and Gaddafi forces, NATO's bombing campaign and the eventual fall of the capital Tripoli. It was a professional relationship and a true friendship that both of us knew would last for years and years.

But our friendship and Marie's life would end in tragedy. A year after the start of our first assignment together, Marie lay dead beside me in the bombed-out ruins of a house in Syria, the country where we first met each other over a bottle of whisky, amid impassioned talk of boats.

CHAPTER ONE

'Paul, I have a plan'

8 February 2012, Coleford, Devon

Blue cigarette smoke drifted lazily through the shafts of early-morning sunlight. I sat, leaning back in a chair, feet up on the table, drinking my fifth coffee of the morning. I had already lost track of the number of cigarettes I'd smoked and it was only nine o'clock. The phone rang. I inhaled deeply, gulped down a huge mouthful of coffee and picked up my mobile. It was Andrew from the picture desk at *The Sunday Times*.

'Paul, Marie Colvin is on her way to Lebanon and wants you to meet her there tonight. She's going into Syria.' He paused. 'The no-visa route.'

I told Andrew that I wouldn't be able to fly to Lebanon until tomorrow. 'No problem,' he said before hanging up. The paper's huge machine immediately swung into action: travel companies began the hunt for tickets and thousands of dollars were wired to airport travel bureaus. Within minutes I received emails with flight details and money orders for bags of cash – all in the time it took to smoke another cigarette.

I was calm. Deep down I could feel the adrenalin dissipating the tension that had been slowly building up inside my body. 'At last,' I muttered to myself.

The no-visa route meant an illegal entry to Syria. The al-Assad regime issued few visas to the press and, even if one were granted, it came with the baggage of state security officials, government-organized trips and close monitoring by the intelligence services. War is never just about bombs and bullets: it's also about media manipulation and propaganda. In short, if you want to get close to the truth, to bear witness, you often have to go 'under the wire'.

The Sunday Times had taken weeks to decide which journalist to send to Syria, which was enough time to let the inner tension mount in anticipation of the dangers ahead. There's always a balancing act that takes place when you're told you're being sent to another war zone. Although screaming with relief inside, you have to retain a modicum of calm on the outside: there are loved ones to consider and cartwheeling around the house is generally not viewed as best practice.

My domestic life was complex. I was separated from my wife and living with my new partner, Bonnie, who, having heard most of the previous call, was already in tears. She knew what lay ahead. She had heard the same call when I headed off on assignment to Syria a few weeks earlier with Miles Amoore, one of the newspaper's rising stars. She knew that once I was inside Syria a deathly silence would fall between us. It was too dangerous to make phone calls or send text messages: editors and journalists were paranoid that simply switching on a mobile or satellite phone gave Syrian security forces the chance to pinpoint your location.

What do you say to someone who knows that you're heading into one of the most dangerous places on the planet? Even as I spoke, my words of reassurance sounded hollow. They were only words. The television in our living room in Devon was filled with images of bombardment, death and misery as Syrian government troops pulverised the city of Homs with heavy artillery fire. No words could soften the sense of pain and hopelessness that Bonnie must have felt as I walked out of the door early that February morning.

I had been working for *The Sunday Times* since the beginning of the Libyan uprising the previous year. I think I ended up spending about twenty-two weeks in Libya. I was now going to break the news to my wife, Kate, and my three children that the whole routine was about to begin all over again.

The hour's drive to my family home gave me time to think. Saying goodbye to the kids was by far the hardest part. Although they had endured it dozens of times before, seeing me off never became any easier for them, or for me. Kate would remain silently furious at my 'devil may care' approach to life and her resentment at my departure was born out of seeing her loved one head off to risk life and limb in the knowledge that she might never see him again. She never tried to stop me though. I'd always had her full support. It just got harder for her every time I left. Her fear of my death or injury and the impact that would have on the kids grew with every assignment. I was always the lucky one because I never saw it the same way as the rest of my family. In my mind's eye, I was always coming back. There was never any doubt.

The atmosphere in Totnes, where Kate and the kids lived, could be cut with a knife. Not only was I now living with Bonnie, but I was about to head off to war again. On the previous assignment only a month or so earlier, rebels from the Free Syrian Army had been forced to evacuate us from Syria on a motorbike. We later learnt that government forces were hunting for us. Now I was going back.

17

My youngest son, Otto, aged ten, told me bluntly, 'Dad, it's going to go wrong this time. I just thought I'd tell you.'

I got the same from Kate. 'Paul, you're pushing it. Your luck's going to run out soon. You can't keep doing this,' she told me.

With so much joy in the air, I tried a chirpy old, 'Well, I'll have my bulletproof underpants with me.'

There was not a glimmer of a smile from any of them. My twenty-year-old son, Max, told me that he too had a bad feeling about this one. The only one who didn't roll the chicken bones in the sand and foresee tragedy was my eighteen-year-old, Kim. He's also a photographer and perhaps he understood it. Either way, it was like attending my own wake.

During my years in the British army my job as a forward observer wasn't the most envied. I had been stationed in Germany at the height of the Cold War, a time when the Iron Curtain had well and truly descended and the imminent threat of invasion from the Warsaw Pact countries, spearheaded by Russia, hung ominously in the air. It was my job, along with my battery commander and driver, to let the main Soviet battlefront pass us by as it made its advance into Europe, leaving us behind enemy lines. From this rather unenviable position, we were then supposed to locate targets and pass back grid coordinates of Soviet troop positions to our heavy-artillery units. In reality, we would probably have had a lifespan of about ten minutes, although even that would have been five times longer than the guys who actually manned the guns.

The army and I were never really best of friends. I had a tendency to go AWOL whenever the whim took me, which was more often than not. On reflection, I spent a greater part of my career under arrest of some sort than I did running around and getting dirty. I was trying to get out or 'work my ticket', as it was known, but the powers that were knew this and, to punish me, they kept me in.

In the end, I resorted to planting hashish in my own locker before anonymously tipping off the battery commander with a handwritten note slipped under his door. He promptly had my locker searched and, after much detective work, the soldiers eventually found the hash. I was court-martialled and given nine months in the glasshouse – the military prison at Colchester. On the day I left the prison, I had an interview with the commanding officer of the prison. It was a mere formality.

'What are you going to do when you leave the army then, Conroy?' he asked, clearly bored with the routine.

'Cartwheels, sir,' I answered, with a straight face and no hint of sarcasm.

The commanding officer, without pause, said simply, 'Get him out of here, Sergeant Major.'

And that was it. I was now a civilian. I could kill a man with almost any everyday object, I had the ability to make explosives and booby-trap a room, I could identify a Soviet T-72 tank at night and I knew the killing range of most modern weapons. And so it was that I took the next obvious step for a man with these credentials: I became a sound engineer. I spent two years in dark studios. My face went white and my eyes blackened: I developed engineer's tan, as it's known.

The years flew by and I crammed in what I could, blanching at the sounds of the words 'stability' or 'pension'. I lived in caves in Crete, picked tomatoes professionally, rebuilt medieval churches and toured the world with bands, becoming something of a connoisseur of almost every banned substance in the process. But everywhere I went I always took cameras with me – video and stills. I built up a passion for the subjects I shot.

In the late 1990s I ended up in the Balkans, having filmed an aid convoy that was distributing aid to the starving people of

Kosovo. The donated aid was a pretty shambolic pile of old tat. For months, the residents of one village looked like they were at a Bay City Rollers convention. I was captivated by what was happening in the Balkans. When the aid convoy left, I stayed on for six months to shoot stills and make a film. The deed was done. I had found my calling and I was once more off into the badlands.

8 February 2011, Totnes, Devon

I checked my kit in silence. Last time we'd been smuggled across the border into Syria, the smugglers we were with told us we could only take one bag each and that we would have to leave our body armour behind because it was too cumbersome to wear on the back of a motorbike. So I packed accordingly: two camera bodies with two lenses, a laptop, satellite phone, memory cards, battery chargers, satellite transmitter, spare phone and my Lebanese phone. I rolled up a few socks, a T-shirt and some underpants and stuffed them into the remaining spaces inside the bag.

Next, I called Marie. She was already at Heathrow when she picked up the phone. 'Paul, we're going. I'm getting on a plane. Where are you?' she said with infectious excitement.

Marie was on fire. We had covered most of the Libyan conflict together and she was keen to get the team back up and working again.

'Hurry up,' she kept saying. 'We gotta get in soon. We're behind everyone on this one! Oh, and by the way, see if you can get me some money from the office. They won't give me any because I still haven't done my expenses from Libya.'

'What, you have no money? The office isn't giving you any cash?' I laughed in disbelief at the prospect of Marie heading into a war zone without money. I promised I'd try but didn't think I'd have much luck.

I found myself chuckling when I hung up. Marie's passion for the story was contagious. For her, reporting really wasn't about beating the competition, although she loved to be the first in and last out of any conflict. Instead, she was driven by a deep sense of moral outrage at the suffering of civilians who are inextricably caught up in bloody conflicts around the world.

In a famous speech she had given at St Brides on Fleet Street, a church traditionally associated with journalists, a few years earlier, she argued passionately for the need to send reporters to dangerous places. She believed war reporting was a way of speaking truth to power, of holding governments to account by telling the public what their governments were doing in their name. For her, war reporting was about bearing witness to the plight of ordinary civilians so that she could record it for the world and reveal the brutal consequences of decisions taken by men in high places. It sounds grand, but she believed that without war correspondents governments could conduct themselves as if in a vacuum: their lies and propaganda could be conveyed without challenge, allowing them to carry out atrocities far from the prying eyes of the world. In her words, it was about sending back the first rough draft of history and cutting through the sandstorm of propaganda that flares when armies, tribes or terrorists clash.

When we were about to enter Syria, the television screens in Britain were full of grainy, shaky video images taken by Syrian civilians and activists. This amateur footage – of bloody corpses, of women and children screaming as they prayed for protection from government bombs – only fuelled Marie's desire to enter Syria to report on the war's awful toll on civilians. Remarkably, where other war correspondents had gradually grown immune to the horrors of war, their senses dulled and emotions blunted over time by their harrowing experiences, Marie had succeeded in retaining her sense of outrage throughout her illustrious twenty-five-year career. It was what drove her to cover conflicts when she was well into her fifties. And it was what made her one of the best at doing it, earning her comparisons to her journalistic heroine, the legendary Martha Gellhorn.

As we chatted on the phone, Marie could barely contain her desire to get on with it. It wasn't only that the paper was sending us to Syria but that we'd been told to head right into the heart of the revolution – the city of Homs and its besieged neighbourhood of Baba Amr. Syrian civilians in this tiny rebel enclave had endured a medieval siege for weeks. In the last few days, Syrian government troops had pounded the area with heavy artillery and rockets, sowing carnage among the civilian population.

Another shot of adrenalin surged through my veins. In January 2011, I'd tried to reach the neighbourhood with Miles. We'd crossed the heavily mined border, dodging Syrian border troops, but a large build-up of pro-government troops on the outskirts of Homs had blocked our path north, preventing us from reaching the city. I knew Syria and I knew how hard it was just to move about, to stay alive.

I called *The Sunday Times* to ask if I could have some money to take to Marie. My request was politely refused and I was asked to stay out of it. Marie was constantly in trouble with the office over her expenses, which she would unfailingly forget to file for months, sometimes years, much to the irritation of managers. For all her prowess as one of the world's greatest war correspondents, Marie was also a Luddite when it came to technology. She would have preferred to live in the age of the typewriter and telegraph than that of the laptop and mobile phone, which she often switched off to avoid pesky, unexpected calls from editors.

I phoned my parents. They put on a brave front. As usual, they gave me the same warning. My dad would say, 'Be careful, you know how your mum worries.' And my mum would say the same: 'Be careful, you know how your dad worries.' It had been going on like that for years. I knew they both worried like hell.

And that's basically how it happens. A glum-faced family stands around a ticking-over Land Rover saying its last goodbyes. It isn't pleasant, never pretty, and always leaves you with a lump in your throat and a tear in your eye as you pull away slowly, waving and stretching to catch a last glimpse of your tightly huddled family. I was leaving behind a growing number of anxious and troubled people.

The drive to Heathrow was almost a relief. I now needed to focus on the job ahead. I parked at Heathrow, picked up my single bag and entered the terminal. My first stop was the Travelex to pick up $6,000-worth of expenses. It's always fun to watch the sideways glances of suspicion that the cashiers give when you pick up large wads of cash and then proceed to stash the notes in all available pockets, bag pouches and jacket linings.

It felt good to be on the move as the plane took off, a sort of relief that the ball was rolling in the right direction. I glanced around at the families, businessmen and young travellers who were all heading to their prearranged destinations. They had travel plans, agendas, loved ones at airports and happy reunions with faces sorely missed. I mulled over my own prospects. Sometime in the next week I would hand over my destiny, freely and wilfully, to a bunch of smugglers whose real names I would never know. Then there was the sobering thought that, at some point, there would be lots of people working very hard to stop me from reaching my destination or, worse, trying to kill me. I ordered another drink as I considered my prospects.

On arrival at Beirut airport, I cleared passport control without a problem. But I was soon faced with customs and the spot checks at airport security. This can sometimes be difficult. Unsurprisingly, a lot of countries don't like satellite transmitters. I was lucky. I watched as a television crew struggled through with a mountain of kit. The Lebanese customs officials immediately pounced on them. I waited until they began questioning them, watching as gloomy despondency descended over the journalists. Just then, a group of backpackers approached customs. I mingled with them, strolling casually past the officials and into Lebanon.

I called Marie. She answered first time, which was unusual, if not unheard of.

'Marie, I'm in. Where are you – at the Bristol Hotel?' I asked.

'Fuck no,' she replied. 'Have you ever been to that place. Too old-fashioned for me'

'Yes, Marie. I lived there for three weeks when me and Miles went into Syria last time.'

'Jesus, you guys have no taste! I checked us out and booked us into the Rotana. It's five star. I can't believe you guys stayed at the Bristol for three weeks. Get in a cab and call when you get in.' She hung up the phone.

Exhausted after the flight, I grabbed the nearest taxi. 'Holiday?' the taxi driver asked, as winter rain beat against the windscreen. I nodded. In Beirut, there are so many rival factions – each with its own intricate network of opaque loyalties – that it's never wise to advertise the fact you're about to cross illegally into Syria. I played the dumb tourist for half an hour before finally arriving at the Rotana.

Marie had chosen well. In the field she can rough it with the best but, given the option, she liked a little style and opulence before a job. She also refused to enter war zones without her expensive silk underwear, which she said made her 'feel good'. The problem was that her expensive knickers would always go missing. In 1999, as militiamen looted and pillaged the capital of East Timor, Marie returned to her hotel after a day's hard reporting to find that the building she was staying in had been trashed. The marauding militia had smashed her television and broken the room's furniture but they had miraculously left behind everything else of value – her voice recorder, radio, clothes and body armour. Oddly, the ferocious militiamen hadn't left completely empty-handed: Marie's luxury silk bras and underpants were all gone. Clearly these militiamen had good taste.

I called her room. No answer. She'd obviously passed out. At check-in, I had been mysteriously upgraded to club class because the receptionist's name was Paul. He informed me he always upgraded any guests with the name Paul. I found myself in a grand suite, drinking a large Scotch.

For the first time in thirty-six hours I allowed my mind to relax. Since the initial call from the paper, life had been a whirlwind of frantic activity. The whisky had now warmed my body, my mind no longer raced and I began to take fuller stock of the situation. Here I was again in a foreign country, no visa for the next war-torn country we were to report from, our cunning, guile and a bag of money the only tools at our disposal.

It was all about the planning: get it right and the rest would fall into place. We could busk it once we made it into Syria, but at the moment that was a long way off. I had managed to get into Syria a month ago, but circumstances on the ground can change rapidly and what had worked then might no longer be a viable option. It was to be a land crossing over the mountains, as the Syrian coast was heavily patrolled and the seas were rough and unpredictable at this time of year, precluding any entry attempt by boat.

My mind was starting to drift and I thought of the planning sessions Marie and I had worked on last year whilst sneaking in and out of Libya. I smiled inwardly: the master plan had been our most audacious ever. We had planned it fastidiously over a six-month period during the Libyan conflict. On our first meeting, while attempting to get into Iraq from Syria eight years earlier, Marie and I had bonded over tales of war reporting and sailing. The two passions we shared were not only the basis of our tight-knit team, but also formed the bare bones of the master plan.

20 May 2011, Dafniya, Libya

For two months Marie and I had advanced with the Libyan rebels as they pushed Gaddafi's forces further from the centre of Misrata to the outlying rural district of Dafniya. The battle had reached near-stalemate and we found ourselves, more often than not, sitting in shallow trenches or olive groves with time on our hands. The retreating government forces continued to bombard rebel positions with huge salvos of missiles and artillery, but we sat tight and continued to report. We were worried, though: if the battle lines remained stalled in Dafniya, then we feared we might miss out on any advance on Tripoli by rebel forces based to the west of the capital city.

A large part of Marie's professional life had been devoted to Libya – she had met Gaddafi on numerous occasions and had travelled, under government supervision, to many parts of Gaddafi's private fiefdom. As a young reporter invited into his home in 1986, Marie had even broken the news that the Americans planned to bomb the building, days before they actually did. Her good looks and charisma charmed the increasingly insane and brutal dictator, but she had a genuine passion for the Libyan story and she certainly wasn't going to miss out on what was possibly the last chapter of a tale that spanned forty-two years of Gaddafi rule.

Marie and I had found ourselves a small depression in the ground in which to shelter from the withering artillery attacks. The front line was about fifty metres away, which didn't make us any safer: most of the missiles landed hundreds of yards, and occasionally miles, off target. It was now suppertime and the solid chunk of stale, flat white bread and the open tin of tuna looked as appealing as ever in the yellow glow of the hunter's moon. Marie had fallen very quiet for the last ten minutes. She appeared to be deep in thought, so I left her to it and struggled to snap off a piece of bread.

She finally spoke. 'Paul, do you have the map, the map of all Libya?'

'Yes,' I replied rather glibly. 'Why? Going somewhere nice?' I mockingly observed our surroundings with exaggerated turns of my head.

'Asshole,' she chuckled. 'Give me the goddam map.'

Marie took the grubby, creased lump of paper I retrieved from one of my pockets. 'Jesus,' she said, holding the map in the air between her finger and thumb with a look of disgust on her face. 'Where the fuck have you been keeping this thing, Paul?'

'Best you don't know, mate.' I sniggered. 'Anyway, why do you need a map? We only ever travel on one road and we've been doing that for months.'

Marie ignored me as she peeled open the map and spread it out on the ground next to our dinner. She studied it for a moment, found what she was looking for and turned to me.

'Look,' she said, with her finger on the map pointing to the Libyan capital, Tripoli. 'There are three roads into the city: from the west, the east and south up from the desert.'

I nodded, unsure where this conversation was going.

'What do you expect is going to happen when the attack on Tripoli begins?' she asked, a wry smile on her face.

'Erm, sheer mental fucking chaos?' I proffered.

Marie beamed back at me. 'Yep, dead right. Now how the fuck do we get to Tripoli if all the roads are blocked and it's sheer mental fucking chaos?' she asked.

I shrugged.

Marie paused for effect, building up to the moment when she would reveal all. She slowly moved her finger from Tripoli and slid it across the map, where it came to rest on a piece of blue nothingness. Her finger had stopped in the middle of the Mediterranean Sea. She turned and looked at my baffled face.

'Paul, we sail in. We go in by boat,' she said, growing visibly more excited as she spoke. 'Every other journalist is going to get trapped in the rush for Tripoli. The roads will be manic. There'll be battles in every part of the surrounding area and we'll just drift on in – by boat!'

I looked at Marie in awe. 'Fucking genius, it's perfect.' I had immediately fallen utterly in love with the idea. That we might sail into Tripoli as others were bogged down in fighting around the city was such a tremendous concept that I hadn't really thought through the details and so wasn't prepared for what came next.

'There is a catch though, Paul: we need a boat,' Marie said. 'Do you still have yours and if so where is it?'

'Indeed I do. Northern Spain, not that far away,' I muttered, while struggling to calculate the distance in my head. 'I could get it to Malta in about a week's sailing if need be.'

And there we sat, missiles flying overhead, stale bread and tuna for dinner, map spread in front of us and huge idiotic grins pasted on our proud little faces. We had a plan.

Marie had grown up in Oyster Bay on the Atlantic coast. Sailing was in her blood. Many a night I'd listened to her fantastic sailing adventures. The latest one was a lucky escape that she had while sailing with her partner, Richard. The weather predictions, she claimed, were for light winds and blue skies. Now, sailing being sailing, this proved not to be the case. A sudden squall had caught them off guard and they soon found themselves in trouble. Firstly, the mainsail was ripped by the fierce winds – survivable but a pain. Next, the roller reefing that pulls in the foresail jammed – not so good. To add to this run of bad luck, the bilge pumps stopped pumping water from the hull – scary. To top all of that, the engine failed, leaving them with an almost completely unsailable boat. When I asked Richard about the trip he said that it was the only time in his life that he had considered calling for help. As it turned out, the combined efforts of all the crew got them into harbour intact.

July 2011, Devon, England

A week later Marie and I withdrew from Dafniya and headed back home. We had spent two months under siege and were due a little rest and recuperation. But we never really stopped. Once back in the UK there were hour-long phone calls as we began to put the boat plan into place. Marie recruited Ella Flaye, daughter of her partner, Richard, to help crew the boat. She would stand guard while Marie and I slipped ashore into Tripoli to report on Gaddafi's downfall.

The war in Libya was still stuck in stalemate: the rebel advance had stalled and Gaddafi's forces had dug themselves into well-secured defensive positions. NATO planes were bombing government targets on a daily basis but the disorganised rebel forces had failed to capitalise on the air power available. The same ground was being fought over and then lost in a seemingly unending cycle.

In Devon, I plotted passage plans for the trip to Malta, where we intended to berth my yacht ahead of our seaborne entry into

Tripoli. From Malta we could reach Tripoli within twenty hours so long as we had fair winds. All was progressing as planned but, deep in the back of both of our minds, stood the elephant in the room: we had not yet asked *The Sunday Times'* editors for their permission. So far this had been a rogue plan, a black op that nobody else knew about but, with the rebels expected to resume their creep towards the capital any day, the time had come for the paper to sign off on our master plan.

After another intense flurry of calls between the two of us, we decided it was time to act. She was due in for a meeting at the paper's office in London and would present our boat plan to the editors then. On the day Marie put the plan to them I couldn't keep myself from playing out the various scenarios in my head. Would she be laughed out of the office? Perhaps removed from the building, wearing a jacket with very long sleeves, by large, unsmiling men in white coats? It was anyone's guess.

At roughly five o'clock my phone rang. It was Marie. I stared at the phone, unsure if I wanted to hear the response. I finally pressed answer and held the phone to my ear.

'Captain Conroy,' came the words down the line, 'prepare to cast off and proceed with all due haste to Malta.'

'You're fucking joking,' I spluttered.

'Nope,' replied Marie. 'They love it. Said they would get you another boat if yours gets blown up.'

14 July 2011, Sant Carles Marina, Spain

I stood proudly on the pontoon as my younger brother, Neil, completed the final preparations before casting off. He knew the boat – *Kitani*, a 35-foot Waterwitch wooden-hulled yacht that had been built in the early sixties – better than anyone. We had sailed her from Devon across the Bay of Biscay, where we had to slug it out through a storm for three days before hitting land in La Coruña, Spain. Since then Neil had more or less lived on her for three years and had kept her in a state of full seaworthiness. He was to crew her with me for the seven-day non-stop sail to Malta.

After a five o'clock gin and tonic in the cockpit, we slipped our mooring lines and proceeded south-by-south-east. We picked up fair winds across our starboard beam, set the sails accordingly and relaxed with a fine bottle of red plonk and chorizo stew. Ahead lay the tranquil Mediterranean Sea. The winds from the North African coast were pleasantly warm and life seemed very good indeed. We continued in this manner for seven days, eating freshly caught fish and sharing night watches with a wee dram of something malty. It was the finest sail of our lives.

When the week was up – and we were exhausted by the constant reeling in of fish and popping of corks, which seemed to grow more strenuous the further south we got – we spotted land off the port bow. Neil promptly claimed the island for Queen and Country as we prepared to drop anchor in St Thomas Bay, a beautiful inlet that lies south of the capital, Valletta.

We had a glass of rum to celebrate, then Neil announced he was off to seek out the natives and find something to smoke. I called Marie and told her that phase one of the plan had been a complete success. She put the phone down a happy lady. Neil returned two hours later, smiling. He had found a Rastafarian-run bar, The Zion, on the beachfront and had quickly made friends with the patrons. He too was a happy chap.

After a week in the sun doing odd jobs on the boat, fishing and swimming while preparing her for the voyage to Tripoli, Neil dropped me off on land in the rubber tender. It had been our best voyage together. We hugged as I got into a taxi to the airport. He was clearly delighted with the prospect of resuming his role as the ship's captain and with his part in the plan to infiltrate Tripoli by sea. It was the last time I would see Neil alive.

I returned home and waited. It seemed as if the war in Libya would continue in stalemate for eternity. Nevertheless, Marie and I communicated constantly, updating each other about the rebels' progress or lack of it, as was more often the case. Bored with waiting, Marie announced that she was going racing in the Mediterranean for a week or two aboard a yacht skippered by Griff Rhys Jones. She warned me that Tripoli would probably fall while she was away sailing. And it did.

I received a 'Get to Libya immediately' call from *The Sunday Times*. I was to meet up with the paper's Afghanistan correspondent, Miles Amoore, who had flown in from the border with Pakistan to cover for Marie. Together, Miles and I reported on the fall of a strategically vital town thirty miles west of the capital called Zawiya, the invasion of Tripoli and the storming of Gaddafi's palace in Bab al-Aziziya, in a ferocious two weeks of rolling battle. Marie was unable to get off the yacht and missed the fight for the capital but joined us in Tripoli only days after it fell. Much as she tried to conceal her fury at missing the fall of the city, she failed.

Our master plan had been usurped by the unexpected speed of the rebel advance and we were crestfallen. All the planning and effort we had put in had come to nothing, but we continued reporting from Tripoli for the next month before returning to the UK. On my arrival at Heathrow airport I forgot to turn my phone back on. Halfway down the M4 motorway I stopped to listen to any messages. The phone went crazy: there were dozens of missed-call notifications from my father and it was with trembling hands that I called him back. Neil, my brother, shipmate and soulmate, had been found dead in the rubber tender in St Thomas Bay. He'd had a massive heart attack at the age of forty-five.

10 February 2012, Rotana Hotel, Beirut, Lebanon

I woke fully clothed on my bed, wondering where the hell I was. I remembered, as I searched for cigarettes. I walked to the window of my hotel room and gazed out over the Beirut skyline. Before me stood a city reborn from the ashes of a ferocious civil war. Silently I pondered the challenges that lay ahead of Marie and me in Syria.

The clock was ticking. The countdown had begun.

CHAPTER TWO

Ballistic Wonderbra

10 February 2012, Beirut, Lebanon

Marie called me at about ten o'clock that morning and we arranged to meet for breakfast at ten thirty. I settled in for the wait.

At midday, I saw Marie enter through the back door of the hotel, which had a separate annex to the rear. She looked amazing: freshly dyed and styled hair and an incredible suntan – no doubt the result of her most recent ocean-racing adventure. I let her walk past me before shouting her name. She spun around, spied me and beamed widely. Marie, with her blonde hair and tall, thin figure, always managed to look elegant no matter where she was. She was as comfortable in the skinny jeans and shirt combo that she would often sport in war zones as she was in the glamorous dresses she wore to glitzy London galas while back home.

But it wasn't only her looks that seemed to suit any occasion. It was also her personality. She could capture you with a story, tell jokes and laugh into the early hours with her easy-going manner and effortless charm. Below this upbeat veneer lay a deep empathy with others and a lack of self-consciousness that made her a plea-sure to spend time with. It was partly her ability to adapt so smoothly no matter what social environment she found herself in that made her such a superb correspondent. She felt equally at home in the company of London socialites and British aristocrats as with Kurdish warlords, North African dictators and Afghan taxi drivers. Or Scouse photographers for that matter.

She gave me a big hug and we laughed. It was good to see her again. Seeing her made me realise how much I had missed her company since we had last been together in Libya in October 2011. Her sense of humour in a war zone was unsurpassable. Her epic tales of ocean adventures, told on dark moonlit nights in the desert as we sat out under the stars, killing time before the next battle or attack, made her the ideal person to travel with into conflict zones. But, apart from being a fun colleague to work with, she was also someone with whom I had built up a strong friendship.

Forged during combat, friendships quickly run deep. The public face of Marie – the one that wrote in newspapers, appeared on talk shows or gave speeches in public – was that of a battle-hardened, veteran war correspondent who wore an eyepatch. But there was so much more to her than that. When my younger brother died on my boat in Malta, Marie was straight on the phone to me. She offered emotional support but she had also already spoken to a long list of people in Malta who could move my boat and look after it for me. In any crisis, she was right there by my side with advice and support. In short, she was a true friend and it felt great to be embarking on another assignment with her.

20 October 2011, Libya

I had been told to link up with Marie again so I had grabbed my bags from my house in Devon and, within twenty-four hours, I was with her in Libya, looking for the body of the country's former ruler, Colonel Muammar Gaddafi, who had just been executed by rebel forces in his hometown of Sirte. They had moved his corpse to the port city of Misrata, whose people had arguably suffered the most during the revolution, having been subjected to the full force of the dictator's wild revenge.

An old contact from earlier in the year when Marie and I were in Misrata took us to see Gaddafi's body. Rebels had driven it to the old African market on the edges of the city, where it was placed in a walk-in meat refrigerator. Already scores of people, including families with small children, had started to queue up to see the body. The atmosphere was like a carnival. We recognised several of the rebels guarding the freezer. They waved us in past the crowd.

There lay, in Ronald Reagan's own words, the 'mad dog of the Middle East', his bruised and battered body – still fresh at this point – guarded by the local Misratan rebels who had captured and killed him. His face was oddly serene, given the torture he'd undergone prior to his death. The body was certainly Gaddafi's, but a Gaddafi stripped of power, a Gaddafi shorn of mystique, reduced from king to corpse. As I took photographs, I marvelled at how this man had so brutally ruled a nation, crushing any sign of dissent for forty-two years before finally succumbing to the fury of the very people he thought adored and admired him. His death was an ironically inglorious one for a man who had spent his life in pursuit of adoration.

After getting the photographs I needed, we located the house where Gaddafi had stayed during the battle for his hometown of Sirte. Finding the house where the Libyan ruler spent his last night was a scoop for *The Sunday Times*. The foreign desk was delighted.

The next day, as we made plans to fly back to the UK, Marie received an email from the newspaper's foreign editor. She looked a little crestfallen: she had been told to head to Tripoli to cover the political situation there. 'Are you coming?' she asked.

'No fucking chance. I'm not shooting committees,' I replied. My hatred of committees was a hangover from our siege days in Misrata, where I refused to photograph old men drinking tea under neon lights while a war raged outside. She packed and left. That had been our last meeting.

10 February 2012, Rotana Hotel, Beirut, Lebanon

Marie looked at me earnestly in the lobby of Beirut's Rotana Hotel. 'We gotta go, we really have to get in soon,' she said.

'I suggest a coffee before we try,' I replied. She laughed and sat back down. 'Have you spoken to Leena yet?' I asked.

Leena was the fixer Miles and I had used when we entered Syria on our previous assignment. If you needed something, anything in Beirut, then you needed Leena. She had been a producer and a television presenter during the civil war in the 1980s and she seemed to know everyone worth knowing in the city. In short, she was our way into Syria. In her early fifties now, Leena no longer went into the field – a promise she'd made to her worried daughter – but she still had a superb understanding of political developments inside the turbulent city.

'We spoke yesterday,' Marie replied. 'She's coming to meet us at the hotel today. She thinks maybe we can go in tomorrow.'

I nearly choked on my coffee. 'Tomorrow!' I said, smiling – not wanting to dash Marie's hopes while trying to inject a touch of reality into the situation. I reminded her that it had taken Miles and I three weeks to reach the border.

Marie stared at me questioningly. 'Oh? She sounded pretty positive when I spoke to her.'

I nodded. 'Same with us. Miles and I were on daily standby – for three weeks. We were going crazy. All I'm saying is that things work differently and slowly here. You know that, you've spent enough time in Beirut. It hasn't changed.'

Marie seemed to drift back to the past for a few moments. She grasped a memory, smiled and then said, 'Well, I've got time for a little shopping then.'

Marie, in a desperate search for long johns and high-energy snacks, left in a flash. I set up my laptop in my room. My plan was to make contact with some of the activists still transmitting out of Homs on Skype and Twitter. It wasn't hard. Within half an hour I was in direct contact with Omar Shakir, who was destined to become a very good friend. He briefed me on the current situation in Baba Amr. It was terrifying: the Syrian president, Bashar al-Assad, had ordered his forces to launch massive artillery strikes on the small neighbourhood. Civilians and rebels alike were penned in and they had no means of moving the injured or dying. Government tanks were making forays into Baba Amr but small units of rebel fighters, known collectively as the Free Syrian Army, were fighting them off. In short, all hell had broken loose and people were struggling to survive. Other sources on Twitter and Skype confirmed Omar's information. At one point, I found myself watching a live feed that showed the shelling he'd been describing.

Marie arrived back from her shopping trip. She had also visited the home of Jim Muir, the BBC journalist based in Beirut. Jim, an old friend of hers, had briefed Marie on the situation on the ground and both our pictures matched: continual shelling, tanks, snipers and a medieval siege that was taking place under the world's nose. A world which, for the greater part, seemed to be ignoring it.

Marie rummaged in a bag and produced a pair of long johns. I looked quizzically at her and she smiled. 'Jim Muir,' she explained. 'I got Jim Muir's long johns. A little big, but hey.'

We both retired to our rooms. Marie began work on a piece she had to write for Sunday and I continued to research the situation in Baba Amr. A few hours passed. The news coming out of Syria continued to describe a rapidly deteriorating situation. As I watched the devastation on the television, Marie told me that Leena was ready to meet us.

In the hotel bar, Leena broke the ice. 'I think the boys can get you in tomorrow, so be ready to go by seven a.m.,' she said.

Marie's face lit up while mine retained a mildly sceptical look. I'd heard this before so I refused to get too enthusiastic. Leena went through the routine. 'One bag each,' she said. 'Don't give anyone any money as that will be sorted on the way out.'

Marie asked how much but Leena just told us to make a donation to the cause, whatever we felt necessary. 'You will go the Bekaa Valley route, same as last time, and if you want to take body armour you must wear it under your jacket,' she said.

This was the first mention of body armour. Mine was back in the UK because last time we were told we couldn't wear it. I hated the stuff but, having seen hundreds of people killed in Libya by tiny pieces of shrapnel that body armour could have stopped, I now wore it as a matter of principle. Leena said I could borrow hers. We spoke for an hour or so altogether as Marie gently interrogated Leena for more information.

'That's fantastic,' said Marie once Leena had left. 'Tomorrow, game on.' I rolled my eyes a little. Marie caught the glance. 'What's up, Paul, why the eyes? Don't you believe her?'

'I've heard it before,' I said. 'Seeing is believing. Everyone here likes to please, so nobody ever says no. It's always yes, and you only find out if it's no when they don't show up.'

'God, you're a miserable bastard,' she laughed. 'I'm off to finish the piece for Sunday and pack.' She disappeared upstairs in a flurry of excited anticipation at tomorrow's move. I walked rather more sluggishly to my room, doubting, almost guaranteeing, that we wouldn't leave tomorrow morning.

I had been back in my room for ten minutes when there was a knock at the door.

'It's gone, it's all fucking gone and I didn't touch anything. It's just gone,' Marie kept repeating.

'What's gone?' I asked, trying to calm her down.

'My whole piece. Gone. It was there one second ago and now I can't find any of it.'

Marie was panicking. I rarely saw this side of her, so I knew it must be bad.

As I took the laptop from her so I could start looking for the missing article, her phone rang. She looked horrified as she saw the name on the screen: the editor. 'Shit, it's Sean. He wants the piece now.' She tried to calm herself before picking up.

'Hi, Sean,' she said, a false note of controlled serenity in her voice. 'No, it's all good. Paul's just transferring it now.'

She glanced over to check my progress. I shrugged as I tried manically to find her piece.

'No, Sean, I've definitely written it. It's just a technical glitch. It will be with you in ten,' I heard Marie say.

'Run fast and get the power supply for your laptop. If it runs out of power we may lose everything,' I shouted at her as I noticed the battery sign flashing in the corner of the screen.

Marie flew out of the door. Her phone started to ring again. I picked it up from the bed where she'd left it and answered it. 'Marie's phone.'

It was Lucy on the foreign desk. 'Ah, Paul, hello. Marie tells us she's had a bit of a glitch and is just transferring her piece.' Lucy paused. 'Paul, has she really written it, honestly?'

I confirmed that she had and that I was just transferring it, ready for email. Lucy sounded somewhat short of convinced and hung up. I found the missing article seconds later. I'm not sure how, but there it was. Marie flew back into the room.

'I have it.' I smiled. 'All you need to do is press send.'

She took the laptop and left the room running. About twenty seconds later she was back again. 'It's gone,' she said, horrified.

'Bollocks. Give it here.'

Somewhat sheepishly she handed over the computer. I was perplexed. I had seen the article with my own eyes. I could think of only one answer. I went to the menu and hit 'edit undo'. The text reappeared and Marie breathed a sigh of relief. She'd obviously hit the delete button by mistake. Marie left my room again, holding the computer like an unexploded bomb in front of her, walking very, very slowly.

The next morning at seven o'clock I found myself sitting in the near-deserted hotel lobby with Marie. It's one of the hardest parts of any assignment – the waiting. It grinds you down, saps your energy until you transmogrify into a frustrated, lethargic subhuman. It kills me. I hate the waiting game: it forces you to think about what might lie ahead. Doubts escalate and your fears are amplified until you begin to wonder what the hell you're doing there in the first place.

Eventually, Marie received a text. She struggled to disguise the disappointment on her face. It was obvious we weren't going today. We would have to wind down and prepare to do the whole thing over again. It's a morale-sapping process – the soul-destroying wait for the go call.

April 2011, Benghazi, Libya

Journalists often find themselves having to find ways around seemingly impassable obstacles. While on assignment in Libya a year earlier, Marie and I encountered a similar situation to the one we were now facing in Beirut. We had arrived in the eastern city and rebel stronghold of Benghazi only to discover that the real story had moved on to the more westerly port city of Misrata. Benghazi was truly liberated, and with liberation came the birth of the dreaded committee.

Previously in Benghazi you could do whatever you wanted. There was a war on so there were no rules. You could jump in with a rebel unit, race to the front and be back in time for your evening meal. But now the committees were sprouting everywhere, weighing everything down with bureaucracy. We wanted to reach Misrata, a city under siege that was suffering beneath the full force of the Gaddafi regime's destructive rage. The only way in was by ship and the only one heading to Misrata was an International Organization for Migration boat. In order to board the boat we needed various letters of permission issued by new committees with dull-sounding titles.

During our day-long hunt in search of the right committee with the right piece of paper, we received news that the boat was leaving the next evening. It was now essential that we bypass the committee stage completely. Early the next morning, carrying a small backpack each, we made our way down to the harbour. We hadn't bothered to check out of the hotel. The plan was to go to Misrata on the boat and return with it. We'd be gone a few days at most. We had no real strategy other than to jump aboard.

At the harbour, we hid behind some containers and watched as volunteers loaded boxes of aid and food supplies. I turned to Marie.

'Let's make friends with the captain. If we can get aboard and meet him then we're on. They can't throw us off,' I said.

Marie's eye sparkled. 'So we're just going to sneak on board and make friends?'

'Correct,' I said. 'You game?'

Without replying she moved towards the gaping hole in the ship's hull where containers were now being shuffled into position. We paused, waited until nobody was looking directly at us and sneaked aboard the huge Greek roll-on roll-off ferry. We headed up the stairs, giggling as we went, and stopped only once we arrived at the canteen deck. A member of the Greek crew passed by.

'Excuse me, where is the captain?' I asked, trying to assume an air of authority and belonging. The crew member paused and nodded towards a set of sliding glass doors.

We entered the canteen area. In the far corner, alone, sat a bulky, contented character, drinking a beer and eating his lunch. We approached the captain.

'Kalimera, tikanis, kalla,' I said in fluent Greek.

'Yas as.' The captain beamed at me. 'You speak Greek very well my friend,' he continued, proffering a seat with the wave of his hand.

Marie simply gawped at me. 'You speak Greek?'

'Liego, liego,' I answered.

The captain laughed. He shouted to a waiter, who brought us two beers. We chatted amiably about his boat, his job and his family. He told us that his wife thought that he was still running the ship as a tourist boat in the Greek isles. Apparently she had no idea he was in a war zone taking aid to the starving people of Misrata. After an hour of polite chitchat we hit him with the big one: would he take us to Misrata with him?

He smiled a huge grin, nodded and replied, 'Of course! You are my guests, and you must come.'

I caught a glimpse of Marie's face. She was beaming a smile I will always remember, like a young girl who'd received a much-dreamed-of present at Christmas. We were in. We were going to Misrata and no committee in the world could stop us now.

11 February 2012, Beirut, Lebanon

However, this time, back in Beirut, it wasn't a committee blocking us from crossing into Syria. Instead, it was the full force of the Syrian army deployed along Syria's western border with Lebanon. Then there were the minefields and the smugglers, wary of people using their lucrative routes into Syria.

We eventually received news from Leena. We were to meet the head of the smuggling operation whose men would guide us across the border. Leena had described the meeting as something akin to an interview. The chief smuggler had met me before but he now wanted to check out Marie.

In the afternoon, Leena picked us up from the hotel to meet the man known to much of the western press simply as 'the beardy one'. Given that we were meeting the beardy one – the head honcho – I imagined that the whole thing would be shrouded in the utmost secrecy: a dark backstreet, perhaps, in a hidden, secluded location far from prying eyes. Nope. The meeting took place in Starbucks. It was something of an anticlimax. Marie kept glancing at me and mouthing the word Starbucks as she struggled to keep a straight face.

We drank coffee and waited for the beardy one, watching the city roll by outside the glass-fronted café. The streets of Beirut were alive. We were in a prosperous part of town, with an ambience like Knightsbridge, far from the images of war and destruction that the name Beirut conjures up. Beautiful couples strolled hand in hand.

Obviously the breast-implant industry had found a new, welcome market in this city once torn apart by civil war.

Mr Beardy arrived with a flurry of handshakes and greetings. He sat down and laid out an amazing array of mobile phones on the table in front of him. If phone count was any measure of status then Beardy was definitely 'the man'. I counted six.

We chatted for a while. Marie was in full professional mode, reading the situation perfectly. She made the right noises at the right times and Beardy relaxed. It seemed that Marie and I had passed the interview. It was agreed that Beardy's men would pick us up the next day to make the crossing. We drank more coffee while Beardy answered his constantly ringing array of mobiles until he made his goodbyes and left.

To celebrate, Leena invited us to the international press club gathering that evening. We agreed and found ourselves in a rather classy private bar in the Hamra district. There were familiar faces among the press corps who had gathered for a drink and a catch-up. I met Bryan Denton, a freelance photographer, who shoots mainly for the *New York Times*. We had spent a month together in Misrata when the siege was at its worst and most of the world's press had abandoned the city. Now, he and all the other journalists we spoke to that evening warned us of the dangers.

Bryan was a serious shooter. He had covered many wars and was a veteran of Afghanistan, but his face was etched with concern when I told him of our impending trip to Syria. He told me that he wouldn't even consider going in at this point. He said it was too volatile and pointed out that there was no place to retreat to should things go badly wrong. The Free Syrian Army held no territory that could be considered safe, unlike the rebels in Libya, who had at least been able to hold ground.

Lindsey Hilsum, Channel 4 News International Editor, chatted to Marie and admitted openly that entering Syria was a cut-off point for her – she would not cross the border. Lindsey, who has an incredible record reporting from conflict zones around the world, urged caution. She looked concerned as we drank, bullshitted and told stories well into the night. It seemed that out of the friends and fellow journalists we'd met so far, only Marie and I were making plans to enter Syria.

The next day, Marie went to visit Paul Wood of the BBC, who had recently returned from a crossing into Syria. He warned her about the precariousness of the situation. We received a similar brief from Stewart Ramsay of Sky TV, who had returned from Syria the previous night. He told us that things were pretty hot on the ground and he too urged caution.

I met up with Bryan Denton the next day. His concern was so great that he brought along some spare field dressings and a first aid kit, just in case things went badly wrong inside. We drank coffee and bought a short-wave radio so we could monitor the BBC World Service within Syria. I shook hands with Bryan and we hugged before parting. 'Good luck in there, man. Keep your head down, do your job and get out,' were his final words to me.

The evening before our departure, Marie and I went through the codes that we had set up to keep the office and Leena informed of our status while inside Syria. Airport meant the border, Beirut meant Homs. 'The weather is sunny' meant that all was well, 'cloudy weather' that we had a minor problem and 'storm coming' that all hell had broken loose and we were getting out.

We had listened to all the advice from those we trusted, those who had been in and out. I told Marie that it was possible to make the trip. I had made the same journey three weeks earlier. Yes, it was a little hairy but it was very doable. We discussed it for hours and came to the conclusion that if Assad was slaughtering civilians in the town of Homs, then someone should be there to cover the onslaught. After all, this – reporting on the suffering of civilians and bearing witness to the bloody impact of war – was what Marie was all about. It was what we did. Our minds were made up.

At least we thought so. Morning the next day came and went down to the marble lobby. We sat watching the same cleaners, mechanically cleaning the same floors, the same receptionists, struggling to smile at the same loud, obnoxious guests, and the same sense of growing despair as no furtive smuggler mysteriously appeared in the lobby. And then a phone call. Marie scrambled anxiously for her mobile. I watched, trying to read her face. Frowning, Marie nodded twice and then, just as the tension was becoming unbearable, she smiled and hung up. I prepared myself for bad news.

'Marie, please tell me,' I pleaded. 'I can't do another night here.'

She smiled at my comical, yet sincere face. 'Eleven o'clock this morning,' she said, pausing for effect. 'Today, confirmed.' Again that wonderful deep chuckle from Marie as my face relaxed.

Back in my room time ticked by at geological speed until, eventually, my Lebanese phone rang, making me jump. I pressed answer and held my breath.

'Paul, I'm outside now. You must come, you will see me,' an unknown voice on the other end said before hanging up.

I looked around. There was a problem. There was no sign of Marie. I called her. 'Marie, it's happening, the driver is here, actually physically here,' I said. 'No, I'm not bullshitting . . . no, he wasn't very chatty but at least he exists.'

Marie promised to be down in five minutes, so I made my way across the marbled lobby. As I walked, I took in the sights: corpulent corporate-types sat smoking cigars and quaffing whisky. There were a few travellers huddled around *Lonely Planet* guidebooks and a proliferation of bland-looking businessmen wandering around aimlessly. I silently said my goodbyes to them – to the polished marble, to the friendly staff and to the piped music that worms its way into your soul. I was leaving it all behind. There was no regret. As soon as I venture through the polished glass frontage of the hotel my life will change, I thought. I never expected by how much.

Outside, I scanned the street for the driver. He had a dark blue Mercedes saloon. I caught his eyes looking straight at me. This has to be our man, I thought. Closing in on the car, I spied a smile. The face seemed familiar and then it hit me. It's Hussein, I realised, a driver that Miles and I had used many times on our last assignment here. We hugged. He was laughing.

'Paul, why are you back here? Didn't it scare you enough last time?' He beamed. 'You're an idiot. Please, why don't you be a good, well-behaved journalist and get a visa like everyone else and maybe people won't shoot at you.'

'Because I missed you, Hussein. I just had to come to see your smiley face.'

'Where is Miles?' asked Hussein quizzically, looking at the hotel door.

I explained that Miles was back in Kabul and that Marie and I were the team for this assignment. Hussein nodded before saying, rather bluntly, that Marie must have a huge set of balls to be border-jumping into Syria. Speaking of Marie, where the hell is she? I asked myself. I called her and again she promised to be down in five minutes.

Hussein smiled. 'It's okay, I have a wife too,' he said, a cheeky grin on his face.

Half an hour later, introductions over, we moved through the thick Beirut traffic. We had to stop by Leena's to pick up my borrowed body armour. Marie had hers on underneath her jacket and I groaned at the prospect of living in the stuff. At Leena's house, I saw a young man waiting patiently on the street with the armour in a bag. I gasped when I picked it up. Leena, about a foot shorter than me and a little bustier, had what I can only describe as a bulletproof bra. I tried it on and that's exactly what it looked like. It was about four sizes too small and it barely covered my ribs. Christ, I thought, I'm going to war in an armoured Wonderbra.

We continued to weave through the traffic. Outside the car windows, the concrete and glass modernity of downtown Beirut slowly disappeared, fading into the unkempt, poorer suburbs of the city. The overwhelming impression was one of crumbling poverty. I explained to Marie that on my last trip Hussein's son had taken us deep into the Bekaa Valley before handing us over to the smugglers. I was just about to explain the next step when Hussein pulled into a garage. He made a phone call in Arabic and asked us if we wanted coffee. I could see Marie's face growing concerned as Hussein shuffled off to get us a drink.

'Paul, did this happen last time?' Marie asked.

'No,' I replied. 'Last time it was a car all the way through the valley.'

I understood Marie's apprehension. On these jobs, the more you know the more you feel you have a degree of control over your fate. We were surrendering ourselves to an unknown group of smugglers. It was a leap of faith and it was unnerving.

Hussein arrived back with the coffee, explained that a car would take us to the Bekaa Valley and told us that we would then be led into Syria. For about twenty minutes we drank and smoked, waiting for the changeover vehicle to appear. Hussein received a call. He pointed at a small minibus parked up about a hundred metres away. We grabbed our kit and approached the vehicle. Hussein helped load our bags, spoke to the driver and shook hands.

'Good luck.' He smiled as he walked away. 'See you next week.'

The minibus was shabby and rickety. Brass trinkets covered the dashboard. More worrying than the décor and roadworthiness, though, was the driver. He appeared to be – and almost certainly was – certifiably mad. The moment Marie and I climbed in he turned and looked at us.

'Syria?' he asked in Arabic.

We both nodded silently. He put two fingers to his temple in the shape of a gun and mimed someone being shot in the head. Marie turned and looked at me.

'Jesus Christ, Paul, this guy is nuts. Who is he?' she asked, as if I'd met him before.

I shrugged my shoulders. 'Almost certainly not a smuggler,' I replied, a touch hopefully. 'Probably just someone they know who's a safe pair of hands to get us through the valley.'

If a person's driving technique can be interpreted as a measure of their sanity then Marie's 'nuts' diagnosis soon held true. Never exceeding fifteen miles per hour, he wove in and out of the traffic shouting randomly at anyone standing on the pavement. Eventually, he slammed on the brakes and screeched to a halt, hurling us forward against the seat in front. A soldier climbed in, smiled and sat down next to me.

Marie, who was in the seat behind me, muttered, 'Paul, what the fuck's going on? He's picking up soldiers. Is this guy actually a smuggler? He's scaring me.'

'Probably a taxi, Marie. They're using a taxi as cover,' I muttered back, not wishing to say too much in case the soldier spoke English.

We climbed high into the mountains that loomed over the city. Snow covered the sides of the road. The minibus was soon packed with people the nutty driver had enticed from the roadside. They included five women, three soldiers and a policeman. Marie was asleep or at least pretending to be asleep rather convincingly. The driver turned the heating on full blast to stave off the winter chill outside, making it unbearably hot inside. But I couldn't take off my jacket. I was acutely aware of the impression I might make on my travelling companions were I to reveal my bulletproof Wonderbra.

As we began the steep descent from the mountains towards the town of Baalbek, in the Bekaa Valley, our fellow travellers began to dismount at intervals along the way. The valley was famous, or infamous, for many reasons. It was, and possibly still is, one of the world's top producers of hashish. It was also home to Hezbollah – a Shia political group with a huge armed militia backed and funded by Iran that now held the balance of power in Lebanon. This affected us as Hezbollah were against the uprising in Syria and actively supporting the president, Bashar al-Assad. Hezbollah weren't happy that Lebanon was being used as a launch pad into Syria by the press and, more importantly, by smugglers ferrying in weapons and medical supplies destined for rebel forces in Syria. This made us targets even though we were still inside Lebanon.

In Baalbek, we dropped off our last passenger and headed north, slowly winding our way up the mountains that would eventually lead to the border with Syria. The driver, still nuts, would occasionally turn to us, laugh and say, 'Syria,' before turning away and chuckling to himself. I hated him by now. He made my nerves jangle. Marie was awake in the back but she remained silent. When Marie falls quiet I know that her mind is turning over all the possibilities. If she was anything like me, then she too was nervous.

The minibus slowed as the mountains grew steeper and the passing villages grew smaller and poorer. Eventually we arrived on a wide-open plain. Ahead, we could make out the final mountain range that separated the two countries. In the far distance, we could see Syria.

Marie's voice rose from the back of the vehicle. 'Paul, is this the way you came last time?'

51

'I think so. Maybe we were on the road to our right that runs along the ridge,' I said, pointing at a road in the distance.

'I don't trust this guy,' said Marie. 'He's too nuts to be a smuggler.'

'Maybe that's why he is a smuggler,' I said, trying to allay her concerns.

We continued along the flat plain. I scanned the area, looking for any familiar landmarks that might tell me whether we were in the same place that I'd departed from the last time. Using the sun as a compass, I figured that we were heading north. But occasionally the driver would make sharp swings west or east. After a while though, I was convinced that we were indeed heading in the same direction and that the sharp deviations were part of a route avoiding army or Hezbollah checkpoints.

'Marie, I think this is the same route in as last time. This guy is an absolute crackpot, but I think we are headed to the same village. '

Marie relaxed a little in the back. She was smiling again and I could hear her muttering to herself about the driver. Ahead of us I saw a dust cloud. We were off the main road now, bumping along a stone and sand track. As we approached the vehicle coming in the opposite direction, the driver pointed at it and said, 'Syria.' Within a minute our two vehicles had met. We handed the driver $100. The transfer between the vehicles was swift. As we moved from the minibus into the back of a light blue, battered pickup truck, I was shocked to see a western journalist clambering out of the back. He looked rough and dishevelled.

'Roberto,' he said, holding out his hand. We shook and I introduced myself.

'Where you headed?' he asked.

'Baba Amr,' I replied.

He laughed as he got into the taxi. 'Enjoy the tunnel then,' he said ominously, and then sped off before we could ask him what he meant.

Marie looked at me as we crammed ourselves into the pickup. 'Did he just say tunnel?'

I nodded. I hate tunnels and think all potholing should be banned and all its practitioners re-educated against their will.

Still, things were on the up. I was anxious to recognise familiar buildings from my last trip and this drove out any other thoughts for now. The new driver improved the mood too. He was dressed in military trousers, a green T-shirt and he seemed reassuringly sane. He would occasionally look at us and smile. There were no outbursts and no mock execution hand signs. It may sound strange to say, but he seemed like a smuggler should be: calm, relaxed and confident. We liked him.

We travelled another twenty minutes or so and the driver turned off down a small track. At the end of the track stood a standard square concrete house. For a moment I didn't quite get it. I just thought it was a changeover spot and then it slowly dawned on me. I knew this place. I'd been here before. If my observations were correct then the Syrian border was about a mile away. The driver smiled and gestured towards the door.

'Welcome,' he said in English.

Marie looked at me. 'This is it, Marie,' I said. 'These guys are the real deal. The adventure starts here.'

Marie smiled as she sat and began to take off her boots. Whilst doing so she looked at me quizzically and asked, 'What was that look you gave when Roberto mentioned the tunnel?'

I explained that I had previous form when it came to tunnels. Whilst in the military I'd gone off on another of my AWOL holidays, given myself up after a few weeks and ended up in the same cell as two squaddies called Smith and Lattice. They had got drunk in Germany one night, broken into the armoury and liberated a general-purpose machine gun. The pair of them had gone a step further and nicked an army Land Rover too, before driving off into the night to 'invade Poland'. They sped up the German autobahn and then, tiring of their high-speed getaway, parked for the night. In the morning, they woke up surrounded by a German SWAT team, which included a helicopter circling above them. They were duly arrested. Legend has it that, when questioned about their activities by their German captors, one of them replied, 'When you invaded Poland you got medals. When we did it we got arrested.'

We dug an escape tunnel out of boredom, I explained to an astonished-looking Marie. I removed the bricks one by one over a series of weeks, throwing them away in the pigswill from the prison. We made a hole big enough to crawl through.

On the designated night of the escape, we pulled back one of the beds and the false wall that we'd built to hide the tunnel, which was simply a piece of cardboard painted to match the yellow walls of the cell. I crawled out first, followed by Smith, but when the slightly heavier-framed Lattice tried to make his way out he got stuck. Unfortunately, we had made the hole too small for our biggest man. Out of a strong sense of moral obligation to each other, we abandoned that night's escape attempt. The next morning the hole was discovered and we were all thrown into solitary confinement. Many of the guards told us privately that it was the most audacious escape plan that they'd seen in years of working in the guardroom.

Marie gawped at me, slack-jawed. 'Jesus fucking Christ,' she replied, shaking her head. 'Let's get inside.'

CHAPTER THREE

'A pensioner, a woman and an idiot'

13 February 2012, Lebanon/Syria border region

Marie and I walked to the entrance of the house. 'This is where Miles had to eat his dinner at gunpoint,' I told her.

'Jesus Christ! He ate his dinner at gunpoint?' she asked in disbelief.

'Yeah, we had dinner here when we got rushed out of Syria last time. Miles had eaten everything apart from a few lumps of pure fat. One of the rebels told him to eat it. Miles refused, so one of the guys pulls out a pistol, points it at Miles and tells him to eat.'

Marie looked concerned and glanced at the entrance to the house. 'Was he serious?' she asked.

'Not sure, but Miles ate the fat. I filmed him eating it too.'

'Jesus Christ, Paul, you're a weird friend,' she said. 'Seriously, you think these guys we're with are up to the job?'

'They're pros, Marie. They don't rush things. If we wait, it's for a reason. They won't be pushed to take stupid risks. They got Miles and me in and out last time. They're good,' I replied.

The building we were looking at was of a classic rural Lebanese design: a rectangular concrete construction with no frills and no paint (bare concrete seemed to be the new white in rural Lebanon). Additional smaller buildings were scattered around the main rectangular block. Covering the muddy plot of land were the trappings of an agricultural lifestyle: old tractors, engines, plough blades and an ancient generator rattling away supplying power to the house. There were also children – lots of them – who had now come to stare at the two strange westerners clutching their boots in their hands. They were surrounded by weird-looking chickens.

The door to the main building opened and a man wearing a combat jacket and a *keffiyeh* – a traditional Arab headscarf – beckoned us over. His face was weather-beaten and brown. He had the keen eyes of a fighter.

Entering the house felt like leaping back in time. The rectangular room had bare walls with cushions propped up on the floor against them. A diesel heater in the middle of the room provided the warmth, ghastly neon tubes the light and a television blasting away on full volume provided the noise. Little had changed since my last stay.

Even more astonishingly, the people inside the room hadn't changed much either. The same headman lay sprawled on the floor, Kalashnikov assault rifle within easy reach, with his head on a cushion and his eyes riveted to the television. Lying next to him was Mohamed. He'd acted as our translator for a two-hour interview with some deserters from the Syrian army. The interview had been like pulling teeth but it was poor Miles who had had to go through the agonising process. Mohamed had a big heart but his English was terrible. I'd spent the whole two hours chuckling at Miles' obvious pain, occasionally sticking my tongue out at him to test his straight-faced stamina levels, all for an interview I knew Miles would never use. At least it had killed time.

Now, as the men offered to take our coats, my heart froze. Damn it, I thought, they're going to be treated to the sight of my bullet-proof Wonderbra. As I removed my coat, all the faces in the room turned to gawp at me. They muttered among themselves in Arabic and there were a few suppressed laughs. I ripped off my Wonderbra and attempted to regain what little dignity I could.

They greeted us warmly and produced a welcome pot of the ubiquitous sweet tea. It was only then that I noticed another westerner in the room. He was, at a guess, about sixty-five-years-old and balding. He was a big guy. He'd remained silent, but now he offered me his hand.

'Jean-Pierre Perrin, from *Libération*, a French daily. You are?' he asked.

'Marie Colvin and Paul Conroy, *The Sunday Times*. Great to meet you, mate. How long have you been here?' I asked.

His face dropped. 'Twenty-four hours exactly,' he said, nodding towards the clock. 'I got here at four yesterday afternoon.'

'Jesus Christ,' Marie swore, aghast. 'Oh my God, that's terrible. Why haven't you moved?' Her face showed genuine compassion: she'd suffered the same frustrating situation many times over the last twenty-five years and she understood the agony of 'the wait'.

Jean-Pierre gave a classic Gallic shrug and said nothing. Marie gave me a troubled look. I could read her mind. This room was good for a cup of tea and a rest but it was certainly not the place to spend a full day or, God forbid, a whole night. Marie kicked into action. She called Mohamed over to translate and then approached the headman, who remained sprawled on the floor, watching the television.

Marie addressed Mohamed. 'Tell him thank you for the tea but also tell him we don't want to live here. We want to get into Syria . . . today.'

Mohamed translated. The headman obviously picked up on the humour and laughed. He replied via Mohamed. 'You will go in today, *Insh'Allah*,' Mohamed said in broken English.

Insh'Allah means 'God willing' in Arabic. It's a term that follows almost every response to every request in the Middle East. To constantly put one's destiny in the hands of a higher being can get a little infuriating, especially when you're trying to plan the future.

All eyes in the room were glued to the television. The men were watching Arabic channels broadcasting amateur video footage from inside Syria. The bodies of the dead – of the men, women and children robbed of dignity in their final moments of life – were now being broadcast to the world. There were images of tanks blasting round after round of high-explosive hell into civilian homes while Russian-built armoured personnel carriers spewed forth prolonged bursts of heavy machine-gun fire at anything that moved. The fear carved on the faces of the civilians was heart-rending. The Assad regime, with its entire military might, was squeezing the air from the tiny lungs of Baba Amr. At this rate, there would be nowhere left to report from, such was the level of carnage on the screen in front of us.

The hands on the clock moved at a murderously slow rate around the aged and yellowing clockface. It was now evening and any hope of moving appeared to be slipping through our fingers. It was all getting rather depressing until we heard the sound of a motorbike pull up outside, followed by the hushed murmur of voices.

Marie and I exchanged glances. Could it possibly be?

The door opened and there, silhouetted against the setting sun, was the rebel who had driven Miles and I from Syria when we made our escape the last time. It was the same rebel who had forced Miles to eat raw fat at gunpoint. He was built like an ox, fully bearded, with a keffiyeh wrapped around his face and a Kalashnikov slung over his shoulder. He recognised me instantly. We hugged and kissed in the traditional Arab way before he unwrapped his keffiyeh and placed his gun on the floor.

He looked at me and laughed. 'You go back into Syria, then?' he asked, in very pidgin English. I nodded. Then suddenly he pulled out his pistol and pointed it straight at me. 'You are hungry?' It was a reference no doubt to Miles' unfortunate fat-eating episode. I laughed and pointed at a packet of biscuits while miming a full belly. He seemed satisfied with this response and holstered his pistol.

He surveyed the room. He caught sight of Marie and Jean-Pierre. He smiled. Something humorous had obviously caught his imagination and he muttered to the others in Arabic. The whole room burst into laughter. We sat, watching gormlessly. He seemed to have a nutrition fixation so I predicted another fat-eating session.

Mohamed translated. 'He says things must be serious in Syria: at first they send young journalists but now they send us a woman, a pensioner and an idiot who wants to go back.'

The bearded rebel spoke again, his demeanour more serious this time. Initially he addressed the headman, who was now sitting upright and more alert, and then Mohamed, our semi-English-speaking translator.

'He says, get ready, we will go to Syria now. You must pack your bags and be ready to move,' Mohamed translated.

There was a dramatic change in the atmosphere inside the room. A sense of urgency instantly replaced the laconic, tea-supping ambience. Everybody shifted into a higher gear. J-P could hardly believe it.

'I have waited twenty-four hours,' the Frenchman groaned. 'And now you wait only two and we go.' I detected a hint of injustice in his tone.

'Cheer up, mate,' I replied. 'At least we're moving.'

Marie pulled me aside. She looked serious. She was forever assessing and calculating every move. 'Hey, Paul. It's not dark yet. I thought you guys did it in the dark last time.'

'I think it's because it was so urgent then,' I replied. 'They prefer the daylight for some reason. Actually, it's not even daylight: it's dusk. Look out of the window.'

I gestured to the small window with wrought-iron bars over the glass, the only window in the room. The sun had fallen behind the mountains and we were now entering a dull half-light. The blue haze that settles in before total darkness was an asset, I thought to myself. In military terms, these were the perfect conditions because motion is very difficult to detect at these light levels. The smugglers had in fact timed their move well. The Syrian government's security forces were very twitchy at night and would shoot at any sound, as we'd discovered the last time we'd crossed. But in these conditions the soldiers would still rely on a visual point of reference, which gave us the upper hand.

Marie relaxed a little when I told her that twilight was a good time to sneak past border patrols. She knew I'd spent six years in the military planning for exactly this kind of operation. And she had a built-in and very accurate bullshit detector. Most importantly of all, we trusted each other completely with our lives.

The Frenchman, J-P, looked a little shocked to be on the go and was slightly lumbering in his movements as we prepared to make the move across the border. I had total and implicit trust in Marie's capabilities in the field and how she instinctively handled situations. She was calm under fire and reacted well to danger. I knew Marie would never fall apart on me; we could communicate without words. J-P, on the other hand, was an unknown to both of us. He had worked in Afghanistan with the Taliban, but that was now many years ago. The last time I made this foray into Syria, Miles and I had received an intelligence tip-off just before we crossed. I had already told Marie about this before we left England but thought that now was a good time to let J-P know too.

'J-P, there's something important,' I began. 'A few weeks ago a Lebanese intelligence officer passed us some information they'd intercepted over the Syrian communication network. Basically, he told us that there were orders for any western journalists caught around Homs to be executed on the spot and their bodies thrown on to the battlefield. Statements would be issued by the Assad regime saying they were killed in crossfire.'

J-P considered this for a moment. He asked if he could quote me on it without giving away my source, before deciding that he'd still like to press ahead with the crossing into Syria regardless. To give him his due, he certainly had balls.

A very physical reaction occurs when faced with extreme danger and I could feel the chemical changes beginning in my body. Adrenalin was being pumped into my system, my senses were heightened and I was far more aware of my surroundings than before. Then there was the fear. It's a natural, built-in warning system but it's something you actively have to keep a lid on or it can spin out of control. The combination of adrenalin and fear is a unique blend that is difficult to describe. It is something I consider healthy. Marie agreed. She was always the first to admit when she felt frightened and I would seriously worry if anyone told me they didn't get the fear at times like these. It's an asset rather than a handicap when you're about to cross an enemy front line: it ensures that your mind and body remain alert.

I was well aware of what awaited us out there. On the Lebanese side, there was the ever-present danger of Hezbollah patrols. Hezbollah were natural allies of President Bashar al-Assad and his government. They were also enemies of the Sunni rebels who were taking us under their wing. The border area we were passing through was Hezbollah's domain. They were well trained and well armed and had little sympathy for journalists using Lebanon as a staging post on their way to Syria.

On the Syrian side, we had to contend with the regular Syrian army, which was always on the lookout for arms smugglers coming in from Lebanon. They shot to kill and rarely took prisoners. This was a brutal combination that had caused the deaths of hundreds who had tried to make this crossing in recent months: wounded civilians, smugglers and rebels alike had all been legitimate targets in the eyes of the pro-government security forces that were strung out along the border. To add to this cocktail of danger, the area was also heavily mined. Mines were hidden killers; war's invisible soldiers. Death would stalk every footstep of our crossing.

As I waited to mount the vehicle, I thought back to the border crossing I'd made into Libya a year ago, when the revolution had first ripped through the rogue North African state as rebel forces fought to topple the mad dictator, Colonel Muammar Gaddafi.

5 March 2011, Egypt/Libya border

The scene at the Egypt–Libya border had been one of abject misery. Thousands of sub-Saharan migrant workers were fleeing the fighting in Libya and the border crossing had become a bottleneck for those seeking sanctuary in Egypt. Small camps had risen up anywhere that provided shelter from the blistering heat. People lay on cardboard in the dirt. Everywhere you looked were the zombie-like faces of the dispossessed, staring blankly through traumatised eyes.

I navigated the chaotic scene to the departure kiosk at the border post. On the other side of a metal fence were thousands of people queuing to enter Egypt. On the exit from Egypt into Libya there were, unsurprisingly, far fewer. Well, one in fact – me.

I waited half an hour for the Egyptian customs officer, who had clearly taken an extended lunch break. He ambled back through the chaos, careful to avoid the human detritus huddled on the floor, and let himself into his kiosk. He sat, lit a cigarette, inhaled deeply and looked at me. I offered my passport and said, 'Libya.' He returned my gaze with one of dull disbelief. He shrugged, stamped my passport and slipped the passport back through the glass with a 'Good luck'.

No one really knew what was actually happening on the Libyan side. Rumour had it that armed gangs were robbing everyone and chaos abounded. I had been told that it would be seriously foolhardy to risk crossing into Libya. There was only one way to find out. I started walking along the two-kilometre stretch of road that led across no-man's-land. Either side of me, Egyptian tanks aimed their barrels towards Libya.

It was blazing hot. The heat sapped my energy as I walked into the unknown. Eventually, Libyan border control loomed in the distance. The tension in me mounted as I continued the dusty walk towards the isolated post. When I got there, the post seemed abandoned. All the doors to the offices were broken open and the green flags of the Gaddafi regime lay strewn in the dust.

Out of nowhere I heard a voice shout in English. 'Hey! Hey, man! Are you a journalist?'

I turned to see a man dressed in a mixture of combat fatigues and civilian clothes. He had long hair, a headband and a long black beard. In his hands he carried the ubiquitous AK47 assault rifle. He appeared to be smiling as he approached me. My mind began to whir: was he one of the armed robbers I'd heard so much about?

'No, I'm a photographer,' I replied, hoping that this information would slip me a step lower down the food chain than a journalist. 'How are you?' I asked, reaching out my hand to shake his. He returned my gesture with a high five.

'A photographer,' he said, before pausing a moment. 'Then where the fuck are your cameras, man?'

I nodded towards my bag. At customs posts you do not take pictures. You hide cameras: customs and cameras are an unhealthy mix. I could hear myself saying goodbye to my precious tools. This is it, I thought. Robbed in my first few minutes in Libya.

'Then take some fucking pictures, man. No point in having cameras if you're not taking pictures,' he said, before adding merrily, 'Welcome to free Libya.'

I was stunned. I fumbled for my camera, eager to please this solitary machine-gun-toting border guard. It was the first time that I'd ever been ordered to take pictures at a border crossing. I snapped off a few shots of him posing with his AK47, another few of the ramshackle border post and then thanked him for his help. He laughed, fired off a few rounds into the air and waved me into Libya. I walked through the customs post and I was in. It was that easy.

13 February 2012, Lebanon/Syria border region

Now, as I stood waiting with Marie and J-P for my ride into Syria, I found myself hankering after such an easy crossing. As the three of us bundled our bags into a pickup truck and climbed on board, I knew that this was not going to be a 'Welcome to free Libya' kind of crossing. The tension in the cold evening air was palpable. J-P seemed most affected. His breathing had grown heavy and he appeared distracted. Marie was outwardly as calm as ever. She also looked the part: her black jacket pulled tightly over her body armour made her look like a stocky commando; her tight black jeans and a black rucksack completed the look. She always seemed to pull these things off with a panache that I lacked. I looked like a tramp, with my tatty old combat trousers and green jacket.

The pickup fired unhealthily into life and started bouncing its way out of the farm and on to a tarmac road. There was total silence in the back. We were all lost in our own thoughts, each of us dealing with what lay ahead in our own, solitary ways. About one kilometre down the road, the pickup slowed to a crawl. In the distance, the familiar crack of automatic-rifle fire echoed through the dusky night. The shots, no more than a kilometre away, brought home to us exactly what we were just about to attempt.

We arrived at another neo-classical concrete farm building and parked outside. Again, I recognised the place from my last trip. Dismounting from the truck, I was greeted by a smiling face. It was Hussein – the guide who'd taken Miles and I over on the last crossing. He greeted me like long-lost family. It was reassuring to see a familiar face.

Marie, who was gathering her things from the truck, saw our bearded, fat-eating rebel friend and took the opportunity to talk to him.

'Is it safe?' she asked, nodding towards Syria.

The bearded rebel smiled. 'Of course it's safe.' He laughed, before disappearing on his motorbike into the hazy gloom of the evening light, still chuckling softly to himself.

J-P stood silently, observing events unfolding around him.

A group was beginning to form: three men with AK47s and another three, armed with pistols, were chatting among themselves in a circle. There was a short discussion and then Hussein, my old smuggling buddy, approached me. He said nothing – he had no English – but he gestured for us to follow him and then pressed a finger to his lips. This is it, I thought. We were about to cross no-man's-land. We had no one with us who spoke any English and we had no idea what plans had been put in place for us once we made it into Syria.

We started out on a track that led from Hussein's house. Three armed rebels stayed on point, followed by Marie, J-P and myself, with one rebel guarding the line to the rear. I could hear very little other than the sounds of feet on earth and heavy breathing. There were short bursts of machine-gun fire in the near distance, forcing us to crouch low, our hearts pumping while our guides desperately tried to figure out where the shots had come from.

We cut off the path we'd been following and stooped low under some wires that fenced off a field. We skirted round the edges of the fields, acutely aware that the area had been heavily mined. We tried to follow directly in the footsteps of the lead person, afraid in case we stepped out of line and triggered a mine.

More gunshots rang out, forcing us to press ourselves against the earth. This time the bullets were much closer. To our left, about a hundred metres away, we could make out a Syrian army patrol base. We crept silently through the fields around the post, our bodies and minds raked with fear, praying that the soldiers in the watchtowers failed to spot us. My mouth turned dry and my breathing grew heavy, sending out thick clouds of steam on the cold air. I forced myself to breathe in through my nose and out through my mouth to regulate my breathing and calm my nerves. Every sound seemed amplified: the snap of a twig, the rustle of a rucksack or the tripping sound of someone stumbling seemed to scream, 'We are here, come and get us, you must be deaf not to hear us.'

We pressed on, scrambling through ditches and up embankments in what seemed like a cacophony of noise. Several bullets snapped suddenly over our heads. We crouched down and waited, blood thumping in our ears again. We are the hunted, I thought. If anything happened now we would be trapped in no-man's-land. Our only chance would be to head south, back into Lebanon. But, without a guide and without knowledge of enemy positions and minefields, we would be at the mercy of lady luck.

Hussein signalled for us to move again, this time across an open field. We were exposed on all sides and the buildings ahead seemed far away. The field was thick with mud and our feet were soon heavy with solid red earth that clawed us back, slowing us down. Eventually we reached the ramshackle buildings. It felt safer there. Suddenly, a single flash from a torch about ten metres ahead came out of the dark. The figure of a man emerged. He had his hood up, which made him look like a black ghost in the twilight. He gave the all clear for the next move. We sprinted across some uncultivated land between two clusters of derelict buildings, fully expecting the machine guns and grenades of hidden Syrian forces to open fire on us. Yet nothing happened. We made it to an empty street in a small, seemingly deserted village. A tiny light glowed eerily up ahead of us. We approached it in silence. The light turned out to be a rebel on a motorbike – our pistol-toting, fat-eating friend again. He had the engine off so we only had a dim red light to guide us in.

We huddled around the rebel as a whispered conversation took place. One of the other rebels motioned for Marie to climb on the back of a motorcycle. The rider kick-started the machine and disappeared down the street without his headlights on. As I watched Marie disappear into the darkness on the back of the rebel bike, I inwardly saluted her courage.

The rest of us continued on foot, sticking to the shadows of the buildings to avoid detection. I could hear J-P alongside me, his breathing laboured. He sounded exhausted, so I signalled silently to him to see if he was okay. He nodded. Red tracer rounds from automatic weapons pierced the darkening skies, shooting up long arcs above us. We soon spotted the dark shape of a vehicle in the distance. Once alongside it, we threw our kit in the back and silently climbed in. The truck moved off slowly, again without lights. Over the noise of the engine more shots rang out. I asked myself how long it had been since we started walking. It could have been ten minutes or an hour. I'd lost all sense of time. Flooded with adrenalin, my body had begun to shake.

The truck travelled at a torturously slow speed as the driver tenderly nursed the gears to keep noise to a minimum. In the back, J-P and I tried to catch our breath. He was wheezing badly, reawakening my fears that he was not fit enough to make the journey. My own breath was still coming in large gasps and my mouth was so dry I could hardly open it. For once in my life I actually thought I needed water more than a cigarette. We were still vulnerable: the stretch of road we were on ran parallel to the border and it was heavily patrolled by pro-Assad troops in armoured personnel carriers. I watched the road ahead and occasionally saw a single flash of light from the roadside. As we slid silently past, soldiers of the rebel Free Syrian Army (FSA) loomed out of the shadows, patrolling the road and giving the all clear to their own vehicles.

Without warning, the truck turned off the main road and we started down a rougher mud track. Our destination was an FSA safe house. Within a few minutes we caught a glimpse of the soft glow of light from a small building through the straggly orchards. The truck glided to a halt outside a house which looked very much like the one we had just left. As we dismounted from the truck, Marie appeared at the doorway. Without waiting for me to enter, she walked straight over and gave me a huge hug. We were in Syria. The relief was palpable.

'Jesus, Paul,' she said, laughing nervously. 'That was fucking insane.'

I smiled back and hugged her again. 'I told you it was a bit hairy scary.'

'I could almost smell those guys we were that close,' she said, referring to the Syrian border soldiers we'd just crept past.

We walked together to the building and I told her my concerns about J-P. He sounded like an old accordion when we were moving across the border.

'Marie, I need to smoke badly, very badly indeed,' I gasped, removing my boots.

'You've come to the right place then.' She chuckled.

We entered the room. It was a reassuring sight: a thick cloud of static smoke hung in the windowless room. Within seconds I was bombarded with offers of cigarettes from FSA soldiers huddled around the diesel heater. I accepted them all, sat down, lit up and began to process what had just happened. My pulse rate began to drop and my breathing returned to near normal. There was nothing complicated in the way my brain now worked: all it had to do was to ensure that I sat there in silence, intermittently uttering the word 'shit'. I looked across the room at Marie and J-P. They seemed to be undergoing the same mental debrief.

A solitary low-wattage bulb lit the room. It was a room of shadows and whispers, but it felt secure. Tea was produced – hot, sweet and delicious tea that seemed to stabilise my random collection of thoughts. The FSA soldiers appeared nervous. Their assault rifles were never far from their hands and their senses had clearly been honed by months of living within Assad-controlled areas. Any sound that penetrated the room from the outside caused everyone to fall silent and reach for their weapons. Bursts of static from the VHF radio punctuated the silence. The rebels gathered around the radio, trying to decipher the barely audible signal.

Marie turned to me. 'Paul, we can't afford to get bogged down here. We have to keep moving. Remember, there are journalists who've been stuck in towns along the border for months and haven't gotten anywhere near Homs.'

Marie was back on top form. The fear of the border crossing having dissipated, she was now on the story. She was calm and focused. She chose the rebel who seemed most in command and approached him. Of the two of us, Marie had the best Arabic and she was now putting it to good use. The rebel commander stood like a naughty schoolboy as Marie made it more than clear that we needed to get to Homs. He nodded, picked up his radio and started shouting aggressively to the poor sod on the receiving end. He then attempted to pacify Marie by saying 'Homs' a number of times while giving her the thumbs up. These guys were obviously not used to being ordered about by a female. I suspect they were simply shocked into action. Marie seemed satisfied and casually started making notes in her notepad.

After ten minutes, we heard a vehicle pull up outside, followed by the sound of slamming doors and then footsteps approaching the room in which we were huddled together for warmth. Framed in the doorway stood another heavily armed rebel. He greeted everyone in Arabic, looked at us and asked, 'Homs?' We all nodded eagerly. He motioned for us to get ready to leave before addressing the rebel commander who'd made the radio call. As in most Arabic conversations I overheard, it seemed as though some huge argument was under way. The reality was often completely different and on this occasion the two men ended the conversation with a hug and a kiss. We stood awkwardly awaiting the next command before he nodded for us to go outside.

Marie could hardly bend due to the body armour and extra clothing she was wearing, making each boot removal and refit a ten-minute debacle. I could hear her cursing and swearing in the dark as she attempted to do up her laces. I dreaded every stop that meant removing my boots. Because of his age and size, J-P was no quicker when it came to putting on his shoes. I prayed that, should there be any attack on our position, it would come at a time when we all had our footwear on.

The vehicle we mounted was a minivan similar to the one we'd taken from Beirut to the border. I was confident it would fail a British MOT test. In the front sat the driver, armed with a pistol. Next to him was a stocky, thickly bearded rebel with an AK47. In the back seat were two more rebels, both with AK47s. Again the tension mounted. We had no idea where we were heading but we could feel the cool silence of the driver and guards. There was no fear, only a tangible sense that they knew that what we were about to attempt was high risk. The FSA had many safe houses along the border area, but our little van would make great target practice for any Assad armoured column that we might encounter.

The vehicle spluttered into life, willed on by a stream of Arabic and occasional English expletives. The driver nursed the van out of the orchard. A single light flashed at us, giving us the all clear to mount the tarmac road. We knew that every kilometre travelled was one more kilometre from safety and another towards the killing fields of Homs. After two kilometres, the van turned right on to a muddy track. I knew from the stars that we'd made a northerly turn and that we would be heading towards the besieged town of Al-Qusayr. We inched our way along the track, the ruts in the ground an indication that this was a well-used route currently considered safe by the rebels.

The FSA guards were like hawks, continually scanning the trees and road ahead for signs of an ambush. Unlike some of the Libyan drivers that Marie and I had used during the revolution there, these guys knew what they were doing.

15 April 2011, Misrata, Libya

I remembered how, in the Libyan city of Misrata the year before, Marie had insisted that she wanted a proper driver who could keep his head under fire. Instead, we were given a bloke called Hakim, who was a young testosterone-fuelled boy racer. We were trying to find the new front line that the rebels had opened up the day before. The newly opened route to this front was of strategic importance. We wanted to travel it. Marie had pulled Hakim to one side and briefed him on what we wanted: to travel slowly, watching out for any ambushes that might have been set on the way.

We left Misrata early and reached the coast road by ten. Hakim had obeyed orders so far, but he soon grew bored and began to drive faster. Marie was getting pretty pissed off. She was annoyed that we'd been given Hakim in the first place and now he was ignoring everything she'd briefed him on earlier.

We turned off on to a tarmac road that took us due south. It was a road that, in theory, would lead us to the main battlefront at the town of Dafniya. Marie continued to urge caution. Although the road was allegedly clear of Gaddafi forces, you never quite knew in Libya: the fighting was so fluid and the fronts shifted the whole time. Hakim, who was lost in his own little world, sped down the road. And then it hit us – a blistering volley of small-arms and heavy machine-gun fire from a field and a hedge to the right. It ripped up the area around us. Hakim froze and jammed on his brakes, leaving us no option but to rapidly exit the vehicle.

I grabbed Marie and placed her behind the engine block. I took cover behind a wheel. The bullets screamed past, their terrible whistle flying inches above the car. We were pinned down. I spotted a drainage ditch about ten metres from the car and shouted to Marie that we had to make cover. I knew that if these guys had a rocket-propelled grenade we were done for.

Crawling around to the engine block, rounds landing inches away, I told Marie about the plan to reach the drainage ditch. She needed no encouragement. She crawled to the back of the vehicle and I told her that I'd shout when it was safe for her to run. I stuck my head up and drew fire while Marie ran to the ditch. Then I crawled around to the back of the truck. I sent Hakim next. He made it too. Encouraged by the bad shooting, I sprinted and then dived into the ditch. It was low enough to avoid any incoming fire, unless they brought out mortars.

Marie looked at me. 'Hey, Paul, I guess that's one way to find the front line: just drive into it.'

She had more words for Hakim. 'Hakim, you do not fucking well drive full speed down a road that we are unsure of, and you certainly don't stop and freeze when the bullets start firing. In the future, if there ever is one, you listen to me or Paul. Understood?'

Hakim nodded guiltily. He knew he'd got it wrong. It would take a long time for him to recover from Marie's fiery lecture. We were pinned down for two hours in that position until a unit of Libyan rebels, hearing the commotion, arrived to check out what was happening. A battle ensued and the rebels eventually drove back the Gaddafi unit that had attacked us.

13 February 2012, Syria

Now, as we bumped over the muddy track, pushing ever deeper into Syrian territory, I thanked the stars that Hakim wasn't with us. The rebels we were with seemed sharp and professional. Not once did they fail to scan, watch or listen for any signs that things were out of the ordinary. They had a VHF handset and appeared to be in constant touch with a control centre somewhere. On occasion, they stopped the vehicle and took up defensive positions, but generally it was a smooth ride: slow, but certain.

At one point, we came across a small building. The rebels had lit a fire to keep warm and I counted at least twenty-seven armed fighters. After a quick word with our driver, they began refuelling our vehicle from jerrycans. Each man smoked as they did so. I joined them.

Marie seemed happy with the progress. 'Paul, I like these guys. They're not hotheads like the Libyans. They actually seem to have a plan. I don't know what it is yet, but at least they seem to have one.'

We continued our journey in short bursts through the inky black night. It was a unique experience, driving with no lights. Your night vision kicks in quickly and I could make out breaks in the trees and wide-open fields on either side of us. Eventually, we reached a small farm building with its lights on. Our escorts indicated for us to get out. They seemed relieved and for the first time since we'd left they chatted among themselves. I was convinced this would be our lay-up for the night. We'd crossed the border, made it into Syria and were now about to sleep. Day one, mission accomplished, I thought.

We took off our boots and entered the rebel farmhouse, unsure, as ever, about what to expect. It seemed that we had moved up a level: there were two gloomy 40-watt bulbs and a diesel heater that would melt steel. Inside the room were four FSA soldiers who each stood up and greeted us in turn. One spoke perfect English and told us that we could stay the night with them. We would be safe as the nearest Assad unit was over a kilometre away, the rebel told us. Great, I thought. A whole kilometre.

We sat, drank coffee and generally tried to get a sense of what was happening in the area. The picture we got was that the FSA was still very much a defensive force. It lacked weapons and ammunition and it also lacked secure communications, which was one of its largest problems, preventing the rebel outfit from being able to coordinate as efficiently as its fighters would have liked.

While we chatted, we heard another car pull up outside. The door to the room opened and there, to my complete amazement, was Abu Sallah. He ran straight over to me and hugged me like a long-lost brother. Each of us was as delighted as the other at our unexpected meeting. Abu Sallah and I had become firm friends on my last trip into Syria. He was one of the fighters who had helped get me out of Syria when news spread that Assad's forces were looking for us. To see such a familiar face, out of the blue like this, gave me confidence that we were with the right people. I explained this to Marie and she looked relieved that we were among people we knew.

Abu Sallah invited us to stay at his house. It wasn't far from our current location and I would know more people there. Arriving at the house was like a grand reunion. Faces I'd said goodbye to in a hurry only a month before were now gathered around with welcoming smiles and hugs. In many ways it was akin to coming home. We were immediately elevated to five-star status. Marie was given her own room, and mattresses were laid out for J-P and myself.

J-P, rather strangely, elected to sleep in the reception room of the house. It was cold and empty but I guess he needed sleep. I noticed that he'd changed from his everyday clothes into a pair of long johns and matching top.

'J-P,' I said, 'we're in a house less than a kilometre from an Assad tank and infantry unit. Are you sure you're comfortable in pyjamas?'

Another Gallic shrug greeted my warning. Damn, I thought, I'm living in what I'm wearing for the whole trip. If Assad's forces chose to strike that night at least I'd die with my trousers on.

I left J-P to his bed and rejoined Abu Sallah in the main room, where a game of cards had just begun. As we played, a hot, sweaty and exhausted-looking rebel burst into the room. Everyone stopped and listened as he spoke. There were a few murmurs and someone made a VHF radio call to someone else. The soldier who'd burst into the room slumped down in the corner. The card game continued.

Abu Sallah turned to me and smiled. 'Paul, can you run very quickly?' he asked.

'Erm, yes, not too bad,' I said, a tad suspicious. 'Why?'

Abu Sallah grinned. 'We have just got news that Assad's forces are attacking this house tomorrow. We might have to do some very fast running.'

'Are you taking the piss?' I asked.

'No,' he replied and went back to his game of cards.

It was now four o'clock in the morning, so I clambered into bed. I struggled to sleep. It wasn't the noise of the card game keeping me awake, but the image of J-P in his long johns making a dash across the fields as government forces stormed our house.

I woke a few hours later to the sounds of vehicles and the noise of a small army gathering outside the window. Abu Sallah entered the room with a beaming smile on his face. 'Paul, get up. The general is here with all his men. He wants to meet you and have some photographs taken.'

I scrambled out of bed and ran to knock on Marie's door. 'Marie, the general is here. He wants photos taken, and he wants to meet us.'

'General? Which general?' she asked as the sleep faded from her eyes. 'Right, you take some shots and I'll talk to him. This could be the next move forward.' She was smiling as she spoke, her brain running at full speed as she thought about how to make the most of a visiting general.

I went outside with my camera to take some photographs and shoot some video. There were hundreds of FSA soldiers hanging out in the garden. Almost every weapon possible was on display. It was an amazing sight to see. I was busy shooting away when I caught a glimpse of Marie being introduced to a man who I assumed was the general. I continued to shoot stills of the FSA unit and then, half an hour later, Marie appeared. It had clearly gone well. Triumph was written all over her face. The general then made a speech that I duly filmed. I was itching to get the news from Marie but a rebel had taken it upon himself to direct the shoot and it seemed to take an age before the general finished his speech to camera.

I grabbed Marie as soon as I could. 'What's happening?' I asked impatiently. 'You're looking pretty smug with yourself.'

Marie beamed at me. 'We've got a lift to the town of Al Buwaydah, with General Reeda, this morning. It's about fifteen kilometres from Homs and he'll introduce us to the right people to get us into Baba Amr.'

I could have hugged her. Marie had that touch with these guys. She was tenacious and, where a lesser mortal might back down or be intimidated, Marie would coax and persuade until she got what she wanted. We were to have breakfast with the general and then leave for Al Buwaydah.

We ate in a circle in the main room – a meal of yoghurt, cheese and tinned tuna with sweet tea. I'd eaten enough tinned tuna in Libya to last a lifetime and I was averse to the sight and smell of it, but Marie still loved it and she tucked in. The coffee came round and I refuelled. I had a feeling we might need the caffeine today. After only a few hours' sleep and the previous night's border crossing, fatigue was beginning to set in.

Breakfast over, we were told to grab our bags and mount up in the general's personal Transit van. J-P looked terribly haggard. The place he'd chosen to sleep had turned out to be a major thorough-fare, with rebel fighters coming and going throughout the night.

We had crossed the border at night and survived, but it was now a completely different scenario. We were to travel through enemy lines in daylight. The prospect was terrifying. The darkness of the night brings a sense of comfort: you feel protected. A journey in broad daylight does the opposite. All main roads in the area were under the complete control of Assad's security forces and so we'd have to weave cross-country for thirty kilometres until we reached our next destination – the town of Al Buwaydah.

We had four fully armed FSA guards with us – the general's personal bodyguards – plus the general himself. The men fell silent as we departed. Everyone was aware of the risk and we were content to keep our thoughts to ourselves. About a mile from the house where we'd met the general a motorcycle appeared on the track ahead of us. We kept a distance of about five hundred metres from the motorcycle, whose driver acted as our scout. Occasionally we'd stop while he checked a bend in the road before giving the thumbs up for us to proceed.

The van soon left the potted mud tracks and started driving across ploughed fields. The sense of imminent danger increased. All four bodyguards scoured the horizon with binoculars. I occasionally caught Marie's eye, which told me all I needed to know: she was alert but her mannerisms were tense, as were J-P's. I could feel the apprehension rise among all of us. You try to distract your mind but the reality bites as every gunshot or explosion drags you, kicking and screaming, back to earth. You then start the tiresome process of mental preparation all over again.

We hid behind bushes when the sound of heavy machine-gun fire grew too close for comfort. The thunder of artillery in the distance also served as a constant reminder of the threat we faced. As we drove through villages, the bodyguard to my right called out the religious affiliation of the area. 'Christian, Allawite, Sunni,' he said. 'We're careful about the Allawite. They have allegiance only to Assad. We do not stop here.' Damned right, I thought. Why the hell would we do that?

We followed the motorbike across terrain that no two-wheel-drive van should ever attempt. The recent rain had made the going treacherous and I hoped that if we got bogged down it would be nowhere near an Allawite village.

We were now driving through forest tracks, with the expert driver weaving an impossible route through the trees. Marie uttered one of her only words of the journey, a pure sweet and simple 'Fuck'. It broke the tension in the vehicle. Even the general turned round and smiled. We broke the cover of the forest and turned once more on to a mud track. We took another turn and for the first time in hours we were back on a tarmac road. The scout ahead waved us through.

We passed a few houses, then a few more and soon we were in a small town. Snaking through the narrow backstreets with the sound of heavy artillery fire in the distance now constant, the bodyguard nodded to our right. He said one word – 'Homs' – before shaking his head slowly. His face was the image of true sadness and my heart bled for him.

The vehicle made a final turn in the narrow backstreets and pulled gently to a halt. The general and two bodyguards dismounted and banged on two steel gates. Within a minute they opened and the men disappeared into the house. Marie turned to me.

'How are you? That was scary as fuck, eh?'

'I think I preferred minefields at night. Far more relaxing than that,' I said, exhaling from the twentieth smoke of the day.

'Do you reckon this is a stopover?' Marie asked.

'I reckon. If we drove any further we'd be in Homs. That shelling is close, very close,' I replied.

This did nothing to reassure Marie so we fell back into silent reflection until shouting from the house prompted one of the bodyguards to lead us through the gates. Well, this is it for today at least, I thought, as we followed him inside. The steel gates were heavy and solid. They led into a small garden with a house set back among struggling shrubbery. We took off our boots, entered the house and were directed into a room immediately to our left. It was empty. The cushions and the diesel heater were identical to the ones in all the houses we had visited so far. The general came in and sat with us next to his bodyguards and a small boy.

'We must wait,' said the general.

So we sat, drank tea, smoked, attempted jokes and killed time. Half an hour passed before we heard the metal gates open and the sound of voices filling the garden. Marie and I exchanged glances. We both smiled. We were nearing the top of the FSA food chain and we both knew it.

About six men entered the room. There was an outbreak of

kissing, hugging and general greeting. When everyone had finished, one man stepped forward. He spoke little English but managed the words, 'So, you want to go to where?'

Marie looked him in the eye and held his gaze. 'Homs, Baba Amr.'

The commander smiled wryly, thought a little and said, 'Then I think we can help. Please, sit down and relax.'

CHAPTER FOUR

The lion's den

15 February 2012, Al Buwaydah, Syria

We sat facing the commander in silence. We knew he wanted to help, but still the feeling of being sat in front of the headmaster pervaded the atmosphere.

'If it's about smoking in a war zone I'm snitching on you, Paul,' Marie said out of the side of her mouth.

The commander addressed one of his bodyguards who immediately turned and raced out of the room. He then turned his attention on us.

'Please wait,' said the burly figure dressed in combat fatigues. 'We have a man who talks perfect English. He will come now. My job is to get food and medicine into Baba Amr and to get very sick people out. Please tell me why you want to go there. But wait until our translator arrives – it's not just your English I don't understand.'

The town of Al Buwaydah where we'd stopped was typical of most rural villages in the area. Religiously, it was. Sunni, but physically it was almost identical to most rural villages in the area, small and dominated by single-storey cement-constructed houses that were built in a maze of small alleyways and obscure cul-de-sacs.

The town was poor and life here appeared to have suffered since the start of the revolution. A shellhole there, a crater here proved that the place hadn't escaped President Assad's notice. If the guns were turned on this town in full, however, then there would be little anyone could do. Al Buwaydah was built on an open plain. There were already shells falling here and there would be nowhere to hide once they began to fall in earnest.

Marie was light-hearted and in good spirits. Her mood since we'd arrived at the house in Al Buwaydah had been bright and optimistic and she took the break in the stressful journey as a chance to unwind.

'Hey, Paul, remember looking for Gaddafi's body in the desert?' she asked, laughing her familiar deep chuckle. The rest of the room – mainly bodyguards who spoke a little English – swivelled to face us as she continued. 'Didn't the picture editors ask you to get a photo of Gaddafi's unmarked grave in the desert?'

I grinned at the memory. 'Yep,' I replied. 'An unmarked grave in the desert. I remember I was tempted to photograph the hotel garden.'

23 October 2011, Misrata, Libya

Libyan rebels captured and killed Colonel Gaddafi on 20 October 2011. A few days later, Marie and I were asked to track down the site of the mad dictator's secret burial spot. We had a serious advantage over all the other grave-seekers: we knew the man who had buried Gaddafi. Salah, a forty-year-old lightly bearded rebel commander, who was lauded as one of the Libyan revolution's legends for his fierce courage and skilful leadership, appeared happy to see us again when we walked into his headquarters in the port city of Misrata. After an hour of chat, Marie popped the big question.

'So, erm, where *did* you bury Gaddafi? Can you can tell us, Salah?' she asked, hopefully.

Salah, as we knew, had sworn on the Koran that he would never reveal his secret. Obviously wanting to help, but being unable to tell us directly, he simply smiled back at Marie.

'You have been there before,' he said mysteriously. 'I took you there when we were fighting – the place with the tents on the ridge, about fifty kilometres south of the city, in the desert. You came along with me. Remember?'

My heart sank. Salah was actually telling us the place where Gaddafi was buried. Marie was smiling but I could read her mind: she had absolutely no clue where he was talking about. Salah could be telling us the location of the lost city of Atlantis and we still wouldn't have found it, even if we'd already been there. Marie looked at me. I grimaced back and mouthed the word 'more' at her. Salah, unaware of Marie's total lack of a sense of direction, thought that he'd just given us the location of the grave while still keeping his holy vow. Despite Marie's best efforts to wrestle more information from him, Salah wouldn't be pushed any further.

So the next day we rented a 4×4 and a driver. I had scanned through Google Earth the previous evening, looking for anywhere fifty kilometres south of Misrata that could be the sort of place where one would bury the body of a dead tyrant. We spent the next three days in the scorching desert heat searching out possible gravesites. At one point, I found myself kneeling on the ground examining piles of stones to see if any vehicles had driven over them recently. Needless to say, the whole mission was a failure. Our driver rebelled and refused to do any more of this 'stupid desert driving' and, in the end, we had to settle for a picture of Marie looking pensively out over the desert at dawn, a symbol of our fruitless search. It was the only picture of mine that the newspaper printed that week.

15 February 2012, Al Buwaydah, Syria

As Marie and I chatted about the final days of the Gaddafi regime in the small room in Al Buwaydah, waiting to hear whether we'd be allowed to enter Homs, the door to our room opened. The commander and a man in his late twenties entered. Everyone seemed to know the young man. They pointed at him, saying, 'English, English.' He had a soft, gentle smile and introduced himself as Wa'el. He sat between the commander and the three of us.

The commander began to talk. He spoke to Wa'el in very fast Arabic. Wa'el listened carefully, never once interrupting, which is always a good trait in a translator.

Wa'el finally explained, 'The commander says you are very brave to come this far and he salutes you but he wants to know why you need to go into Baba Amr. It is very dangerous: every day we lose our colleagues and people die trying to get in and out. He is extremely worried about you.'

Up until now, Marie had relied on my experience from my previous foray into Syria but now I deferred to her. This was now her territory. Her face was animated and her voice brimmed with passion.

'Commander,' she said, 'this is a very important story to get out. The world really needs to know what's happening here in Syria. We can't just sit by and watch murder take place. The world desperately needs to see what's happening inside Baba Amr. Please, if you don't take us in, then this carnage will slip past into history. Assad can crush you right now. You need people to see this. People will listen to me and they will see Paul's pictures. We can help: we can show the world; we can bear witness.'

Wa'el translated very carefully, stopping on occasion to confirm parts of Marie's speech and ensure he was translating it verbatim. The commander appeared genuinely moved by Marie's words. His eyes were gentle and kind but they were also flecked with the deep sadness brought about by war and the heavy losses he had suffered in recent months. Marie's speech obviously worked. He relayed, via Wa'el, that he would be proud to help us get into Baba Amr but that it would take some time to organise and that we must remain patient. We nodded in agreement. The commander then asked if I would take some pictures of his rebel brigade later that evening.

Marie turned to look at me and said, nodding towards Wa'el, 'Paul, this guy is good. We should get him as our translator.'

I nodded in agreement. Good translators were essential and hard to come by: I once had a translator in Iraq who openly admitted to me that he simply made up much of what he translated.

Marie turned to Wa'el. 'Hey, Wa'el, how would you like a job working with *The Sunday Times*?'

Wa'el paused a moment, looked at us and then said earnestly, 'Only on one condition: you do not pay me. I must serve my country. I will not accept any money. If you try to pay me I will resign.'

Marie tried to interrupt but Wa'el cut her dead. 'These are my terms. Take them or leave them. I will go to Baba Amr with you and I will bring you out alive.'

The room thinned out. The commander promised to return and fetch me once it had grown a little darker and I could photograph his brigade.

As we waited, we spoke with Wa'el. It turned out that he had quite a story to tell. He had once been a commando in the Syrian army but, as soon as he finished his military service, he'd grown his hair long, worn a beard and rebelled against his military experience. When the fighting broke out in Homs he decided to join the rebel cause. On one occasion, he was travelling with a group of FSA soldiers when government forces sprung an ambush on their column. Two of his companions were killed in the firefight that followed, but Wa'el made a lucky escape, fleeing into the countryside. He spent seven days living wild in ditches and foxholes, sleeping in the daytime, moving only at night and attempting to avoid the army who were now searching for him. He eventually made it home and was now serving the Free Syrian Army by acting as a conduit between the various FSA groups in the area. As a man of fierce principles, Wa'el refused to pick up a gun. He was, as he put it, a 'vegetarionist' and also, he whispered when the others were out of earshot, an atheist. He smiled a beautiful smile when he told us this last piece of information. Marie laughed. 'Wow, a vegetarionist atheist. That takes some doing in Syria!'

We all sat and smoked for a few hours, listening to Wa'el's remarkable story, until a vehicle arrived. We heard the heavy gates swing open. The commander had returned, having assembled his brigade on the outskirts of the town so that I could photograph his men. As soon as we left the building, we heard the worrying rumble of artillery shells bursting in the distance. The commander nodded towards a long plume of smoke drifting lazily across the beautiful orange sky. 'Homs,' he said. 'For fourteen days they do not stop now.'

I could feel the proximity of the explosions. They couldn't have been more than ten kilometres away. We drove in silence to a location about three kilometres outside the town, using a bewildering network of dirt tracks, fields and vast expanses of mud to avoid Syrian troop movements. Eventually, arriving at a small, abandoned factory, I caught my first sight of his brigade. They all wore balaclavas or keffiyehs to hide their faces. But the most conspicuous thing about them was their lack of weapons. I estimated that only half the rebels were armed.

The brigade lined up for a group shot. I framed the beautiful orange sky in the background as the awful plume of smoke slipped like a black scar across the sky. Against this backdrop were the men, full of bravado as they lined up, ready to fight and, if need be, die for a country broken by war.

After the shoot, many of the men approached me. They had taken off their balaclavas and scarves. I could now look into the eyes of this band of volunteers. Most of them were defectors from the governments' security forces, they told me, pulling out their army or secret police identity cards as proof.

'No Al-Qaeda here. We are all Syrian, all soldiers. We do not want Al-Qaeda here. We do this because we love our country,' said a twenty-year-old fighter, responding to media reports that Islamist extremists were trying to hijack and exploit the revolution for their own cause. I believed the young rebel.

Marie seemed excited when I returned to the house. She'd managed to gain permission to enter the only field hospital in Al Buwaydah, serving the besieged population of Homs. It was being run by a vet, she told me. I grabbed another camera and we headed outside to a waiting car that Marie had organised. One of the commander's bodyguards drove while Wa'el sat in the passenger seat. Marie was now truly flying. This is what it was all about for her – reporting on the ordinary people caught up in war. Much is written about journalists being war junkies or adrenalin addicts. I would challenge anyone in the world to accuse Marie of being one of these. Yes, she would jump borders and risk life and limb but only ever for the story; for the very people we were now about to visit. She had little time for people who accused foreign correspondents and photographers of being dysfunctional thrill-seekers.

The car wove through the narrow, pitch-black streets. Lighting was a forgotten luxury of the past. Drivers steered as much by instinct as by sight. Outside, we heard the ominous rumble of bombs and missiles as they rained down on Homs, while much closer by were the vicious and sporadic bursts of heavy machine-gun fire.

Through Wa'el, the driver said, 'Every night is like this. Assad's security forces try to stop anyone getting in or out of Homs. They have it surrounded. Many people are injured but today we only managed to get two sick people out.'

Statistically, that seemed like an impossibly small number of people. If only a tiny percentage of a day's shells hit their target, then Homs would be full of the dead and wounded. Marie must have being making the same calculations.

'Paul, it's a massacre in there,' she said. 'The shelling doesn't stop and that place is full of women and children, young and old. We really are going in. No matter what it takes, we are going in. We need to shout and scream to the world about this one. We don't back out now – deal?'

'You don't even need to ask, Marie, but you know this is not going to be as bad as it gets?' I replied.

'I know,' she said. 'I know.'

Once inside the field clinic, which in reality was just another spartan residential house, we were given our taster of the conditions that would face us inside the city. In the corner of the main sitting room lay a man who was semi-conscious and in obvious pain. His left leg was heavily bandaged. I saw his eyes flicker open occasionally before he passed, mercifully, back into what little comfort sleep could offer. Another man sat upright, a chest drain emptying into a large plastic drinks bottle on the floor beside him. The bottle was half full of blood. The ashen colour of death was slowly engulfing his pain-ridden face. Time was short for him: he had a bullet lodged near his heart. Not long now, I thought. The only way out for all these critically wounded patients was the route that Marie and I had taken to reach the area. It was, in many ways, a death sentence in itself for the severely wounded.

Wa'el introduced us to the 'doctor', who was in fact a veterinarian. Out of sheer necessity, he'd adopted the role of doctor in the previous months and now treated those lucky enough to escape from Homs. He was charismatic, laughed a lot given his circumstances and was well versed in gallows humour. He asked me for a cigarette. I told him doctors shouldn't smoke. He laughed and said, 'I'm a vet and the cows don't mind me smoking.'

Back at the house we ate a huge dinner, which was, as usual, laid on by the unseen women of the house. It was a welcome meal: we hadn't eaten properly for some time now. I was surviving on coffee and cigarettes, Marie on coffee alone.

My hunger having overcome my manners, I found that halfway through the meal I had already eaten a full bowl of falafels. In Syria, when you have a son, your own first name changes to Abu, which means 'father of', followed by the name of your first-born son. Hence, I was called Abu Max by all the rebels I met. Noticing how much I'd eaten, the commander pointed at me and announced grandly, 'Your name is no longer Abu Max. It is Abu Falafel.' From then on I was known only as Abu Falafel among the rebels – the Father of the Falafels.

During the meal, the familiar clang of the metal gates outside signalled the arrival of another visitor. The man who entered the room was clearly popular. Everyone stood for him, greeting him with kisses and slaps on the back. He was wrapped for warmth in a thick combat jacket, the customary keffiyeh and heavy-duty combat trousers. Despite these layers he still looked freezing. His name was Abu Zaid. It turned out that he was our guide on the motorbike from earlier; the same one who sped ahead of the general's convoy to make sure the route was clear for us while we were en route from the last town of Al-Qusayr.

Wa'el laughed on seeing him. 'They call him Blondie,' he told us.

When Abu Zaid unwrapped the scarf from around his face you got the joke. He was a deep chestnut colour, wind- and weather-beaten from a life outdoors. He was the most rugged-looking person I'd ever seen: short but built like an ox, with skin the texture of tanned leather.

Wa'el continued, 'Every night he loads his bike with bread and medical supplies and then drives to within two kilometres of the edge of Homs. He then hides the bike and carries a forty-five-kilogram load across the government-controlled highway into the city, delivers the aid and then retraces his route. Every night. Before the war he was a treasure hunter for twenty years. He would dig tunnels into old burial grounds looking for antiques. Twenty years and he never found a thing.'

Wa'el translated what he'd said back into Arabic for the benefit of the others. The whole room burst out laughing. Abu Zaid laughed along too. He didn't seem to know the meaning of the word vanity.

Abu Zaid turned to Wa'el. 'Tell them they will be coming in with me. They will walk crouched down for two miles, pass a govern-ment-occupied school and then, when a vehicle passes on the highway, they must cross it quickly, running fast while Assad's troops are blinded by the headlights. If they see us they will shoot to kill.'

Marie and I caught each other's eye. Marie spoke first. 'Jesus, Paul, that sounds fucking scary but it sounds like the way Stu got in.' She was referring to Stuart Ramsay, Sky TV's veteran foreign correspondent, who'd told us that he had to sprint across an open highway at night to enter the besieged city.

'Yeah, sounds a bit more frightening than the border crossing. The whole plan basically acquaints to, erm, run like hell.'

'What the fuck were we expecting – a taxi?' Marie drawled back.

J-P was trying his best to keep up with the discussion. We told him of the plan and he returned to his silent reverie. That night, after the meal, Marie was taken to another house to sleep, along with the rest of the women. She was treated to a bed while J-P and I grabbed some cushions and slept in a room full of rebels. J-P reverted to long johns and soon the nightmarish image of him fleeing a combat zone in pyjamas returned to haunt my sleep. As a gesture, I slept without my combat jacket on. Even then I felt naked.

Another day passed in the house. We killed time. There was no point trying to pressure the rebels into speeding up our departure. This was their neighbourhood. They made the rules and we played by them. Nonetheless, the waiting, as usual, was a killer. We drank coffee and smoked as various rebel fighters came and went. On day three, the commander summoned us all together. We duly sat down and began to drink more coffee around the diesel heater.

The commander adopted a deep, serious tone. 'Paul, Marie, J-P, we have had a change of plan,' he said.

I groaned inwardly and I noticed Marie slump next to me. We expected the worst: after the optimism of the last few days our plans were about to turn to dust. I lit a cigarette and waited for the final nail in the coffin.

The commander continued, 'We like you but the way into Homs is very dangerous. We will let you use our special way in.'

Special way in? I thought to myself. Once again Marie and I exchanged glances. J-P looked delighted at the news but he didn't have to cope with the image that was forming in my mind. It was the same image that I knew was now creeping into Marie's.

The commander smiled, delighted to be giving us news that he thought would make us happy. 'We will take you into Homs through the tunnel.'

The tunnel, the tunnel, I thought with dread. I was mute, unable to process any other thought. I turned to Marie. 'The fucking tunnel, remem—' I began.

Marie cut me off. 'Yes, the Spanish photographer . . . "Enjoy the tunnel",' she said, referring to the mysterious journalist we'd met as we prepared to cross the border into Syria from Lebanon.

There was silence in the room. The smile on the commander's lips had been replaced by one of puzzlement. He seemed a touch hurt by our subdued response to his cheery message. Marie realised that someone had to say something. She slowly managed to form the question.

'Erm, how long is the tunnel, Commander?'

He was smiling again. 'It's only three kilometres and safer than running across the road. It is a storm drain,' he said jollily. 'You cannot stand up properly and there is not much air but it can be done.'

J-P chipped in with, 'Did he say three kilometres?'

I nodded silently and J-P returned once more to his own private world to digest the information.

But the commander wasn't finished yet. 'The other good news is we will go in tonight. My men will come for you later. Please be ready,' he said with a smile before leaving the room.

Wa'el seemed happier than all of us. 'Don't be so worried,' he said, trying to reassure us. 'The tunnel is the best way in. They even have a motorbike in it.'

'What!' exclaimed Marie. 'They have a motorbike in a storm drain – am I dreaming this?'

Wa'el smiled. 'No, it's true. They have adapted it for moving supplies and injured people through the tunnel. You will see it. You may even go on it.'

I had told Wa'el my break-out story, and now he excitedly told the other rebels in the room about my attempted escape from a British military prison. They joked and I was made an honorary Mujahedeen. We all laughed for a while but slowly, inevitably, our thoughts returned to the tunnel.

'You know, Paul, I don't know what sounds worse: running across the highway at night or walking for three kilometres through a damned tunnel,' Marie said.

'Sounds like we have no choice. The old commander seemed pretty bent on the tunnel idea to me. Tunnel it is, I think,' I said, a hint of resignation creeping in.

We sat in silence. All minds were now concentrated on a tunnel we had never seen, a tunnel we would have to pass through knowing that at the other end we'd be greeted by the full force and rage of the Assad regime's tanks, machine guns, snipers and artillery.

Wa'el left to pack a small bag, leaving us alone with our thoughts. The next few hours were spent in preparation: batteries were charged as we checked and stowed our kit and conversation dropped to a minimum. When making plans to enter somewhere like Homs, there is always a part of me that thinks it will never actually happen. I believe that somehow it will all be called off at the last minute and I will return home, unscathed by the evils of war. As the goal gets closer, that feeling retreats and I slowly begin to accept it might really happen. Our discussion with the commander about the tunnel an hour before had confirmed that, bar a sudden change of circumstances, the moment was finally upon us and it was time to let go of that last remnant of doubt.

Wa'el returned and hilarious laughter broke the contemplative silence in the room. He looked the part: black jacket, combat pants and a black hat. But the laughter was in response to the bag he was carrying: it was a bright blue and red bag with a picture of a character from a children's programme called, strangely enough, *SpongeBob SquarePants*. It was beautifully surreal: Wa'el the earnest ex-commando ready to undergo an extremely dangerous mission with a bag that would delight any four-year-old cartoon fan. It served to lighten the atmosphere in the room for a while.

When the move finally happened it was quick. We heard cars pulling up at the gate and the sound of running feet. One man – a face we'd never seen before – called for us to come outside. Surrounding the two vehicles were our friends from the house and a new group of FSA fighters who seemed very highly strung. A rapid conversation took place between the two groups before we were signalled to get into the waiting cars. Goodbyes were solemn and brief. Within minutes we were on the move, the comfort of the house and our new friends already a fading memory.

I asked Wa'el why things were so frantic. He was sitting in the back of the car and I turned round to face him as he spoke, his face sombre. 'Paul, this is a very dangerous part of the journey. We are in the heart of Assad-controlled territory. All the roads are controlled by Assad's troops, they have snipers on all the high buildings and the checkpoints are moved every day. We must drive through this area to get near the tunnel. Sometimes we get ambushed and many men have died just trying to get to the tunnel. These men never relax: it could happen at any moment.' He paused to make sure his English was correct before concluding, 'We are now entering the lion's den.'

I was almost sorry I'd asked: ignorance sometimes really can be bliss. I turned to Marie. She sat motionless, staring out of the window. I could imagine the thoughts going through her mind. I was probably having exactly the same myself. The idea that at any moment we could be ambushed, that death could strike immediately and we'd be defenceless in its face, stirred up a plethora of emotions. Every turn in the road, every explosion, every bullet whizzing past the vehicle brought me back to the edge. Not for a second could I trick my body into relaxing. It was like walking a tightrope between life and death on a windy day: it could go either way.

The cars pulled up and sharp whispered orders were given in the evening light. The rebels placed me in the back of a cement lorry with a single FSA guard. Marie, Wa'el and J-P were put, I think, in a small white van. The whole changeover took seconds. The tension in the air indicated that what was happening was indeed an extremely dangerous manoeuvre.

Within moments we were on the move again. The vehicles in the convoy drove slowly, without headlights. The sun had set and once again we moved in the dusky half-light favoured by the military and rebels alike. I watched the guard alongside me. Never for a second did he stop scanning the horizon behind the vehicle. He had loaded and cocked his AK47 when we mounted the truck. He was expecting action.

It was a rough ride and painfully slow. Sometimes we stopped for ten minutes at a time while scouts reconnoitred the roads and turnings ahead. I'd often catch myself failing to breathe properly and have to force my breathing back into a regular pattern. What the fuck am I doing? I thought.

The journey took about an hour, a week. I don't know. I lost track of the world I existed in and only snapped out of my trance when the vehicles pulled to a halt and I was told to dismount by my guard. As I climbed down from the truck, I was greeted by Marie, J-P and Wa'el, as well as a bunch of FSA soldiers who signalled for us to follow them. No one spoke a word as we trudged across ground that was strewn with rubble. Eventually we arrived at a blacked-out house where a rebel beckoned us inside.

It was boots off chaos again but we eventually entered another typical Syrian home. It was warm inside and about five FSA soldiers sat smoking around the diesel heater. Tea was poured for us as we took stock of our situation. It was impossible to relax at moments like this. With no timescale to work on, my brain never stopped thinking about the next move. The FSA soldiers did their best to assure us that all was well. They gave us cigarettes, smiled and tried to tell us that the tunnel was nothing to worry about.

'What do you think, Paul?' asked Marie. 'These guys seem to know their stuff pretty well.'

'I feel good about them. They're not chancers. They're all ex-military and seem to know what they're doing. I just can't shake the fact that this is the easy bit and the tunnel is where the fun starts,' I replied.

'Same here,' said Marie. 'We're close to the shelling now. Can you feel it?'

It was hard to miss: the deep rumbles of high-explosive shells reverberated around the room. Except they were no longer sounds, they were now feelings. The small arms and machine-gun fire was also extremely close. Before, the rebels had barely flinched at the sound of gunfire; now they looked and cocked their heads to sense the direction of fire. We were deep within the battle zone of Homs. I was exhausted already but, when I thought that these guys lived this life every day, a pang of shame ran through me. If this was how I felt after only a few hours, God only knows how they were feeling.

There was a short burst of static followed by a message on one of the hand-held VHF radio sets. Immediately, three of the FSA soldiers stood up. They picked up their weapons, checked their magazines and armed their AK47s. This is it, I thought. Wa'el confirmed my suspicions.

'Paul, we're going into the tunnel,' he said. 'We must stay close together and be completely silent. There are government patrols only a few hundred yards away. Do not speak and do as you're told. It's very important now.' He delivered the same message to Marie and J-P.

I must confess that, just then, the idea of sitting at home, drinking a hot coffee and watching television seemed a very attractive alternative to what was about to happen – and I don't even enjoy watching television. We gathered in a small pack outside the house. A quick headcount was conducted before the leader of the small band of rebels began walking. We followed in single file. I put Marie ahead of me so I could keep her in my sight – her blindness in one eye made travel at night treacherous for her. Wa'el followed behind me with FSA troops to the rear.

Initially, we travelled through gardens and between houses but slowly the terrain changed, opening out into fields with deep trenches dug on either side. The ground was uneven and it took a lot of effort to keep up with the FSA guide ahead of us. At one point, I lost sight of Marie and had to scan the horizon for movement. I caught sight of her about a hundred yards away, wandering off in a different direction.

I caught up with her and whispered into her ear, 'Where the fuck are you off to – Damascus?'

'Paul,' she whispered back, slightly embarrassed, 'I can't see a fucking thing. I keep moving in circles.'

I took her by the hand and we caught up with our friends of

the night. The comfort of another person's hand in yours at such a moment is a wonderful feeling. It gives hope when it is most needed.

We trudged on silently as the terrain continued to change. We hugged a treeline that extended into the darkness ahead of us. Spread out in a long line, we reached a two-metre-high wall that was surrounded by bushes. Two FSA soldiers took up position at the foot of the wall, cupped their hands and literally threw people over the wall head first. Unfortunately, Marie got stuck on the top. Her body armour snagged and she began to spin in a circle like a turtle stuck on its back, unable to move. I could hear her laughing as she spun. All it took was a quick push and she was over on the other side.

We continued in this manner for about two kilometres, crossing every obstacle imaginable: rocks, boulders, trenches and even broken farm machinery. Shots pierced the cold air but, as the night drew on, the seemingly ceaseless bombardment of Baba Amr grew more sporadic. We climbed another wall – this time about three metres high – and found ourselves next to a factory, facing us were a line of trees, perhaps ten metres distant, that ran parallel with the factory wall, creating a sheltered piece of land that offered some cover. The FSA soldiers indicated in sign language that government snipers were active. We must proceed slowly and, more to the point, silently.

Almost on tiptoe, we followed the line of trees for about two hundred metres. No one made a sound. Only the crack of small arms fire and the rumble of exploding artillery ordnance broke the cold silence. The tension was immeasurable. We stopped about ten metres from the end of the treeline and crouched in the damp grass. It felt beautifully cool and the pause gave me a chance to catch my breath.

From somewhere in the darkness, the signal was given for Marie and me to cross the open ground. We stood, paused for a moment, nodded at each other, took each other's hand and started running in a half-crouch position to a group of rebels about a hundred and fifty metres away. The dash seemed to take for ever. A few shots cracked through the air. How close? Who knows. We arrived, out of breath, in the middle of a wide open field and joined up with the group of waiting rebels who were kneeling down. In silence, before Marie had a chance to protest, a few of them picked her up and gently lowered her into the ground until she disappeared from sight into the inky blackness below.

And that was the entrance to the tunnel. The rebels had simply dug a hole about four metres wide in the middle of a field. It had no structure: it was, simply put, a large, muddy hole in a field. Before I had time to think, I was manhandled into the hole in similar fashion to Marie. It was soaking wet inside. About four pairs of hands reached up, grabbed me firmly and pulled me down roughly into their subterranean world. At the bottom of the hole, I had to lower myself on to my belly and slither through the mud into a very small entrance that the rebels had cut into the side of a concrete tube, which formed the tunnel proper. It was like crawling into your own waking nightmare.

It was pitch black inside and a rising sense of panic washed over me. I called out gently for Marie. The whispers amplified and reverberated in this strange new world. I heard Marie call back. I attempted to stand but cracked my head fiercely on the top of the concrete shaft. I finally reached Marie, splashing my way through pools of water that lay inches deep on the tunnel floor. We gave each other a hug.

'We made it, mate,' she said, the nerves in her voice causing it to tremble.

'Don't worry, Marie, I've got the fear too,' I whispered gently back.

The tunnel was not quite circular. It was more of an egg shape, tapering off at the top. With only the light that trickled in from the shaft to go by, I could see no more than a metre in front of my face, but a rebel with a very faint torch made it just possible to see inside the tunnel. It was then that we heard the commotion. We turned back to the entrance to see J-P making a fuss with some of the rebels.

'I don't want to go. I just can't do it,' he was saying. 'I'm just too scared. I didn't want to get in here. I should go back now.' His voice was cracking a little.

I spoke to him. 'Hey, J-P, it's okay. Really, it's okay. We're all shitting ourselves, mate. Give it a few moments, get your breath. You are with us and it's going to be fine,' I said, hoping to soothe his understandable anxiety attack.

'I really can't do this. I'm scared, I just can't do it,' he repeated.

'Listen, chum, you can't go back now. The guards are with us and there is no one to take you back. We will stick with you, we won't lose sight of you and if you need to stop then we'll stop too. Deal?'

It was my last-ditch attempt to convince him, it seemed to work and in the process I had calmed my own nerves, restoring a little confidence in my ability to walk the three-kilometre stretch of tunnel that awaited us.

I turned to Marie again. 'How you doing, mate?' I asked, lighting a cigarette to calm myself further.

She smiled a little. 'Feeling a bit better than when I was dragged into the arsehole of the world.' She tried another smile and quipped nervously, 'What the fuck. We got this far, just a little walk and we'll be there.'

That's exactly why I loved Marie. She had just been dropped into one of the nastiest places I'd ever seen and yet she was already laughing. Who could ask for more? Still, the worst was to come: at least for now fresh air still blew in from the muddy shaft above us.

The FSA bundled some supplies down the shaft before we set off. One of the rebels took point. We were told we could use torches once we had left the entrance to the tunnel. It is important to note that not even the smallest of us could stand upright in the tunnel. The position of bent back or bent neck didn't seem too bad to start with. After about 200 metres I got the feeling that this might possibly be a pretty uncomfortable trip, after 400 metres I knew it was and after 600 metres it was sheer bloody hell. No amount of body twisting, back stretching or any other clever little move that I could dream up was going to make it any easier. There was also the air. It was heating up rapidly as we drew further from the entrance and it was obviously less oxygenated. I could feel the temperature rise every few hundred metres and my breathing was now coming in shorter, sharper bursts. The oddly swinging torches people carried played tricks on the eyes. It was impossible to focus as the light kept changing position, bringing on a mild form of seasickness.

As we proceeded silently down the tunnel, the physical toll became a battle of mind over matter. Muscles started to cramp due to our body positions and the lack of oxygen. My head started to play games. It was impossible to work out how far we had travelled. I had no sense of time, nothing to measure anything against.

And then we heard something. The strange noise was distant at first but it grew louder as we walked on. A deep rumble echoed down the tunnel like a monster cornered in its lair, growling as it sensed intruders. The beast kept on coming, louder, more ferociously and faster. Soon the whole tunnel was filled with the sound of the roaring, angry beast. It could smell us and it was relentless in its approach. Its eyes, which were distant yet clearly visible, were pale yellow. The three of us froze as the monster growled its final approach and then fell silent. It was a Russian-built 125cc motorbike.

By this stage, J-P was sitting on an old sack with his head between his legs, breathing sporadically and deeply. Uh oh, I thought, here comes the heart attack.

Marie shuffled over to him. 'Hey, J-P, you okay?' she asked.

'I must go back,' he said, his gasping breaths breaking up the words that he was having difficulty saying. 'I cannot go on any more. I am too old for this. My breathing is bad.'

'Erm, going back may be a little tricky, J-P,' said Marie. 'Seems like it's a one-way ticket today. Anyway, you can't stop here. The air is full of motorbike smoke and you'd be on your own. We can't wait here with you, even if we wanted to.' Marie sounded sympathetic to J-P's plight but also a little irritated.

'Can't go on,' was all that J-P could muster.

Thankfully, Wa'el interrupted. 'We can put him on the motorbike. He won't have to walk any more,' he said.

The motorbike driver nodded his approval and began to turn his bike around in a small, square space built into the cramped tunnel, reversing and pushing it forward a few inches at a time in order to manoeuvre it into the correct position.

'Let Marie go on the bike,' J-P gasped.

This time, I spoke. By now my temper was getting a touch frayed. 'Listen, J-P, Marie isn't about to conk out and have a fucking heart attack. You are. Now get on the bike.'

We eventually loaded J-P on to the back of the bike and waved goodbye as he wobbled off down the tunnel. I suffered a severe pang of jealousy as I watched him being carried away on the bike. Perhaps I could try the heart-attack gig myself, I thought. But J-P's condition was real and he had beaten me to it so I resigned myself to reaching the end of the tunnel on foot.

We started walking again and, for a few minutes, it seemed like the pain had disappeared. It'll be okay now, I thought. Wrong. As the metres grew in number, so the pain returned with a vengeance. The air was worse too: the motorbike, running up and down all day, had stolen precious oxygen, replacing it with carbon dioxide. Fine if you were a plant or tree but generally useless for a human being. My muscles cramped in such a painful and unrelenting way that I seriously began to wonder if I could make it myself. How long had we been in the tunnel? It was a real mystery. I was soaked from head to toe in sweat, so much so that it blurred my vision. The pain clouded all reasonable thought. Each step became a small triumph in itself and the future was measured in splashes. There were no minutes, seconds or metres – only the measure of a boot splashing in water. I dug my nails into the palms of my hand to distract my thoughts from the cramp in my thighs – anything to break the mental and physical stress of the pain now wracking my whole body.

And then I felt it. Initially I thought it was my mind and body playing tricks on me. I waited, not daring to let my hopes rise until I was sure. About twenty splashing paces passed before I felt it again. It was real. I wasn't imagining it. It was air, fresh air; a gentle, soft waft that would normally go unnoticed, but I'd felt it. It could mean only one thing: this tunnel actually did have an end. I now wanted to make it there. The thought of sitting down and giving up had crossed my mind many times but now I wanted out. I picked up my pace a little. Did it hurt a little less? I couldn't be sure but the idea of an ending spurred me on.

Marie's voice echoed down the tunnel to me. 'Paul, I can smell something weird.'

'That's fresh air, Marie,' I joked back.

'How far do you reckon now?' she asked.

'About two thousand splashes,' I answered.

'Paul, you are very strange,' she replied.

The wafts of air continued to get stronger as we pushed on through the tunnel. It was another two hundred splashes later when I heard something. A voice. No, more than one voice – I could hear people arguing. That old saying about a light at the end of the tunnel is nonsense; at the end of the tunnel there is a bunch of arguing Arabs. I was elated,

Marie shouted back, 'Paul, I can hear them arguing. We must be nearly there.' She was laughing, a touch hysterically.

The last half-mile or so was the worst. The sound travelled very effectively in the tunnel so everything seemed closer than it actually was. I kept expecting to bump into a crowd of rebels yet the source of this noise remained elusively far away. We just stomped on. I never went through the pain barrier, as long-distance runners often describe. I just found it and hovered around the wrong side of it. But, in the end, endurance paid off. The voices amplified as we walked on and then there was a glimmer of a torch, more voices, and then more lights.

A hundred metres to go and it would be over, I told myself. The pain would go and we would breathe clean air. Fifty metres, ten metres. I collapsed in the dirt, a bundle of sweat and exhaustion. Voices echoed around me and lights blinded me as people struggled to muscle into the cavern at the end of the tunnel. I was sitting next to Marie where she'd fallen, equally exhausted from the walk. We said nothing. We hugged in silence. We had both run out of words.

People everywhere moved bags and stowed kit. It wasn't exactly the ideal place to relax and savour our triumph. Within minutes of us sitting down, a rebel told us to join the queue to get out. We were in what seemed like one of the tunnel's main service junctions, which seemed to be an old pump house. The way out was via a five-metre steel ladder embedded in the concrete wall. That was all that stood between us and the outside world.

'Paul, you go first so there's someone I know to help me out at the top,' Marie said.

I nodded and began the climb. Halfway up, hands reached down and grabbed my bags, leaving me clear to climb the rest easily. I reached the top and found myself inside what appeared to be the entrance to the pump room. Marie started the climb. She came up slowly but surely and halfway up someone took her bag. I reached down and took her hand, guiding her to the top. Solid ground. We both looked at each other and grinned.

A voice interrupted our shared moment of quiet triumph. 'Welcome to Homs,' said the FSA soldier as he disappeared into the darkness of the night with its sweet, fresh air.

CHAPTER FIVE

The singing rebels of Homs

15 February 2012, Homs, Syria

'Welcome to Homs,' Marie repeated tentatively. 'God, I never thought I'd find those words reassuring.'

'Marie, now comes the dangerous part,' a rebel quipped from the dark, fetid tunnel below us.

It was hard to tell if he was joking or being serious. It didn't really matter either way: his words had done little to ease the sense of apprehension that we all felt.

The two of us – Marie and myself – were squeezed into the corner of a tiny dilapidated room to avoid the frenzied activity around us. Rebels pulled people, food and ammunition crates from the man-sized hole that led out of the hellish tunnel below, cramming the room with even more bodies and crates. The dim light of a rebel's torch revealed the detritus of war carpeting the floor around us: empty ammunition boxes smashed open in haste and thousands of spent AK47 cartridges. If this tunnel was such a well-kept secret, I puzzled, then what had all the fighting from this position been for? I never found out and to this day I am amazed the tunnel remained secret for so long.

Our translator, Wa'el, appeared from the tightly packed melee of armed rebels. He looked as bad we felt. Sweating profusely, pupils fully dilated and his eyes straining in the darkness, he looked deeply troubled.

'Quickly, Paul. I need a smoke,' he gasped. 'Oh, and I have J-P. He is outside getting some air. He seems a little better.'

I hadn't even thought about smoking a cigarette since we entered the tunnel. I wondered whether I'd suffered mild brain damage because of the lack of oxygen. I lit up and handed one to Wa'el.

'Do you know what happens now?' I asked him.

He shrugged his shoulders. 'I guess we wait until they clear the tunnel and we move together in a group to Baba Amr,' he said, his voice tense.

Marie, who hated the sitting and waiting around as much as I did, took command. 'Wa'el, it's critical that we get to the media centre as soon as possible,' she said. 'We don't want to get stuck drinking tea for hours. Try to find the commander and let's get away from this fucking tunnel.'

Wa'el smiled. He had grown accustomed to Marie's straightforward manner. He was now part of our team and he relished a challenge. He left the dark antechamber and disappeared into the night.

Marie and I huddled together for warmth. It was very cold outside and the sweat was starting to freeze on our bodies.

She turned to face me. 'Paul,' she said in her relaxed American drawl, a half-smile on her face, 'we have done very weird stuff over the years but this, this has got to take the biscuit. I can't think of anything else so bizarre and dangerous but now we've made it, it's so much fun.'

I smiled back. I knew what she meant. Although we had only been out of the tunnel for five minutes, I could already see how we would tell the tale when we returned home. At the back of our minds we both knew that it would be something we'd laugh about for years to come.

We sat in silence waiting for Wa'el. The sound of machine-gun fire and the menacing rumble of distant explosions reached us through the cold air of our first night in Homs. J-P had slipped off into another world. He had hardly spoken since clambering out of the tunnel. We were worried about him. How would he cope with what was to come?

Wa'el came crashing through the doorway, breaking off the thought. 'Quickly, get your bags. We must go now. We have a rebel convoy to take us to Baba Amr,' he said urgently.

Within seconds we were ready. We regrouped outside in what appeared to be an agricultural area. Through the familiar small stone walls and furrowed fields we could just make out our surroundings but the dark shadows and high moon made it difficult to identify exactly where we were. Walking in single file, I led Marie by the hand as we set out across the stony, muddy ground, slipping or stumbling on unseen obstacles whenever the clouds obscured the moon.

'I hear voices,' I whispered.

'What?' replied Marie. 'This isn't the right time for a confession, Paul.' She chuckled softly.

'No, real voices ahead and getting louder. Trust me, I ain't losing the plot,' I told her, finding it hard not to chuckle at her wonderful sense of the surreal.

The source of the voices became apparent as we continued in single file behind Wa'el. We soon arrived in a courtyard surrounded by three buildings where clusters of FSA fighters were working hard to load munitions on to trucks. It was a natural staging post. The walls around the courtyard were high enough to keep watch from and the position was discreet enough for large groups to gather without being spotted. It was obviously considered sufficiently safe to operate from, a place where supplies could be brought before being broken down and smuggled into Baba Amr.

Four pickup trucks were waiting outside the courtyard. We were directed to mount up in the second vehicle. Armed FSA rebels climbed in with us. We soon found ourselves cocooned by men arming their weapons, primed for the next phase of the journey into Baba Amr. The other three vehicles in the convoy were all packed with rebel fighters. An unseen signal was given and the first vehicle started to crawl away from the courtyard with the other vehicles following close behind.

This is how I had imagined it would happen: the silence followed by the whispered orders and the sense that we were deep behind enemy lines. I wasn't prepared for what happened next. Without warning, the rebels broke into song. Their loud, brazen voices from the four vehicles pierced the night. I tried to figure out what was going on. Why, I thought, after all the silence and whispers, all the ducking and diving, is now a good time to start making one hell of a racket?

'Paul, why the fuck are they singing?' Marie asked, half amused, half terrified, unable to make her mind up if this was a good or a bad sign. 'We're supposed to be sneaking in. What the hell's going on?'

I had no idea. If we had tried a similar stunt in my army days we would have been hung, drawn and quartered. I couldn't think of a single possible explanation. I turned to Wa'el and looked at him questioningly.

'They are happy that you are here. They are celebrating your arrival,' he explained, with a shrug of the shoulders and a half-smile.

The convoy proceeded into the blackness of the night. When the moon occasionally broke through the clouds, its ghostly light revealed a scarred and battered landscape. There was no sign of human life in the villages we passed through. Nothing moved, apart from the odd stray dog that broke cover and sprinted from the shadows as our musical convoy sped by.

That's when it happened. Leaving one of the deserted villages we first saw and then heard the flaming tail of a rocket-propelled grenade streaking towards our convoy. The round seemed to take for ever to reach us, seemingly suspended in slow motion as it flew over our heads and exploded harmlessly a hundred metres to our left. Next came the bullets, screaming like demonic banshees as they passed through our convoy.

The natural reaction when under fire is to make yourself small. We crouched tightly in the back of the pickup truck with our heads pushed down between our knees, curled-up balls of fear unable to respond to the incoming fire in any other way. The fear was amplified by the troubling thought that our lives depended entirely on the reactions of people whose faces we had never seen. But the rebels reacted to the fire in a puzzling way: they sang even louder and with more gusto than before. At no point did they return fire. They simply continued singing their hearts out.

'*Takbir* [God is the greatest],' shouted an unseen rebel.

'*Allahu Akbar, Allahu Akbar, Allahu Akbar* [God is great],' responded the FSA rebels in all four trucks.

Body armour is better, I thought to myself from my shrunken position as bullets whistled past our speeding convoy. Marie had sunk into a state of bemused silence. Each time the moon illuminated us I caught a glimpse of her slightly baffled face. She returned my gaze with a simple shrug of her shoulders before hunkering back down into the foetal position.

The small-arms fire eventually ceased and we uncurled ourselves from our protective forms. Ahead, perhaps a mile in the distance, we saw the orange glow of buildings whose hazy outlines broke the monotonous gloom and oppressive darkness of the horizon. We were heading in the direction of the buildings and I rather hoped it was a rebel-held position.

The convoy drew closer and I could feel the excitement of the FSA soldiers mounting. A sense of relief flooded through me as I realised that we had taken another major step forward in our journey. We pulled up outside a cluster of apartment buildings. Lights blazed on all five floors. We weren't in Baba Amr yet. If we had been, these apartment blocks would have been blazing in a different way.

Dismounting, we stood and absorbed the scene in front of us. Everywhere FSA soldiers scurried, carrying crates of ammunition, heavy weapons, sacks of flour and large boxes of tinned food. The atmosphere here was more relaxed than any of us had expected. Clearly the FSA felt they had a degree of control over the area. We stood smoking in a tight huddle. Around us, in the orange glow of the street lighting, FSA rebels continued their chores. Occasional bursts of heavy machine-gun fire passed overhead but the fighters ignored them. We watched as the trucks were eventually emptied. Small children peered out of darkened doorways. Even from a distance I could identify the hollowed look of fear on their faces. It was the unmistakable mark left on those suffering from immense trauma.

We were all acutely aware that we had to keep moving that evening. It was critical that we made Baba Amr under the cover of darkness. A daylight entry was a no go.

Marie pulled me to one side and whispered, 'We must make it in tonight, it's Wednesday and we have to file by Saturday at the latest, best by Friday. We really can't afford to get stuck here tonight. I know it's nice to feel safe for a while, but whatever happens we push for the move to Baba Amr. Are you cool with that?'

I nodded in agreement. Time was against us. We had enough material from the trip in to file a story already, but both of us were aware that reaching Baba Amr would bring our piece to life. I agreed fully with Marie's point of view.

Wa'el, who was always on top of the situation, had already arranged a meeting with the commander. We followed him into one of the apartment blocks, behind a rebel fighter. The sound of children playing in the perceived safety of their homes, the clatter of weapons being unpacked, civilians and soldiers moving together between rooms and apartments, revealed how many levels of Syrian society were caught up in this war. The incongruity of women sitting in chairs feeding babies under the orange glow of the streetlight while fully armed rebels prepared for war pushed home the sense that there was now little distinction between soldier and civilian. In the eyes of President Assad and his security forces, there was none: civilians and armed rebel fighters were the same and, as such, would be treated with the same level of brutality.

The rebel fighter led us into one of the many bustling apartments on the second floor. He ushered us on to a sofa. The room was more decorated than any we had stayed in before. Chairs and sofas replaced the carpets and floor cushions, and there were ornate wall hangings, intricate woven carpets and gilded framed verses from the Koran. Coupled with the 60-watt light bulbs that illuminated the room, all this made it feel like a family home.

We were embarrassingly aware that we were covered almost head to toe in drying red mud from the tunnel. We took off our jackets to minimise our environmental impact on the home. J-P was busy making a fuss of sitting down because of the mud on his trousers when an FSA member entered the room. 'He took one look at J-P's distress before asking the Frenchman if he wanted his trousers washed. J-P seemed delighted with the offer. He removed his trousers and handed them over to the FSA soldier turned laundry manager. The rebels offered him a pair of trousers in return. I watched the whole episode open-mouthed. I couldn't believe that he had actually agreed to get his laundry done . . . in a fully-fledged combat zone. I felt uncomfortable removing even my boots and hadn't undressed since leaving Lebanon. There was no way anyone was getting hold of my trousers.

Having gulped down some hot tea and puffed away on a few cigarettes, we soon warmed up nicely. We were informed that the FSA were looking for a vehicle with enough diesel to make the final run into Baba Amr. It was strangely relaxing in the room and the sounds of children playing in the corridors took us briefly away from the war. I could feel my determination to move crumbling with every sip of warm tea. This really wouldn't be a bad place to spend a night. I began to doze off as the warmth from the diesel heater and the exhaustion of the tunnel took hold. Just as I agreed to surrender myself to sleep, an FSA rebel burst into the room. He looked ready for combat: he was clutching an AK47, had a keffiyeh wrapped around his head, revealing only a sharp set of dark brown eyes, and there were four grenades attached to his Kevlar body armour. There goes my sleep, I thought.

The rebel with the grenades spoke urgently in English. 'Miss Marie, Abu Falafel, please, we must go now to Baba Amr. The car is waiting, come quickly.'

Marie, Wa'el and I jumped immediately to our feet and began to gather our kit. It was then that I noticed J-P. 'I want my trousers back,' he said. He looked indignant, standing there in his borrowed trousers, searching for the rebel who'd taken his pair to the laundry. 'No time, mate,' I said, 'we gotta go now. There's no time to find your trousers.'

We were already on our way out of the apartment. I felt sorry for him though as I watched him prepare to head off to war in borrowed trousers. I could hear Marie choking to keep her laughter in check. She was fit to burst but she held back for J-P's sake. Following the rebel with the grenades and headscarf, we went down the dark, winding stairwell into the orange glow of the street below, where two saloon cars were waiting for us.

When Wa'el spoke, it was without any trace of humour. 'Guys,' he began earnestly, 'this really is the big one. They will take you to the media centre in Baba Amr now. You have to know that we must cross the front line and we will only be a few hundred metres away from the Assad army. Not small groups of them any more. This is the main front line from where they attack Homs. There are thousands of them. Many people die making this journey every day so they can't guarantee that you will all make it alive. They want you to know this before we start. You can still say no if you want and stay here and work.'

There were a few moments of silence as we digested this news. In reality, it was something we had all suspected anyway but to have it in words gave us pause for thought. Marie spoke on behalf of us all.

'Thank them for their concern,' she said. 'We appreciate their honesty but, yes, we will accept the risks and we'll go with them.'

Wa'el translated. The driver motioned us into the cars. The bodyguards and drivers armed their weapons and we prepared for the final sprint into Baba Amr. All I could do was hope that our luck would hold for another half an hour. The drivers started their engines, passed a message in Arabic via a VHF radio and then pulled slowly out of the apartment blocks into the sombre, terrifying blackness of the main road.

There is a lot to be said about safety in numbers. On the trip from the tunnel to the apartment block we had numbers on our side. Although unusually musical for a night patrol, we had drawn solace from the fact that we were not alone. Now, stripped bare of our musical compatriots, we felt exposed as the car inched ever closer into the unknown of the front line. No headlights, no moon, only darkness and silence. The silence was unlike anything I had ever felt before. There was the silent bravery of the drivers risking their lives in order to make our journey possible, Marie's silence as she faced the unknown, her gaze locked on to the black road ahead, and there was my own silent terror. I felt numb and cold.

The car accelerated rapidly, bringing Marie and me out of our individual trances with a start. We exchanged nervous glances in the back of the vehicle. There was no apparent reason for the sudden acceleration. The car soon reached its top speed, leaving the ground as we sped across the pitted, broken roads. That's when we heard the piercing whistle of bullets. The fact we could hear them over the sound of the engine and noise of the road meant that the bullets were close. But the driver never let up the pace. With a confidence born of familiarity, he navigated tight bends, small bridges and wide-open spaces at a speed that pushed us back into our seats. The sideways force from each bend compressed us into a tight, nervous bundle in the back of the car. No one spoke. Marie continued her trance-like stare into the unknown. My own knuckles whitened as I gripped the handle of the door in a futile effort to steady myself.

More incoming fire. This time I could hear the deep thud of 14.5mm anti-aircraft rounds above the noise of the car engine. The explosive bullets could stop us dead in our tracks, literally. Every seventh round was a tracer. Watching the bright pink glow of the bullet arc like a sprite towards our speeding vehicle was bewitching. The reality of a direct hit was unthinkable.

We continued our high-speed, bullet-dodging run for another

five minutes or so. Then, as inexplicably as the sudden acceleration, the driver slowed to a near crawl. We were now in a lightly wooded area. We could make out the bare and occasionally broken branches of trees whose skeletal shapes were silhouetted against lighter patches of the night sky.

For the first time since leaving, the bodyguard in the front seat turned to face us. His face serious, he pointed to the right of the car. 'Tanks,' he said softly.

Since leaving the apartments, neither Marie nor I had spoken a single word. The bodyguard's information didn't change this. We both knew enough about tanks to know that you didn't have to suffer a direct hit: the simple force from an explosion near by would be enough to send the car flipping like a broken toy through the cold night air.

The driver edged the car onwards, expertly teasing the accelerator and gears to keep the engine tone as steady and even as possible. The wooded area on our right seemed to take for ever to pass. Inch by inch and yard by yard, we crawled past the hidden menace of the tanks. You don't hear a tank fire and then feel the force of the shell: it's the opposite way round – shell first, then the boom. We would never hear the explosive crescendo if we were hit. We'd be found by a patrol the next day, just another burnt-out wreck on a roadside.

Eventually the menace of the woods and the invisible tanks receded. The driver gently accelerated. It is difficult to say how long we sat silently in the car. Gradually the rural backdrop gave way to clusters of buildings. There were no streetlights or house lights, no signs of life anywhere; only the dead and empty shells of buildings, a reminder of the people who had once lived in them. We were rapidly entering a built-up environment, the open countryside surrendering to the urban sprawl at the outer limits of Baba Amr.

The poorly-lit streets revealed the terror that had rained down on the area. Buildings stood twisted and contorted under the constant bombardment of Assad's unrelenting siege. We struggled to absorb the scale of the destruction wrought on this small Sunni Muslim neighbourhood.

Marie turned to me. 'I guess this is—'

She never finished her sentence. The explosion rattled the car as an ear-splitting boom tore through the night. I caught a flash of light to the right and front of the car, about a hundred metres away.

Marie tried again. 'As I was saying, I guess this is Baba Amr.'

'I certainly fucking hope so,' I said. 'Otherwise we have major and pressing navigational issues.'

Another explosion, this time further away but with the same result – a huge boom followed by a large shockwave that shook the car. We promptly shut up. The streets continued to narrow as we travelled further into the neighbourhood. Rubble lay piled up in the streets. Broken glass and destroyed cars were strewn everywhere. It was a landscape of the hunted and the dead. Every single building was testament to the brutal bombardment. Some simply had large gaping holes where artillery shells had pierced the walls before exploding. Sometimes only half a building remained. But more often than not whole buildings had simply disappeared. Rubble marked their graves. The forces of Assad were ripping this neighbourhood apart, brick by bloody brick.

Ahead of us, a large municipal building illuminated in the eerie moonlight had the appearance of a dissected cadaver, one huge black hole reminiscent of a surgically opened chest that had been exposed to the world. The stripped and twisted steel reinforcement rods were silhouetted against the brooding sky, forming a ghostly skeleton that guarded a rotting corpse. Assad, the British-trained eye surgeon, was stripping the flesh from the bones of Baba Amr with surgical precision.

Homs is Syria's most populated city. It was one of the first towns to attempt peaceful, anti-government protests after the Syrian army's successful suppression of demonstrations in the city of Darra. When the army opened fire on unarmed demonstrators after Friday prayers on 6 May 2011, killing 15 protestors, the fuse was lit. Homs, or more specifically Baba Amr, a tiny Sunni neighbourhood surrounded by pro-Assad, Allawite neighbourhoods, was to become the focal point of the rebellion. Assad wanted it crushed there and then.

By the time we entered Baba Amr, the 4th Armoured Division, an elite unit of the Syrian army, had surrounded and laid siege to the neighbourhood for nearly a year. In command of the 4th Division was Maher al-Assad, the brother of the president. If anyone was capable of taking Baba Amr, it would be Maher al-Assad.

'It reminds me of Grozny,' Marie said as she took in the ruin.

Her voice seemed to speak from the past. Images of the death and destruction she had witnessed during the first siege of Grozny were burnt deep into her memory. She barely made it out alive. She went days without food as the advancing Russian army forced her to flee for her life with the band of rebels she was with. Eventually, after she climbed high mountain passes through thick snow, a helicopter from the American embassy plucked her from the mountainside and flew her to safety.

'Maybe it's worse,' she whispered, still gazing out of the window at the desolation before us.

I was silent. I had witnessed sieges and artillery onslaughts many times before, but the devastation of this tiny neighbourhood where people had once demonstrated peacefully went well and truly beyond the extent of my experience. This wasn't war. It was slaughter.

We advanced further among the wreckage, at times accelerating fiercely across road junctions to avoid sniper fire only to jam on the brakes suddenly and hide behind the next pile of rubble. Often, as we crossed a junction, we could see and hear the flashes of explosive bullets impacting yards behind the car. Nowhere was safe: in the open we were prey to snipers and machine-gunners while on the streets we were open to the incoming mortars and artillery shells that force you to count your life in seconds. In Baba Amr, months and years had long ceased to exist. It was now purely a matter of survival.

We were deeply entwined in the maze of back alleys and tiny roads that make up the bulk of Baba Amr. Turning another corner, we noticed a small light burning in a window ahead of us. The driver aimed straight for it. The car gently drew to a halt outside the building and immediately a door opened. From within appeared another FSA fighter, clad in camouflage, *keffiyeh* hiding his face and an assault rifle gripped firmly in his hand. Murmured words were spoken as the fighter rested on our car, his face inches from our driver's. There was no conversation; only what appeared to be a set of instructions.

We had been at rest for no more than thirty seconds when the unknown fighter waved goodbye and the car reversed delicately in the direction from which we had just come. Again the driver gently nursed the clutch and accelerator to maintain silence as we crawled through the backstreets before hitting the accelerator hard when we came across junctions. It had taken time, but the people of Baba Amr had obviously figured out where the snipers were concealed. Turning another corner into a street that was blocked at one end by more buildings, we came to another halt. The driver cut the engine and a wave of relief spread through the car. Marie and I exchanged glances. We had made it into Baba Amr.

The driver and bodyguard clearly had none of our sense of the dramatic: they were out of the car before Marie and I could finish revelling in our united sense of relief. They tapped on the window and indicated we get out rather sharpish.

Stiff and trembling from cold and fear, we stood outside a three-storey building that was relatively undamaged apart from a large hole in the third-floor wall where a shell or mortar had penetrated. Glancing up and down the street, it was clear that this was no safe house. The broken, charred trees, the burnt-out buildings and the patches of rubble where the street's houses had once stood meant that we were well within reach of Assad's artillery onslaught.

It was a relief to be out of the warm car. The drive and tension had an effect that was almost hypnotic. But the night air, cold and cutting, served to break the trance-like spell, reconnecting mind and body. We began to unload our belongings from the boot of the car.

Marie looked up and down the street, then at me. 'Nice place, huh?' she quipped, her sparkle back.

'Last time I book a cheap holiday on the internet,' I replied, picking up my camera bag and nodding towards the door, where the two FSA men were waiting for us. 'After you, madam.'

As we walked towards the entrance, we heard a second vehicle approaching our position. The two FSA fighters turned quickly, their weapons up and pointing at the vehicle. But they lowered their guns when they recognised the car that J-P and Wa'el were travelling in. We had lost their vehicle on the drive in, and now we also lost the fear that they had been taken or hit.

Reunited, we followed the rebels through a small gate that opened on to a short pathway leading to a heavy, carved wooden door. The FSA guys banged with their fists and the door opened almost imme-diately. Behind the figure who greeted us in the doorway, I could make out a small hallway illuminated by a grim fluorescent light. Standing by the pile of shoes in the hallway we began the inelegant rigmarole of taking off our own boots. We grabbed hold of each other as we hopped from foot to foot, struggling to undo our laces.

To our left there was a darkened stairwell leading to the floors above. Directly in front there was a disused door with boxes and junk blocking it. We were led through another door to our right and were immediately hit by a cacophony of voices. Yet we saw no one. The room in which we stood appeared void of people, illuminated by the same fluorescent light as the hallway. It seemed to be a storeroom. Piles of blankets lay strewn across the floor. There were a few chairs, some boxes and a table. A large window to our right looked out on to the street. This explained why the room was empty. Any shell, missile or mortar impacting on the street outside would turn this place into a deadly, glass-powered food blender.

The figure who had answered the front door now opened a sliding glass door opposite the window on to the street. The vocal drone filled our ears, and the scene that greeted us stopped me in my tracks. Through the thick haze of cigarette smoke hanging motionless in the air I saw a scene reminiscent of a hurricane-relief shelter. Between fifteen and twenty people, wrapped in thick blankets, lay or crouched on old mattresses that covered every inch of available floor space. Each of the blanket people had a laptop. The floor, or what was visible of it, was a tangle of wires, power cables and extension leads. A single tungsten bulb made a poor job of illuminating the rectangular room. The ghostly glow from computer screens cast eerie shadows on the walls. To our left, in the centre of the sea of bodies, stood a low table. It too was covered in wires, empty cigarette packets, saucers that overflowed with freshly smoked cigarette butts and empty coffee cups. On the wall to our left was the other side of the door that we had seen blocked by boxes. Directly opposite was another sliding door leading to the back of the house. The source of the noise was now obvious – Skype. Almost everyone in the room was shouting into a computer or headset microphone.

As I looked more closely, I realised it was more like a scene from a science-fiction film than a hurricane-relief shelter. The room was the headquarters of a hunted and starving band of outlaws who were bound together by their desire to survive whatever plague, tyrannical super-race or alien being had threatened their existence and forced them to live in the shadows of the night. In reality, my science-fiction fantasy wasn't far from the truth. The blanket people were indeed the hunted. They were outlaws – targets of a murderous regime. They were the media and this was their temporary home.

My mind flashed back to my last visit to *The Sunday Times* office. Bright and airy with neat rows of desks and air conditioning, everything sleek and ordered, the office was as you would expect of such an organisation. By contrast, this maze of wires, people shivering in blankets and a total sense of chaos was the sole source of information on life under siege in Syria. The world was watching and everything emanated from this single chilly room.

Everyone looked up from their computer screens when we entered the room. The reflections from their screens, which col-oured their faces a pale blue, reinforced my sci-fi analogy. The noise of the chatter dropped a few decibels as the blanket people adjusted to the sight of us, intruders into their secret world. A slightly awk-ward pause followed before one of the shapes in the darkness rose, shedding his blanket as he stood.

'Hey, guys,' he said in perfect English, 'come in, welcome to the media centre.' He looked directly at me. 'You must be Abu Falafel, and you are Marie.'

He briefly translated the Abu Falafel nickname for the benefit of the others in the room before turning back to us. 'I'm Abu Hanin,' he said, still smiling. 'And these are our people.'

Abu Hanin was to have a profound effect on our lives in the weeks to come, although we didn't realise it at the time. Short and stocky with a completely shaven head, he had a naturally smiling and kind face that made you relax on first meeting him. An impossibly complex and convoluted ceremony followed as we were introduced to all of the media-centre crew. Names were spoken and hands shaken as Marie and I attempted to remember the names of our many new friends. By the end I didn't know a single one and resorted to calling everyone 'Hey, mate' until I could start to link faces with names.

Abu Hanin was something of an enigma. His dress was very western and casual. His mannerisms were also learnt from the West, which made him appear slightly inappropriate for the room in which we found ourselves. Whereas many people in the room had the telltale signs of war written on their faces, Abu Hanin seemed fresh and physically unscathed by the battle raging round him. He appeared media savvy because he recognised Marie instantly and needed no explaining as to what *The Sunday Times* was.

There were some familiar faces too. Arwa Damon, Neil Hannon and Tim Crockett – a crew from CNN – were deeply embedded among the layers of blankets. There were smiles, handshakes and hugs as Marie and I caught up with these old friends from previous conflicts. In such situations, there is something very reassuring about meeting up with colleagues. You tend to think that you can't be that mad if others are in the same place as you. A slightly darker thought also crosses your mind: Phew, they're still alive – that's a good sign.

Marie and I started to settle in, removing sodden, muddy jackets, piling up bags and ferreting out a space to make our own. We were issued with blankets by a smiling Abu Hanin and within minutes we felt at home. The adrenalin from our trip in dissipated from our bodies. I caught Wa'el self-consciously hiding his SpongeBob bag beneath a layer of camera bags. He caught me smiling at him. He beamed a huge grin back, walked across the room and hugged me like a long-lost friend, his eyes wide and sparkling.

'We made it, Abu Falafel, we made it,' he said simply, and continued to make a space on the floor where none existed.

The noise levels rose once more as the Skype conversations with the outside world resumed. All seemed well in our cosy new home. Outside, the deep rumble of explosions caused the walls of the house to vibrate. The chatter of machine-gun fire and the rounds impacting on the walls outside seemed miles away. We now had walls, and walls were our friends. I picked my way through the sea of bodies over to the spot where Neil and Tim from CNN had built their nest. I sat down next to them.

'How bad is it?' I asked Neil, a seasoned cameraman and a familiar face on the war circuit.

He shook his head. 'It's fucking insane. This is as quiet as it ever gets. Make the most of it, mate. At six thirty every morning the shelling starts. Heavy shit, continual and heavy fucking shelling. They start on one place and then sweep the neighbourhood with everything they have – mortars, tanks, artillery shells and missiles. You name it, they throw it.'

'Any near misses?' I enquired.

'Depends on what you call near,' Neil said. 'Take a look upstairs tomorrow. Third floor. Something came right through it and went bang. It took out the whole floor.'

'Not too near, then.' I smiled, before standing to speak with Marie. She had built her den next to Abu Hanin and they were deep in conversation. She was on form. Half an hour after arriving cold, sodden and adrenalin-hyped, she was now busy making plans with Abu Hanin.

'Hey, Paul, I mailed the office to let them know we made it in, so we're all good on that front,' she said. 'I've been chatting with Abu Hanin about heading to the field hospital tomorrow. Apparently it's the hottest target in town and Assad's goons have been blasting at it for weeks. It sounds like our best shot at a story for Friday. What do you reckon?'

'I'm game, Marie. What's the score on getting there?' I asked.

'It's a risk,' Abu Hanin said. 'The shelling is constant. The best chance is when they're shelling another part of the area. We get in a car and drive fast, hope the snipers miss us and then run like hell from the car to the hospital. They have drones too. They watch us from the sky and they can target cars easily. It's risky but we can make it.'

'Okay. So what time do you reckon we leave?' I asked.

Abu Hanin shrugged. 'We wait and we go when we can. It's the only way.'

Marie and I both agreed with the plan. If Baba Amr was as bad as was being reported, then the field hospital would be a good measure of the scale of the siege.

The main room was so full that Abu Hanin offered to let us sleep in a small back room. 'It's nice. You have mattresses and blankets, but,' he said, before pausing, 'you must be up before the shelling starts otherwise that room becomes a very dangerous place to be. It has a window.'

Syria in February is cold. It is not the scorching desert that springs to mind when thinking of the Middle East. Asked if he was going to cover Syria, Andy Malone, a friend from the *Mail on Sunday*, politely refused on the grounds that he would only cover warm-weather revolutions. So it was that both Marie and I took to wearing all the clothes we had with us at night. As well as the pair of over-sized long johns borrowed from Jim Muir in Beirut, Marie had been given a black Arabic garment that covered her from head to toe. Topped off with a black belt around her waist, she looked for the entire world like a Chechen rebel queen.

Half an hour later, after building beds with a quantity of blankets that would embarrass Sir Ranulph Fiennes, Marie and I lay motionless in our room, listening to the constant sound of explosions and gunfire outside. We fell silent as we lay under our mountain of blankets in that small room in Baba Amr, wondering what the next day would bring. I soon heard Marie's gentle snores as she slipped off into the private world of her dreams. The snores grew louder and louder. I put headphones in my ears and listened to a talking book but it seemed sleep would never come. Through the head-phones, I could still hear the shells, the bullets and Marie's deep snores. Wherever she had gone, she sounded happy enough.

CHAPTER SIX

Desolation Row

16 February 2011, Baba Amr, Syria

A loud explosion shook the glass in our makeshift bedroom and shocked me awake. I could hear stones and shrapnel falling into the tiny courtyard at the back of the house.

Abu Hanin rushed into the room, shouting at us. 'Get out,' he screamed, his eyes wide and frightened. 'Get the fuck out. The shelling has started. You will die in here.'

He turned and ran back to the main room where the other activists had spent the night. They had picked the safest room in which to shelter from the bombardment: there were no windows and the double walls protected them from the shrapnel sent flying by the artillery shells exploding on the wide streets outside the house.

I turned to Marie to see if she had heard Abu Hanin's panicked warning. To my astonishment, the initial explosion had failed to wake her up. I couldn't see her through the multiple layers of blankets she was lying under. Shaking her roughly by what I thought was her shoulder (and turned out to be her head), I forced her awake. I heard her growl obscenities through the thick blankets before she popped her head out of the den. She squinted in the daylight.

'We gotta go, Marie. The shelling has started,' I said as nonchalantly as possible, not wishing to spook her as she woke hazily from
her slumber.

'What? When?' she asked, still groggy with sleep.

'About a minute ago. Didn't you hear it?'

She shook her head and looked at her watch. 'Antisocial bastards,'
she muttered as she battled to free herself from the heavy bedding.
'Bloody hell, Paul, I had to sleep on my back last night. I couldn't
move. How many blankets and carpets did you put on me?' she
asked as she fumbled for her notebook.

'Eight.' I laughed, searching for my camera among my own
mound of bedding.

This morning awakening was reminding me of a night we spent
in Libya a year earlier. Marie and I had found ourselves sleeping
rough on an Astroturf football pitch that belonged to a school
turned temporary rebel base. We were surrounded by snoring rebels
from an elite unit who had spent the previous days fighting their
way into Tripoli during a lightning advance on the capital. The fake
grass provided the softest bedding I had come across for weeks.
But, in the early hours of the morning, we were shaken roughly
awake by a rebel fighter and told that government snipers were
shooting at the school from nearby buildings. The rebel told us to
get up and move inside the classrooms.

From the relative comfort of our Astroturf mattress, we looked
sleepily at the football pitch and concrete schoolyard to determine
where the bullets were landing. They were too far away, we decided,
so we rolled over and went back to sleep. The next morning we
woke to find ourselves alone on the abandoned football pitch. It is
incredible what sleep will do to a person's risk threshold.

Now, in Baba Amr, as explosions boomed outside, I willed Marie
to hurry up and get out of bed. In the same room, Wa'el and J-P

were just waking up. Suddenly, another explosion – this one no more than fifty metres away – rattled the windows with incredible ferocity. The proximity of the explosion proved extremely motivational: within minutes all four of us were safely in the main room of the building.

It was still below freezing outside so the room, crammed with bodies, felt snug and cosy. We picked out a place on the floor, careful not to wake those who had learnt to sleep through the bombardments. Many of the activists were still asleep despite the thunderous explosions outside. It was an indication of how battle-hardened these men had become.

Marie asked for a bottle of water and prepared some cold coffee with the jar of Nescafé that lived stashed within her many layers of clothes. She never went anywhere without her coffee jar. After drinking her half, she smiled and passed the water bottle discreetly to me. I gulped my ration down and returned the bottle. It wasn't an expresso but it was coffee nonetheless.

Outside, the bombardment was growing more intense. The gunners of the government's 4th Division were no amateurs: the rate of fire showed they were well-trained artillerymen and they appeared to have an unlimited supply of ammunition. Marie and I attempted to count the number of explosions that we heard in the space of three minutes. We counted 46 before we gave up. There were just too many shells landing to keep count. The remaining blanket people slowly came to life. Even to them, today's attack seemed exceptionally heavy. Some said it was the heaviest yet.

Marie was the first to verbalise what we were both thinking. 'Paul, this is worse than Misrata at its peak.'

I nodded. We had witnessed the Libyan city of Misrata undergoing intense bombardment from Gaddafi loyalists the year before, and it had been a living nightmare. This was different. The rate of fire, the type of weapons and the skill with which these weapons were being used put Baba Amr in another league. As if to underline the point, a burst of explosive-tipped bullets suddenly impacted on the street and the walls outside, followed immediately by the explosive crunch of a large mortar.

'Try moving around this place on your own,' I said, lighting a cigarette while trying to work out how we could possibly work in these conditions. 'I'd give you less than ten minutes before the snipers got you, which means our only options are to stay with these guys. They know the lie of the land: who is where, what is where and, more importantly, how to get there.'

'At least in Libya we could get a driver and go where we wanted and see what we wanted,' Marie replied. 'Here, it's pretty much up to them what we see. I'm slightly uncomfortable with that. Our lives are in their hands and we just have to go with it.'

We agreed that it was going to be difficult to remain non-partisan. We relied on the FSA and the activists for everything. Coupled with our inability to move independently, this would make both reporting and surviving here far more complex than anything we had experienced in Libya.

Abu Hanin, the chief activist, caught us plotting in the corner and joined us. He explained, with the aid of hand-drawn maps, where President Assad's forces were positioned around the city. He told us that Syrian army checkpoints blocked every entrance and exit in and out of the neighbourhood, whether large or small. He was concerned that the already depleted food supplies would soon run out. The tunnel was incapable of supplying all their needs, even when it ran at maximum capacity. The other supplies, brought in on motorbikes by men like Abu Zaid, would feed a few families for a couple of days, at the most. There were thousands of people trapped in Baba Amr. They needed food by the ton. As it stood, they were receiving only the occasional sackload that could be carried in by hand.

Abu Hanin brought life and warmth to the media centre. He had spent a long time in Canada and Britain, living as a student in Bournemouth. His English was perfect and he had a great sense of humour. The previous night, he had told me about the food fantasies that he often suffered during the siege. He longed for Nando's spicy chicken and, unusually for a Muslim, a cold beer. He also had a penchant for Golden Virginia tobacco and spoke fondly of his visits to Tesco to buy his supplies. He made me promise him that, if I returned to Baba Amr, I would bring him his favourite tobacco in a Tesco plastic bag.

While we waited for a break in the shelling so that we could make a dash to the field hospital, Abu Hanin suggested that we meet a family across the road. They had been forced to share a house with another family because shells had destroyed their own home a few days earlier. The house next door to the media centre had also been removed by a direct hit, killing all four women inside. If we wanted, Abu Hanin said, we could travel five hundred metres down the road to an area where FSA fighters battled every day to prevent government tanks from breaking into the neighbourhood. The only weapons the rebels possessed that were effective against the tanks were rocket-propelled grenades. But they had few of these: arms smugglers were charging them $200 per grenade.

'Jesus Christ,' muttered Marie after Abu Hanin had finished. Her voice was low and sad, as if she knew that what we were about to see would leave profound scars on our souls and in our hearts. 'This could keep us working for months.'

The ferocity of the attacks made us even more determined to remain. Neither of us was inclined to take the easy way out by declaring the place too dangerous to work in. We didn't want to ignore the slaughter happening around us and we refused to allow ourselves to be cowed by Assad's brutality. It only made us more determined to get our stories and pictures out to the world.

We sat in a small group, waiting for Abu Hanin to take us across the road to meet the family. Marie was at her best when she had a cause for which she could use her insightful and tenacious journalistic skills. In Baba Amr, as in other conflicts, she found her purpose in describing the humanitarian costs that war forced civilians to pay. She would give them a voice and put them centre stage. But this didn't come without its own costs. Although Marie firmly believed that no story was worth dying for – 'Kinda defeats the purpose,' she once quipped – she had come close to death in Sri Lanka, where she lost an eye in a rocket-propelled grenade attack as she left rebel-held territory. When she was ready to go back to work, she turned down an office job at *The Sunday Times*. She was determined to return to her 'real' job, as she put it to me. Despite her determination, the trauma left its mark upon her. She was crippled by bouts of post-traumatic stress disorder (PTSD) and visited many dark places during her recovery. Undeterred, she fought her way back to the top of her game, winning the category for foreign reporter of the year at the British Press Awards in 2010.

Looking at her now, I could see the physical effects of the past weeks. She looked drawn about the face. I was familiar with this look of exhaustion and with the telltale lapses into bouts of silent thought. She was always thinking one step ahead. Could her story be stronger? Had she done enough to sculpt in words the images that she saw and the stories she was told?

I too bore the physical and mental symptoms of a long, tough haul. My khaki jacket and cargo pants were filthy, caked in mud, water and cement dust. I looked more like a vagrant than a photographer. I was plagued by a ridiculous hairstyle that changed every time I slept. My greying beard was a perfect hobo length and a peculiar odour followed me everywhere.

Psychologically, the effects of the journey had been enormous and the exhaustion was beginning to bite. In this state, it became easy to lose the sharpness of mind that can keep you alive. We slept when and where we could, but these opportunities would become increasingly rare if the bombardment continued to intensify around us. It was now Thursday, so we had two days to collect and file our story and photographs. The pressure was well and truly on.

We were no strangers to the carnage that we expected to find at the field hospital in Baba Amr. The previous year, we had lived in a hospital that treated dozens of war victims every day. There, inside the hospital's makeshift trauma unit, we witnessed the consequences of a dictator's savagery, the worst that humanity had to offer. Over two months, we saw every injury a war could muster. I remember a man whose torso had been blasted and stripped of flesh from the navel down. His legs, missing from above the knees, were reduced to two snapped femur bones that protruded from the gory remains of his body; two white, blood-smeared sticks that continued to twitch and kick as he stared silently at his broken, dying body. I remember the smiling eighteen-year-old with whom I had smoked the previous day lying motionless on a stretcher before me, his skull split open by a sniper round and his brain, which a friend had found afterwards, heaped in a baseball cap next to his shattered head. I remember the boy's brother holding his cold hand, tears running down his cheeks. And so it had continued.

But what affected me most were not the injuries or the corpses that were carried through the hospital's doors every hour. Instead, it was the simplicity with which people slipped off into death, on improvised beds while medical students and volunteers did their best to save them. We witnessed hundreds of such deaths during those two months and each one sapped a little more of my faith in humanity. For Marie, every death made her want to tell the story even more. Marie Colvin did not give up – ever.

Now, as we waited to begin our day's work in Baba Amr, I saw that familiar determined look on her face. Abu Hanin told us to prepare to move. Outside, in the entranceway to the house, we stood squinting in the bright spring sunshine. The warm rays were a welcome relief from the smoky gloom of the media centre. This was our first daylight foray into the streets of the embattled neighbourhood. We were tense as we stood waiting to cross the road. We could hear the constant low wail of missiles and artillery shells flying overhead. There were dozens of them sailing over us every minute. Each wail was followed by a deep rumble as the shells exploded in the near distance.

Ever since losing the sight in her eye in Sri Lanka, Marie had loathed these weapons. She looked at me, her face grey with fatigue and concern. I gently gripped her hand, nodded and told her that it would be okay. She turned to face the street, summoning up the mental courage to cross. Wa'el was next to us, smiling and displaying no outward sign of fear. For me, the unrelenting scream of the shells overhead made me think of the First World War. I imagined the inner fear of the soldiers who stood in their trenches, smoking nervously as they awaited the whistle that would send so many to their death.

Suddenly a shell landed fifty metres to our left, forcing all of us to hit the ground. Rubble and debris from the blast fell on top of us as we lay cowering in the doorway to the house. I looked to my left and saw the crater in the street. Without any logical explanation, Abu Hanin gave the all clear to cross. We sprinted across the empty street and headed for an unscathed building fifteen metres to our right. Screaming shells ripped through the air as we ran.

More shells struck the far end of the street about forty metres away. Having made it safely across, we tumbled into the apparent safety of a concrete doorway. I looked across at Marie. She smiled and winked back at me and I relaxed a little.

The family inside the house gathered around Marie and she began the arduous and, from a photographer's point of view, unenviable task of piecing together their story. I left Wa'el with Marie and went to photograph what little remained of the street outside.

Baba Amr, a Sunni Muslim neighbourhood in a city and country ruled over by an elitist Shia minority, was one of the poorer areas of Homs. The buildings in the street were a mixture of detached and semi-detached concrete houses, all slightly different in design because most had been handbuilt by their owners. After months of heavy bombardment, the street now looked dead. The individual traces of human life were disappearing. Flowerpots, cracked and broken by flying shrapnel, contained only the dried-up and withered remains of once carefully tended roses; washing lines, blown out of gardens, still had faded children's clothes attached to them.

I walked slowly down the street as shells continued to scream overhead. I stepped over the rusting frame of a child's bicycle, which had been bent back on itself by the force of an explosion. I saw a teddy bear in the gutter, rotting in the cold winter rain. The life has been blown out of this street, I said to myself.

Climbing on to piles of rubble, I peered into the gaping black holes of buildings blown open by artillery gunners who had done their jobs well. Through the holes, I could make out the final moments of family life, frozen in time. These homes were now museums of violence and sudden death. The crunch of rubble and broken glass under my boots and the wail of shells flying overhead had become the soundtrack to Baba Amr. This was, as Bob Dylan had once sung, Desolation Row.

I studied the remnants of the building in which the four women had died three days earlier. The inside had been badly burnt by fire, leaving the bare walls black from smoke. Charred personal belongings and household items lay scattered in the ashes, the only clues that this had once been a family home. Although it served no useful purpose, I couldn't help but imagine what it had been like in the house for the four women, huddling together in the dark as explosions erupted in the streets outside. I thought of the fear that they must have felt as they heard the screaming steel above them and felt the shells bursting around them while they prayed for mercy from their God. Then I thought about the direct hit that shattered limbs and tore through torsos, leaving ragged flesh and bones to burn in the flames of Assad's onslaught. I pulled myself back with a start.

Better cut that out, I thought as I continued photographing the street. At times like these, the camera often acts as a shield for me, a form of protection that blocks out the horrors I witness. I couldn't go into a war zone without a camera. I felt sorry for journalists: they had no such protection. They were truly alone.

'Paul, Paul,' Marie called, 'come and get some shots of the kids here.'

I entered the house and was shown into a bedroom. There was no light in the small room. I looked around blindly, unable to see anything.

'Erm, I don't suppose anyone has a torch handy, do they?' I muttered into the darkness.

I heard someone rummaging in a bag. Moments later a shaft of light flitted shakily around the room before stopping to reveal six children. They were sleeping in two sets of three on cushions that had been laid out on the floor. They looked like sleeping cherubs. The innocence of their young faces shook me. Their tiny forms seemed out of place amid the violence of their surroundings and I had to steady my shaking hand as I took the shots. I did my best to shoot by torchlight, knowing that the value of the photographs would have nothing to do with their quality. Abu Hanin soon interrupted me. He seemed a little agitated and asked me to go into the room where Marie, J-P and Wa'el had gathered.

'Guys,' he said, 'it's time to go to the field hospital. There's a lull in the shelling and we should leave right now. I'm telling you straight. It's only five minutes away but there will be lots of sniper fire and the shelling could get heavy at any moment. When we park the car, you have to run for a few hundred metres as we can't park outside the hospital. It's a major target and we're running short of cars.' He attempted a reassuring smile but his nervous eye movements betrayed him.

Marie looked at me and grimaced. 'How long can we stay there?"' she asked Abu Hanin.

'If the shelling gets heavy, maybe all night,' he replied.

'Do they have laundry facilities?' I asked, shooting a sideways glance at J-P. Abu Hanin looked at me like I was mad, Marie exploded with laughter and Wa'el bit his lip. I think the joke went over J-P's head. He just stood there looking awkwardly bemused.

Marie was still chuckling as we squeezed ourselves into the back of Abu Hanin's car. Abu Hanin gunned the engine a few times to ensure that it was ready for the trip. He pulled out from the kerb and immediately accelerated at full throttle down the narrow street, dodging the craters when he could. He turned to face us as we approached the large roundabout at the end of the road that passed in front of the media centre.

'This is a very dangerous junction,' he told us. 'There are many snipers in the tall buildings to our right.'

We hit the roundabout at full speed and, almost immediately, the sharp crack of explosive-tipped bullets began impacting on the ground behind the vehicle. The snipers were fast but, as the people of Baba Amr discovered their positions, prey for the snipers had become scarce. A speeding vehicle was a large and lucrative target in the death stakes. We continued our sprint for roughly five hundred metres until we reached the cover of a building to our far right.

'The jackals go hungry again,' Abu Hanin said with a wide grin.

As we travelled, more of the destruction of Baba Amr revealed itself like an unfolding nightmare. There were no people. The neighbourhood was deserted. It soon began to rain, adding yet another layer of misery. We hurtled across a junction. Again the sniper bullets missed us. We turned sharply left into a backstreet. The pace slackened and Abu Hanin relaxed a little. Every fifty metres or so we passed the rusting shells of burnt-out cars. Cloying black smoke from smouldering houses filled the streets and the roads became almost impassable at times, due to the amount of fallen rubble and debris blocking them. Explosions reverberated around us. Abu Hanin muttered something about lunchtime being over for the soldiers.

'When we park, don't hesitate,' Abu Hanin said. 'Just follow me and run like hell. I won't stop until I get to the hospital. Just keep running. The street the hospital's on is the most targeted in Baba Amr. About a minute until we get there.'

The district we were entering was full of the crumbling wrecks of buildings that looked like they had been shelled many times over. No building had been spared: not a single window had glass in its frames. If the aim of President Assad was to make Baba Amr uninhabitable, then he had certainly achieved his goal in this part of the neighbourhood. The car screeched to a halt beneath what was left of a large second-floor balcony. We prepared, once again, to make a life or death dash through the streets.

'Run. Do not stop running until you reach the hospital. Let's go,' shouted Abu Hanin, slamming his door shut.

He waited while we dismounted from the vehicle and then set off at a sprint. I let Marie go ahead of me so I could watch her and Wa'el did the same for J-P. A shell exploded fifty metres behind us. Perhaps they are aiming at the car, I thought. We continued the sprint, our breath coming in huge gulps, until we reached a street corner. Abu Hanin veered left. Bursts of machine-gun fire erupted, strafing the street and buildings around us.

'Keep moving, keep moving,' he screamed at us. Further ahead of us more explosions ripped up the tarmac, sending shrapnel and concrete flying. The incoming rounds appeared to come from every angle. We sprinted past two rebels carrying a wounded man, his left leg hanging on by a few strands of flesh, his face blank with shock.

Ahead, perhaps a hundred metres in the distance, were two more men. They waved at us frantically, urging us on. But it felt like I was running through treacle. I couldn't seem to gain any momentum. There was another crunch as a mortar impacted behind us. I felt the force of the blast on my back. The men up ahead of us urged us on. Ten metres, five metres and then outstretched hands pulled us into the doorway and bundled us inside the field clinic.

We stood in a hallway, bent double as we caught our breath. Heart thumping, trembling with fear and adrenalin, I found the strength to raise my head and count our numbers. We had all made it. Wa'el grinned as he checked to see if J-P was okay.

'See, not so bad, eh?' Abu Hanin said, smiling at us as we began to get our breath back.

Marie shot a glance at him and shook her head. She mouthed the words 'not too bad' in bewilderment. While we recuperated, there was a loud bang at the clinic door. The two men we had passed on the street outside only minutes earlier came crashing in through the entrance, still carrying their wounded man. A female nurse ushered them into a room to our left. They heaved the wounded man with the shattered leg on to a stretcher. The floor – from the doorway to the bed – was smeared with a thick trail of the man's blood.

We were shown into an empty office and offered tea by a young man wearing scrubs. We were asked to wait and told that Dr Mohamed would join us soon. We all lit cigarettes – apart from Marie who had given up on the orders of her dentist – and looked around. A child's mobile hung in one corner. Someone, probably the child's parent, had painted Disney characters on the walls in an effort to provide some colour. The metal shutters on the window overlooking the main street were streaked with shrapnel holes. The damaged clock on the wall, its hands now frozen, marked the moment that a spinning slice of hot deadly steel had ripped through this child's bedroom.

The door opened and in came the young lad with tea, closely followed by Dr Mohamed Al-Mohamed. Anyone who had studied the Syrian uprising so far, watched the news or visited YouTube in recent months would recognise this doctor. His blistering performances to camera had become legendary. A former army doctor, Dr Mohamed was renowned for his outspoken condemnations of Assad and the crisis that now gripped Syria. He had run underground field hospitals like the one we were now in for months, moving constantly to avoid being hit by artillery fire. He was mild-natured and he smiled at us when he spoke. But his eyes were ringed with dark circles of exhaustion and his smile failed to hide the months of barbarity that he had witnessed.

'This is my third field clinic. The last one was destroyed. My friend, a pharmacist, had his legs blown off in the previous one,' he explained matter-of-factly. 'Soon they will hit here. Every day they hit the roof of this place. They know where we are. We won't last for ever.

'We have no real medical supplies, no anaesthetics, no painkillers stronger than ibuprofen. We have to amputate while people are awake and, even if they live, we have no room to keep them here. We must put them in people's houses in the town and often they die before we get back to check on them.

'Some days we have so many dead that we do not have enough space to keep them. They are buried at night, in secret. Even then the snipers will attack the funerals. We have lost our humanity here in Baba Amr.'

A huge explosion shook the building. Dr Mohamed barely flinched as the plaster dust from the ceiling drifted down on top of us. Someone screamed his name from the corridor. Moving swiftly past us, he pulled me by the shoulder and said, 'Come, you must see this.'

Grabbing my camera and spilling my tea, I raced from the room in pursuit of the doctor. There was carnage in the entranceway to the building. People were dragging bodies through the door, blood trails led in all directions, screams filled the air and, through the smoky haze, I could make out the lifeless form of a body abandoned on the ground.

'He's dead,' said a nurse in scrubs. 'He must stay there. We have no room for him.'

The front door of the building was wide open and people were still desperately trying to drag bodies in from the street. I was struggling to focus. It seemed that everywhere I looked there was either an injured patient or a medic desperately trying to sort the living from the dead.

A female nurse, Um Ammar, who I had met earlier, pulled me

into one of the side rooms. Inside, there were two operating tables that had been crudely fashioned from stretchers, tables and a recycled hospital trolley. Both tables were occupied and in the corner of the room lay two corpses that had been brought in moments earlier. There wasn't even a spare blanket to cover the dead bodies. A dentist called Dr Ali was busy cutting off the trousers of one of the men who lay on the operating table. Deep shrapnel wounds had ripped open his thigh muscles. Blood pumped from the man's wounds as his whole body went into spasm. He convulsed once more before falling still, his open eyes locked on Dr Ali. The dentist felt the man's neck for signs of a pulse. 'Dead,' he said, his voice void of emotion. He shook his head and repeated the word, 'Dead.'

On the other table, Dr Mohamed was desperately cutting the clothes off a young man who was writhing in agony on the makeshift operating table. I focused the camera and shot. I could see the young man grow visibly weaker. Dr Mohamed peeled back the man's clothes to reveal the wound. He had suffered a massive blast injury to the chest but, before the doctor could even begin to assess the damage, the young man had stopped squirming. He exhaled a final breath and ceased to exist.

I caught Dr Mohamed's eyes. For a moment we just stared at each other, the young man's final breath hanging in the air between us. We said nothing; the doctor and his bloody scalpel, the photographer with his camera and the silent corpse in the middle.

For hours the carnage continued. More critically injured and dead were rushed into the family home turned temporary hospital. Space was made for new patients as the dead were removed and stored in a back room that was filling up by the hour. In the rare quieter moments, the doctors and staff sipped at warm tea and smoked together. The stress was apparent on all their faces – from the boy who made tea to the doctors who worked miracles with no more than basic first-aid kits and a few plasma bags strung from wooden coat racks.

I heard more explosions outside, followed by the screeching of car tyres, a sound that heralded the end of these rare moments of rest. I saw another medic trying to help a three-year-old girl with shrapnel injuries to the stomach. She died in agony. The doctor just didn't have the drugs to do anything for her. As another huge aftershock rocked the clinic, he simply walked to the corner of the room, clutched his head in his hands and raised his face to the heavens. Then he began, slowly and repeatedly, to bang his head against the wall.

Marie came to my side. She looked harrowed and drained. Her shoulders were stooped and her voice was slow and weary. 'How are you doing, Paul?' she asked.

I simply shook my head.

'Come on, you've seen this before. Don't let it get to you, mate,' she said, putting her arm around me to give me a hug. 'We have to show this to the world. We *will* make a difference.'

In moments like this, Marie's ability to motivate and comfort despite the horrors around her was inspirational. We had been through this in Libya, each of us pulling the other through. At times she could infuriate: when we were both exhausted and in need of a break, the driving force in Marie often meant we carried on well beyond our physical abilities. But, when what we witnessed began to take its toll, Marie showed the compassion that she normally reserved for the victims of the wars she wrote about.

We stayed in the clinic for about five hours, exhausted and drained from what we had seen and heard. Then Abu Hanin suggested that we visit what he called the Widows' Basement. The word basement stopped me in my tracks.

April 2011, Misrata, Libya

In Misrata, I had attached myself to a trainee surgeon called Dr Tameem. The pair of us raced about the port city in his ambulance, responding to casualties caused by the incessant salvos of GRAD missiles – Russian-made, 120mm multi-launch rockets – fired into civilian neighbourhoods. There was a continuous stream of ambulances ferrying the dead, mutilated and barely living back to the makeshift trauma unit, which was a tent set up in the grounds of what had once been a private clinic.

One night I was exhausted and sat down to rest. My body armour, which was soaked in sweat and blood from carrying the injured and dying, seemed to weigh more than I did. Dr Tameem and I had narrowly escaped direct hits all night and I felt I was about to explode with anger at the seemingly interminable bloodshed. Tameem, a smiling and slightly rotund Libyan, appeared to have deep reserves of energy and an equally strong sense of humour. He caught me smoking and pulled me to my feet.

'Come on, Paul. We have another ambulance. Another big hit. Many dead,' he said, dragging me to the ambulance. It was riddled with shrapnel and its front wing had been blown off in an earlier mission. We climbed in and raced out of the gates of the hospital. Above the engine noise we could hear the deep, powerful booms of the GRAD missiles that were being launched in salvos of 20 or 40. The missiles devastated anything they hit. A single rocket was capable of removing an entire house. In Misrata, they fell from the sky like explosive rain.

The ambulance pulled to a halt at a small crossroads in the centre of a residential area. Cars were on fire in the street outside and thick black smoke billowed from the windows of houses. The bloodcurdling screams of the injured and dying, trapped amid the rubble of houses, filled the night air. I knew from experience what was about to happen. It sent a chill down my spine. The forces loyal to Colonel Gaddafi would shell an area, wait fifteen minutes until the ambulances arrived and then shell it again, often doubling their kill rate. We had, by my reckoning, another couple of minutes before the second wave of missiles hit.

I could hear screaming coming from somewhere further afield. I turned a street corner and the screams grew louder. The street I was on was full of smoke, making it difficult to see. I stood still to listen for the cries, which seemed to come from all around me. Then I spotted it. There was a small gap between one of the buildings and the pavement. I approached slowly. The screaming grew more intense the closer I got. Kneeling, I peered into the darkness of the hole. A very small neon light illuminated what must have been an underground storage unit or car park. In the corner, gathered together in a terrified bundle of fear, were the faces of perhaps a hundred and fifty women and children.

I leapt to my feet, searching frantically for the entrance to the underground shelter, knowing that any minute the second wave of missiles would come thundering down on us. Turning another street corner, I saw a rebel guarding a door. He turned to look at me suspiciously as I ran towards him. He stopped me at the door, he was protecting the woman and children located in the basement, I simply showed him my camera. He nodded and opened the door.

I raced down the stairs and found myself in a large basement. Women and children were huddled in groups, crying, screaming or wailing. The women, dressed in black with their faces hidden behind veils, increased the volume of their screams when they saw me. They stretched their arms out towards me. The children looked terrified. Suddenly, the pressure blast from a huge explosion lifted

146

me off my feet and hurled me to the ground. My ears felt like they were going to explode from the combined pressure of the blast and the frantic, horrifying screams of the women and children.

The blast had blown out the light, plunging the basement into darkness. I turned on my torch, which illuminated a corner of the room. Two women beckoned me towards them. They pointed at a bundle of blankets. I knelt down, pulled back the blankets and found an ancient old lady, her brown leathery skin stretched over her thin brittle bones. I touched her face. She was warm but I couldn't tell if she was still alive. I moved my hands to her neck and felt for a pulse. Nothing. I checked her wrists and again found no pulse. She must have died from a heart attack. I covered her with a blanket and turned to leave. There was nothing I could do for any of the people trapped inside. There was nowhere for them to run to, nowhere for them to hide. I handed my torch to a young girl. The screams of the women and children grew louder as I disappeared up the stairs of the basement.

Outside, the terrifying screech and enormous explosions of the GRAD missiles continued unabated. Finding a dark doorway only yards away from the basement, I took off my helmet and leant against the door. I lit a cigarette. It tasted foul but I smoked on regardless. I felt empty and helpless. I could still hear the awful screams from the basement. I tried to rationalise my reasons for being there: to document, to record and, as Marie always said, to bear witness. But it all seemed so shallow to me. I knew my presence hadn't saved a single life that night. At best, there would be a tiny ripple when my images where published but I could do nothing that would make an immediate, practical difference. I felt angry and pointless as I crouched, waiting for the sky to rain fire and blow the women and children trapped in the basement to pieces.

16 February 2012, Baba Amr, Syria

I hated basements. The thought of entering one again, this time here in Syria, filled me with dread. Marie looked at me quizzically as we listened to Abu Hanin talk about the Widows' Basement. She could tell that my mind had wandered off and she looked concerned.

'Hey,' she said. 'Hey. Are you okay. Paul? You look awful. Is it the basement, the basement in Misrata?' She had heard the story of that night and seen the pictures. Now she astutely picked up on my silence.

I told her I was fine. I began to gather my kit in preparation for another dash through the streets. By this time it was night and the shelling had eased off. We made the run for the car in a far less dramatic fashion than when we arrived. I noticed something I hadn't seen before, lurking in the shadows created by the high moon – life. Small groups of people stood nervously in the streets outside wrecked buildings, amid the rubble and chaos. Baba Amr was clearly not deserted: its residents had simply become nocturnal, venturing out only when night came. They stood like ghosts in the shadows, their hollowed faces watching anxiously as our car passed them by.

After a five-minute drive, we pulled up on a dark, narrow street. Abu Hanin signalled for us to get out. We stood huddled together in a small group, wondering where we were and what we were doing. There was total silence as he tapped sharply on a double door facing us. After a brief pause the doors swung open, throwing shafts of light over our small group. We entered and the doors quickly closed behind us. We were in the so-called Widows' Basement.

It wasn't hard to work out how it had earned its name. We were looking down into a cavernous, poorly lit basement. Below us was a seething mass of women and children, crammed into what had once been a carpentry shop. Lathes and other woodturning tools had been piled to one side to create more space for the shop's new inhabitants.

Slowly, we descended the stairs into the cellar. I readied my camera. If you don't get the shot immediately then it's over: all you come out with are pictures of kids scrambling over each other to have their photograph taken. I stopped halfway down the stairs and began shooting, making myself as small and inconspicuous as possible. I allowed Marie to slip into the crowd first and waited until all eyes were focused on her tall, slim figure. Then I began shooting the remainder of the crowd in their natural positions. I knew I only had a couple of minutes and sure enough thirty screaming children were soon vying for prime position in front of my camera.

The conditions inside the basement were appalling. We were told that about three hundred women and children lived in this room, no larger than 10 × 15 metres. Old women crouched on threadbare rugs or empty flour sacks, staring into space. Younger girls cooked small bowls of soup on gas burners and one old lady prepared flat bread on an upturned wok. These were the women and children who had lost it all. They were a mix of elderly widows who could no longer fend for themselves and the neighbourhood's younger women, widows of the men killed during the siege of Baba Amr.

A young girl with beautiful yet sad eyes that peered from behind a veil stopped us as we walked between the groups of women and children. She clutched a white woollen blanket to her chest. Wrapped in the blanket was her baby. The child was three days old and had been born in the cellar but the lack of food and the stressful conditions meant that the mother could not feed it. With no baby formula available, the only nourishment for the child was sugar dissolved in water.

The cellar was a haven for these women and children but it wasn't a bombproof shelter. A direct hit from a 240mm mortar would kill all of them. It was a place of misery, devoid of any hope. All these women and children could do was accept their grim lot and pray that the missiles they heard screeching overhead wouldn't come for them.

We left the place in silence. The basement was a potent symbol of all that was happening in Baba Amr. I felt anger bubble up inside me whenever I thought of the total disregard for innocent life that Assad and his military were showing. I understand war; I have seen it many times at first hand. But what was happening in Baba Amr could hardly be classified as war. This was the deliberate targeting of women and children. Baba Amr was a slaughterhouse.

Arriving back at the media centre, I began selecting and uploading my images from the day's work via satellite. It was critical to get them out as quickly as possible. If the satellite was suddenly destroyed by a shell or mortar, then all the day's work would have been in vain. While I uploaded my images, Marie, wrapped in a blanket, collated her notes. We were both exhausted and we planned to finish up and get an early night. It was then, just as we let the prospect of sleep slip into our minds, that we received an email and the idea of a cosy, eight-blanket night began to ebb away.

CHAPTER SEVEN

Should we stay or should we go?

17 February 2012, Baba Amr, Syria

Marie gave a discreet nod and beckoned me over to her side of the room. Puzzled, I crossed over and squeezed in beside her, sneakily pinching half of her blanket for warmth. Her laptop was open on her email page. She looked worried.

'What's up, Marie?' I asked, as a dull feeling of dread began to grow inside me.

'Well,' she said ominously, before pausing. 'I got an email from Sara Hashash, a former correspondent from the paper who now lives in Egypt. Her source says that the final assault on Baba Amr is going to happen tonight. They're going to send in infantry and tanks to crush the uprising once and for all.'

A chill ran down my spine as Marie let the full weight of this news sink in.

'What do you reckon, Paul? What's your gut feeling?' she asked, her voice flat with concern.

'Well,' I replied, 'the intensity of the artillery barrage has been rising all week, according to the activists. It's the heaviest we've ever seen and Assad's mob have been softening up Baba Amr for weeks now. At some point they must commit to a final attack. If they really want Homs free from rebels then it has to come sometime.'

Just then, the CNN crew – Arwa, Neil and Tim their security man – entered the room, breaking the contemplative silence that had fallen over Marie and me as we tried to figure out what to do. The CNN lot looked exhausted as they dumped their dusty bags and cameras by the door. Marie shook off the snug warmth of her blanket and went over to Arwa, who was deep in conversation with Neil and Tim. I followed. We sat together as far away from the local activists as we could so as not to cause any panic. Marie briefly explained to Arwa that she had received news Assad was about to launch the final assault on the neighbourhood. Arwa nodded silently as Marie spoke.

'We've heard the same from the FSA guys on the streets,' Arwa said. 'As well as Abu Hanin who's gone to talk with the FSA, we also got a mail from the office. I guess they picked up the same source. Problem is, we've all been hearing all sorts of rumours for days now, so what makes this one any more real?' Arwa looked troubled, unsure whether to stay and risk being killed or to leave and risk abandoning the story prematurely if the rumoured assault failed to materialise.

'Exactly,' said Marie, immediately picking up on Arwa's doubts about the likelihood of a full-scale attack. 'If we go now and nothing happens we'll be screwed if we want to get back in.' Her voice had taken on a more optimistic tone as she realised that others might want to stay too.

Marie had previous form for staying behind in dangerous places when every other journalist had fled: Chechnya, Sri Lanka and Misrata were just a few examples. She once stubbornly refused to abandon hundreds of refugees in East Timor as government soldiers marched on their camp. The United Nations and Marie's colleagues, with the exception of two Dutch female journalists, had decided it was far too dangerous to remain. Marie's foreign desk editor, deeply concerned for her safety, demanded to know why there weren't any other journalists with her. 'Where are all the men?' the editor asked, a question to which Marie famously responded, 'I suppose they just don't make men like they used to.'

As we discussed the pros and cons of leaving Baba Amr, I could tell that Marie wanted to stay. She wanted to believe the talk of an impending assault was merely just that – talk. Marie and Arwa went in search of Abu Hanin to see if there was any more information. I stayed with Neil and Tim to discuss the issue further.

'Okay, chaps,' I said, 'we've all have been in plenty of tricky hot spots. Tim, I guess, being CNN security, you're ex-military?'

Tim smiled and nodded. 'Special Boat Service,' he said.

Neil shook his head. He wasn't ex-military but he was an old hand.

'Okay,' I said. 'So let's look at it from a purely military perspective. We are in a bad situation here: the neighbourhood is well and truly locked down, sealed tight by a ring of tanks, artillery and infantry. They aren't just a bunch of conscripts either. It's the 4th Division. They know their stuff.

'My major problem with this situation is the exit plan, or more to the point, the lack of one. Our only way out is via that tunnel and if that tunnel, or the road to it, falls, then we are well and truly up shit creek with a turd paddle. From what we have seen, the FSA have just enough ammo and men to fend off probes from single tanks but if Assad's mob come in full force then the FSA will disintegrate as a fighting unit. The rebels will be outgunned and outmanoeuvred. I'm sure I have enough images for the paper for this week and I'm pretty sure Marie has a story now. How about you guys?'

Neil nodded and said that they did have a story. He agreed with my assessment. Tim also accepted all the points I had made, agreeing that to stay could prove fatal. He agreed fully that the tunnel was the deal-clincher – it was the only sure way out of Baba Amr. I relaxed a little, reassured that if it came to convincing Marie it was too hot to stay, then I had the backup that I might well need to win my case for leaving.

The following hours saw the tension in the house mount. Mysterious strangers emerged from the shadows and engaged in hurried, whispered conversations before leaving as quietly as they had arrived. FSA fighters, fully armed and battle-ready, descended on the house. They drank tea, smoked and checked their weapons. Marie and Arwa reappeared and confirmed that the general feeling among the FSA was that the attack was expected. We were to sit tight for the moment. The activists were now absorbed in deep conversation. What had begun as a rumour now looked like a real possibility.

We packed our kit and then sat back down, powerless to do anything other than kill time. The tension was palpable. Although the atmosphere in the media centre was surprisingly calm, the thunderous explosions and unending bursts of heavy machine-gun fire that reverberated through the room had acquired a more immediate sense of foreboding. At about nine o'clock, Abu Hanin entered the room. He looked exhausted.

'Listen,' he said to our small group, 'we believe it is going to happen tonight. All our intelligence points that way. I am breaking my twelve-man team into two groups of six. One half has volunteered to stay and be martyrs; the other six will leave with you tonight.

'You cannot stay here. If you do, you will also be martyrs and we cannot allow that. When Assad's troops enter we will continue to transmit when possible. When that's over we will pick up guns and fight until we die. We need you alive to tell the world what you have seen here. Do you all understand?' He was pleading with us. This was a man who knew that the end was coming. He wanted us out, without question.

We all silently nodded in agreement.

'Then be prepared and be ready to move. We thank you all,' he finished, his expression full of sorrow as he turned to leave.

Marie pulled me aside. 'Paul, do you really believe it or do you think we should stay?' She really didn't want to believe that Assad's forces were about to launch their long-feared ground incursion on the tiny rebel enclave.

I told her about the conclusion that Neil, Tim and I had come to earlier. We may all be wrong, I told her, but the stakes we'd be gambling for would be too high if we stayed. 'Look around you, Marie. They are leaving. There is a reason for that,' I said, nodding towards the activists who were stripping the room of computers and cables as we spoke.

She agreed, somewhat reluctantly, that we should join the leaving party. 'We may regret this, Paul. We really may regret leaving,' she said before turning to pack her few belongings.

'Cheer up, you miserable sod. At least we're getting out in one piece,' I replied, just loud enough for her to hear.

I could hear her chuckling as she started searching for all the bits and pieces she had lost. Marie was a disaster when it came to losing her belongings. In Libya, I would take every fixer we used to one side and inform him that it was his duty to check for Marie's possessions every time we left a room or a car. It was a running joke between us. I remember how she joined up with me in Tripoli a few days after the rebels had taken the Libyan capital, only to realise that she had forgotten to collect her bag from the car, which was now on its way back to Tunisia. The bag had her laptop, satellite transmitter and all her clothes inside – not a great start to any new assignment. Within an hour, the ever-resourceful Marie had reappeared with a new laptop, borrowed from someone, somewhere, as the battle for Tripoli raged around us. This laptop only lasted a few days before she left it at a makeshift rebel base.

The activists were now forming up with their kit. One carried a satellite dish and two others held a large camera they had taken down from the roof. Slowly, everything around us changed. The place that had acted as the world's eyes and ears inside Baba Amr became a waiting room.

A harrowing thought struck me. These men, who had protected and fed us, had, in the last half-hour, made an awful decision: they had selected who among them was to live and who was about to die. It was now entirely possible that many of our friends from Baba Amr would be dead come morning.

I thought about Abu Hanin. There had been no trace of his usual radiant smile when he left us. It was heartbreaking to realise that, while arranging our escape, he was also preparing for his own probable death. Throughout the evening's events, Abu Hanin had maintained a strong and quiet dignity. There was no panic, no melodrama and no apparent fear in the former Bournemouth student as he prepared to make his last stand. Inside the room, those selected to leave and those who had chosen to stay sat together smoking. Death hovered in the air, but no one spoke about it.

As if to confirm the reports of a ground assault, Assad's forces shelled Baba Amr long into the evening. We knew that there could be no escape attempt while the bombardment continued, and the shelling only heightened the already charged atmosphere. However, when the intensity of the shelling subsided to a reasonable level, it all happened very quickly. An exhausted-looking FSA rebel ran into the house and spoke animatedly with Abu Hanin. Both men nodded and shook hands before the rebel left. Abu Hanin then summoned us to share the plan. In two minutes the journalists and half the activists would leave in two separate vans and head directly to the tunnel.

Everyone silently grabbed bags and piled them into the waiting vehicles outside. Short but heartfelt goodbyes were uttered in the darkness. The two groups of activists knew this could be the last time that either saw the other. These men had been through hell. They wore pained expressions as they bade farewell to friends who had shared the horrors of death and the daily fears of annihilation.

Having hugged the activists who were staying behind, we stopped at the entrance to put on our shoes. We were soon ready to move. All that is except J-P. The Frenchman simply stood stock-still in the doorway.

'What's up, J-P?' I asked, somewhat concerned by his lack of activity at such a crucial moment.

'My shoes, my shoes,' he replied mournfully. 'Someone has taken them.'

'Erm, I'm sure they haven't been stolen, J-P. Have another good look around.'

J-P continued his search by torchlight, eventually finding one of them. A rebel suggested he try upstairs. Minutes later he reappeared, clutching both shoes, a huge smile on his face.

'Okay, J-P. Mount up, mate. We gotta move now,' I said, emphasising the 'now'.

He clambered into the van, muttering at the same time, 'Why would anyone steal just one shoe?'

Abu Hanin stopped us on the way out. His face was resolute as he hugged us both. He thanked us sincerely for coming to Baba

Amr. All we could offer in return was a simple thank you for all he had done on our behalf. We promised to keep in touch. He smiled and began to walk away before stopping and turning to face us once more, as if to impart some profound last words.

'Paul,' he said, 'don't forget my Golden Virginia in the Tesco bag.'

'Don't worry, I won't, mate. I'll bring a Nando's and beer too,' I replied as I climbed into a small white minibus with a bullet-shattered windscreen.

I felt a burning sense of humiliation rise inside me as I sat in the back of the minibus. We were leaving these men to a fate that no one could predict. The sense that we were abandoning them appalled me. I finally understood Marie's innermost desire to stay and bear witness.

Marie climbed in next to me. The CNN crew squeezed on to the back seat alongside J-P, while an FSA guard entered the back. Two others – the driver and a bodyguard carrying his Kalashnikov – climbed into the front. The activists crammed themselves into the white van in front of ours.

Both vehicles pulled away simultaneously before making a tight U-turn outside the media centre. Silhouetted like ghosts against the weak light from the media centre's hallway, the activists waved us off. The sickening feeling of abandonment worsened as we accelerated towards the first turn at the end of the street. Sniper shots rang out in the night air as explosive bullets struck the ground close to our vehicles. Astonishingly, the driver started fiddling with the stereo system as we raced through the streets of Baba Amr. Seconds later, ear-splitting Arabic techno music filled the van.

I don't know what it is about Syrians, music, travel and war, but they all seemed to be inexplicably linked. On entering Homs we had been escorted by singing rebels and now our mad dash to safety was being accompanied by high-powered Arabic techno. Given the nature of our trip, it seemed tactically irresponsible to be sending out thumping rhythms into the night.

Marie, visibly disgusted at the driver, shouted into my ear, 'Paul, this is insane! Tell him to turn it down.'

Leaning forward and tapping the driver's shoulder, I indicated that he drop the level a touch. He grudgingly obliged, but only by half a decibel, before continuing to sing along to the music. If I'm being shot at then at least I like to know I am. We could have had rocket-propelled grenades whizzing past our van and we wouldn't have known it. In the darkness, ears become more important than eyes. The sky was black and menacing and it was impossible to make out any of the terrain. We were speeding – deaf and blind – into what we knew were enemy lines. The only geographic marker we had to guide us was the burning fuel line that had been blown up a few days earlier. It continued to blaze in the distance, casting a flickering orange glow in the sky.

Eventually, arriving at a crossroads, the driver mercifully turned off the music and brought the vehicle to a gentle halt. A brief discussion, which sounded suspiciously like an argument between driver and escort in the front seat, ensued. There was a momentary pause before we continued, taking a left-hand turn down a street. But we had only driven about twenty metres down the road when the armed rebel escort in the back of the vehicle began to lambast the driver in bursts of angry Arabic. Slipping the vehicle into reverse, the driver backed up to the crossroads and another fierce debate began, this time between the rear escort and the driver. We started moving again, taking the right-hand turn instead.

'Methinks we are somewhat lost,' I said, turning to look at Marie.

Marie, shaking her head in bewilderment, replied, 'No shit, Sherlock,' before closing her eyes in resignation.

We were later to discover that, had we continued down the left-hand road for a further four hundred metres, we would have bumped into a Syrian army checkpoint manned by about two hundred soldiers.

Not only had we lost faith in our driver but we had also lost contact with the other vehicle full of the activists from the media centre. The FSA escort in the front seat tried desperately to raise someone, anyone, on the radio. The driver then started to shout. Was he happy, sad or angry? We didn't have a clue until he gave the universal thumbs up. Oh good, I thought, he knows the way out. Marie's face was a mask of thundering anger. I understood her silent fury: she had survived everything a war could throw at her; to be killed by a wrong turn would have pissed her off mightily.

Through a mix of luck and determination we finally caught up with the other van, which was parked near the cluster of buildings that we had stopped at on our way into Baba Amr a few days earlier. The activists collected their kit from the vehicle before we organised ourselves into a single line, ready for the walk back to the tunnel.

Our clandestine escape was rapidly descending into farce. Admittedly, the guys from the media centre were activists, not soldiers, the FSA only admitted deserters with a military ID, but someone could surely have offered them at least one basic lesson in tactics. One activist, about three people ahead of me in the line, carried the satellite dish, which looked for the entire world like a large, bright white target. This I could forgive but, about ten people further on, I witnessed one of the most bizarrely memorable sights of my life. It took a little while for my brain to compute but there, in territory occupied by government forces, in the middle of our bold and audacious escape attempt, was a guy in flashing LED trainers. One foot flashed a brilliant white while the second transmitted a rather eye-catching red, lighting up the path towards the tunnel – the secret lifeline to Baba Amr – like a runway. I nearly wept. Many of the escapees were wearing white sweatshirts and jackets and they were chatting among themselves as if they were taking a gentle stroll in a park. The noise was terrifying and the visuals were beyond comprehension, so I resigned myself to the probability that we would all shortly be dead.

The activists' lack of tactical awareness did little to improve what turned out to be a long, exhausting and terrifying affair. They sang their way back out through the tunnel and they made a racket walking from the tunnel to the waiting vehicles. Almost every step of the way, I silently expected to be blown out of existence.

It was an incredibly tense escape, but it could have been far worse had it not been for Neil, the CNN cameraman. Having climbed down into the tunnel, we packed all the camera bags on to a trailer attached to the underground motorcycle, which J-P rode pillion. The bike drove off ahead of us and we struggled on foot behind. Upon reaching the point where the motorcycle was forced to stop and turn around, I looked for my bag and, failing to spot it, simply assumed that it had been carried onwards by one of the activists. It was only when Neil arrived at the end of the tunnel in a state of sheer exhaustion and asked whether the extremely heavy bag in his hand was mine that I realised I had left it behind. The poor sod had carried it halfway through the tunnel for me. It would cost me many beers to make up for his ordeal.

When we finally reached the rendezvous point, having marched a short distance from the exit of the underground tunnel, the rebels bundled us into the back of a closed truck. It was pitch black in the truck and we were squeezed together like cattle. Some of us stood while others crouched into small balls, unable to adjust our positions due to the sheer number of people crammed into the vehicle. Amazingly, given the lack of space, somebody slipped me a lighted cigarette. Others also managed to light up and, very quickly, the van was full of smoke.

I sat on the wet floor pondering the last few hours with my knees squeezed to my chin and the hood of my jacket pulled over my head for warmth. If the attack did come tonight then our decision to leave would be proved correct. A fully fledged assault on Baba Amr would have certainly meant the end for all of us. Within a day or two, the area would become a garrison town. On the other hand, if the assault didn't materialise, then we had left the very place we had worked so hard to access. Regardless, we would find out in the morning whether our leaving was a mistake.

The ride back to Al Buwaydah was bone-jarring and soon became an endurance test. Locked into its foetal position, my whole body began to cramp. I could straighten my back and twist my ankles but that was it. Finally, the driver dropped us back at Commander Abu Hassan's house, where we had stayed before entering Baba Amr. It felt like a homecoming as we gathered at the gate, mentally and physically exhausted, cold and in serious need of sleep.

We entered without ceremony, found some blankets and curled up on the cushions to sleep. Marie walked the fifty yards to the women's house, where a large and comfortable bed awaited her. I drifted off to sleep, the sounds of artillery fire comfortingly far away.

I woke with a start to a hand shaking my shoulder. Was it an attack? I wondered. Did we have to run? Within seconds I was fully awake and ready to move. I looked up to find Marie's face a few inches from mine, whispering, 'Paul, Paul, wake up.'

She looked awful. Her face was tired, her eyes were bloodshot and she wore a worried frown. This was the face few people saw. It was the fatigued face of a woman working in relentlessly high-pressure conditions inside a war zone.

'Paul, they didn't attack this morning,' she said, her voice fraught. 'Commander Hassan told me that all is normal in Baba Amr – still massive artillery attacks but no land forces. Paul, we fucked up.'

I sighed, relieved that Abu Hanin and our friends were still alive and that the remaining people of Baba Amr had been spared to live another day. I was conscious that we had left for logistical and safety reasons but I was now beginning to regret our decision.

'Marie, we made the right move,' I said hesitantly, in an effort to soothe her. 'That attack could easily have happened last night. We did the right thing.'

'Okay,' said Marie. 'We can talk about that later. I haven't slept at all. I've been writing my copy all night and now we have a problem – the BGAN. It isn't working. Can we try yours?'

The BGAN was the satellite system we used to transmit emails and images back to London. Without a working BGAN we wouldn't be able to file anything – no stories, no photographs.

'We'll get one working,' I said, struggling to unwrap myself from the blankets while simultaneously lighting a cigarette. 'Relax for five minutes. I'll get my kit together and we'll get on the roof and try mine.'

'It's been a fucking nightmare,' she said. 'I had it working and then it stopped. I think Assad's boys are jamming the signal.'

We walked the fifty metres to the women's house and climbed the concrete stairs on to the exposed roof where Marie had set up her BGAN. From our position on the roof we could see for miles. The bright crisp sunlight offered a stunning panorama. To our south were the gently rolling hills that led back to Lebanon. Bathed in an early-morning mist, they were an image of tranquillity that would have had Constable running for his sketchpad. Below, in the narrow back lanes of Al Buwaydah, children played noisily, climbing walls and throwing stones at terrified cats. In the patchwork of gardens and backyards, women hung out laundry and scrubbed clothes in bathtubs of water. Old men sat and smoked pipes in the sun. For a few brief moments, my mind was at peace.

In the distance, we could hear the familiar boom of an artillery barrage. First the sound of the guns firing, followed by the explosions as they impacted inside Baba Amr. I turned to face north, in the direction of the guns, and the beautiful vista vanished. Black plumes of oily smoke hung like sinister clouds over the city of Homs, a stark contrast to the beautiful mist and rolling hills to the south.

It was a perfect location to set up the BGAN transmitter. I had transmitted from far worse positions and never failed to get a connection, but something was wrong. I set up my own BGAN and still nothing happened. We couldn't even get a basic signal. I could reach only one conclusion: Assad's forces were indeed jamming us. The Syrians were well equipped with good electronic counter-measures and monitoring equipment thanks to Russia and Iran, who had not only supplied Syria with large amounts of weaponry and ammunition but also with the technology needed to jam and monitor electronic activity. Iran and Russia had even supplied operators to run the complex systems.

Worse still, Iran had provided Syria with the curse of modern warfare, the drone, or pilotless aircraft. These could beam back real-time images of the battlefield and fire missiles at ground targets they detected. They were the affordable and expendable eyes in the sky of the modern army. They allowed Assad's forces to circle Baba Amr and pick out targets for the artillery guns with ease. We had heard them buzzing above Baba Amr every day. With a drone overhead, there was no place to hide.

'We're stuffed, Marie. I can't get the BGAN working,' I said.

Marie looked crestfallen. She had a fantastic piece to file. We knew the alternative was to phone the office and dictate the copy. This wasn't as easy as it sounds: the only communication we had with the office was via a satellite phone, which was one of our most traceable pieces of kit. The longer the phone was switched on, the more opportunity the government had to pinpoint its location. It was our most dangerous option.

Marie spent the morning dictating her piece to Lucy Fisher on the foreign desk in London via the satphone. It took hours: batteries went flat, signal was lost and we had to change location often to avoid possible detection. Around midday, just hours before deadline, Marie finally filed her story. The colour returned to her cheeks and she declared with a weary grin that she was off for a 'little nap'.

During that Saturday morning, Marie had also informed the newspaper's foreign editor, Sean Ryan, that we planned to travel north to a city called Hama. Bashar al-Assad's father had reduced Hama to rubble during a popular uprising in 1982. Many thousands had died in the terrifying onslaught that the president's father had unleashed on the city. Fears now ran high that President Bashar al-Assad was about to re-enact his father's massacre of Hama. He had already ordered his forces to lay siege to the city's population and they had begun to shell residential areas indiscriminately. Sean okayed our plan.

We asked Commander Hassan if he could get us into the city. He agreed he would try to arrange transport for the Monday coming. He explained it would be tough: the roads between Al Buwaydah and Hama were unusable due to the heavy presence of government troops. He also had very little information about the state of the city. It was only fifty kilometres away but rebel lines of communication were poor, especially among units fighting in different parts of the country.

We spent Saturday and Sunday resting from the previous week's endeavours. We knew going to Hama would be a hard and dangerous slog and we needed to recharge our mental and physical batteries. I went foraging for cigarettes with an FSA rebel on a motorbike. I found a present for Marie – a real jar of Nescafé. When I asked about wrapping paper, the shop owner stared blankly back at me, so I ended up wrapping the jar in an even rarer piece of toilet paper.

It was a relief to be out of the house for a while and I asked the driver to take me on a tour of the town. It wasn't beautiful but I found it extremely peaceful and relaxing to potter around on the motorbike, especially after the incessant shelling in Baba Amr. There were few paved roads. We passed a small café where a group of leathery-skinned old men were smoking and drinking coffee while old ladies brushed away the eternal dust from doorways. On occasion, young kids would cheer the FSA rebel as he ferried me around the backstreets, his Kalashnikov slung over his shoulder. They chased us for a while before going back to torturing the local cats.

As the days passed, Marie and I began to worry. We questioned Hassan on an almost hourly basis, but he had no news from Hama. Wa'el had gone home to visit his parents, but before he left he assured us that Hassan was the right man to get us into the city. However, if he said it was impossible then we must listen to him, Wa'el told us. He wouldn't put our lives in danger if he thought it was too hot. Wa'el also voiced his own concerns about going to Hama. He knew nobody there and had no information about the state of the activist network inside the city. He was more comfortable in Baba Amr where he knew people and, more importantly, people knew him.

The tension mounted as we waited. We kept discussing the trip to Hama. Were we missing out on the real story by giving up on Baba Amr? In the end, the decision was made for us. Commander Hassan came to the house early on Monday morning and told us that Hama was off. He had tried since Saturday but had failed to communicate with any of the rebel groups based there. He refused to send us on a blind mission.

Marie and I sat together around a diesel heater in Hassan's house. We drank tea morosely while we pondered our next move. Marie, who was already extremely disgruntled by our exit from Baba Amr, spoke first.

'Paul, you know what we have to do, don't you?' she said, her head tilting to one side, her voice a whisper.

I nodded. 'Yep. It's just that the thought of that fucking tunnel breaks my heart. I really thought we'd never see it again,' I said, as a surge of apprehension welled up inside me.

'Do you have enough cigarettes for another week there?' she asked, breaking the gloom with a sly, cheeky smile.

'Just local smokes. They would be better off loading them into 120mm rockets and using them as chemical weapons,' I said, counting the last of the Marlboros I'd brought in from Lebanon. 'But do you think we can get anything new on Baba Amr, though? Getting around is tough. There's only the field hospital and the Widows' Basement, which we've already covered. We need to find a new angle. I don't want to go back and do the same story.'

'Hey, you miserable sod, we'll find new material. You know that,' Marie replied.

I nodded with a half-smile.

'It's agreed, then? Back to Baba Amr it is,' she said softly. Our eyes locked across the diesel heater. I felt sick.

We called in Wa'el and asked him to find out whether Commander Hassan could arrange for our return to the besieged neighbourhood. Wa'el appeared relieved. He had never wanted to go to Hama. J-P had overheard our conversation about returning to Baba Amr and declared himself out immediately. He studied us as if we were insane. He would return to Lebanon, he told us.

My mind wouldn't settle. Normally, I would be preparing myself mentally for the trip ahead, but I was listless and unfocused, and I couldn't pin down what was wrong. An hour later, we received a message from Hassan. The trip back into Baba Amr was on. We would head in later that day. We spent Monday afternoon kitting up. Everything was charged, bags were repacked and we were ready to move on Hassan's orders.

We gathered around our favourite diesel heater in the living room of Hassan's house. We were both nervous. You wouldn't be sane if you weren't. We had entered besieged cities before but this was the first time we had re-entered a besieged city, having only just escaped from it. Maybe that's what was niggling me. This time we knew exactly what lay ahead.

I hadn't felt like this when we entered Misrata the previous year, nor had I seen anything similar in Marie. There was no nervous hesitation: she was on top form back then. Now I was picking up on small signs – the glances, the bouts of silence and the nervous, unsure laughter.

20 April 2011, Misrata, Libya

Initially, Marie and I had intended to go into Misrata for a two-day reconnaissance mission, to see if reporting from the city was tenable. Neither of us had taken anything other than the bare essentials: cameras, laptops and satellite gear and, in Marie's case, her one little luxury in any war zone – La Perla knickers. We left behind the basics – toothbrushes, soap and clothes. After all, we would

Marie Colvin on Tripoli Street, Misrata, during the siege of the Libyan city.

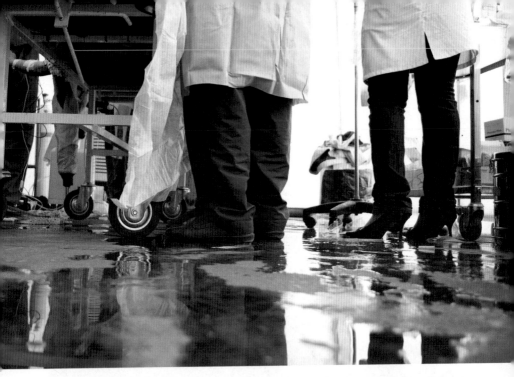

Bloodstained floor – doctors are inundated as a steady stream of injured threatens to overwhelm the meagre emergency facilities in Al Hikma hospital, Misrata, Libya.

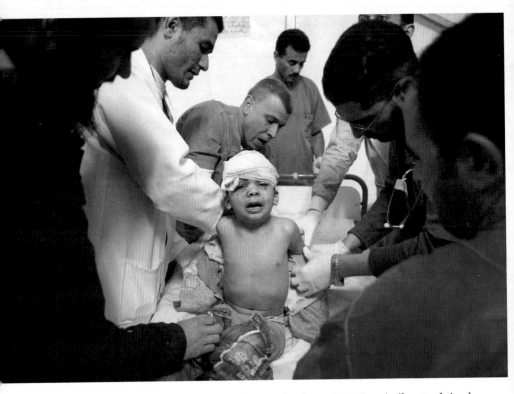

A young boy suffering from shrapnel wounds after a GRAD missile attack in the besieged city of Misrata, Libya.

Paul Conroy with Libyan rebels moments after the fall of Gadaffi's palace in Tripoli.

Marie Colvin and Paul Conroy living on the astroturf outside a school building shortly after Tripoli fell under rebel control. *Miles Amoore*

Members of the Free Syria Army defend a headquarters close to the city of Homs.

Women and children shelter in a former carpentry warehouse, one of the few basements in Baba Amr.

Marie Colvin explores the ruins of a house next to the media centre where a week earlier four women were killed in an artillery attack.

The main room of the media centre in Baba Amra where Marie Colvin and Remi Ochlik were killed by a regime rocket attack. *William Daniels/Panos Pictures*

Syria, Baba Amr Distress call by Doctor Mohamed Al-Mohamed & Scenes of Al-Assad crimes. 17-2-2012

Marie Colvin and Paul Conroy document the slaughter in Baba Amr as more victims arrive in the field hospital.

Dr Mohamed Al-Mohamed, who has run field hospitals since the beginning of the uprising, deplores the slaughter in Baba Amr.

A member of the medical team at the Baba Amr field clinic mourns the death of another civilian.

Remi Ochlik with members of the FSA days prior to entering Baba Amr where he was killed, eight hours after arriving at the media centre. *William Daniels/Panos Pictures*

The house (far right) where Paul Conroy, Edith Bouvier, William Daniels and Javier Espinosa hid out for five days after the deaths of Marie Colvin and Remi Ochlik. *William Daniels/Panos Pictures*

My name is Paul conroy.

Screengrab from the severely injured Paul Conroy's message to the rest of the world about the terrors of Baba Amr.

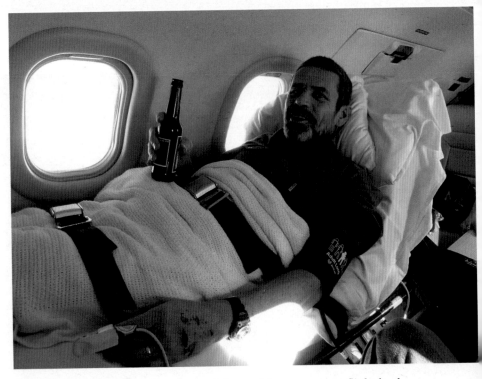

A taste of paradise as Paul Conroy celebrates his escape on a flight back from Lebanon to the UK.

only be gone a few days, right? Wrong. We ended up reporting from Misrata for two months.

We were on our friendly Greek captain's ferry, gazing out from the ship's oily decks, when we caught our first glimpse of the port city. Black plumes of smoke twisted into the sky above the smouldering buildings. The low rumble of heavy artillery hung in the cool Mediterranean air. Marie fell silent as she looked on. We all did. The few journalists who had made the trip with us stared at the burning city, lost in thought as they painted their own private pictures of the chaos and destruction that lay before them. Fear is rarely a topic of conversation among war correspondents – no one shows it and its name is never mentioned – yet it was manifest in the silence of all those who lined the decks that cold, overcast morning.

Chaos is synonymous with war. The two have a symbiotic relationship that is as old as conflict itself. In the harbour of Misrata we found both. As the rusting steel bow doors of the roll-on roll-off ship lowered on to the concrete dock, chaos appeared. Hundreds of eager volunteer dockhands, rebels and civilian alike, who had lined the harbour to greet the ship, now ran aboard and began the arduous task of unloading its precious cargo – the medicine, food, fuel and generators of which the long-suffering people of Misrata were in dire need. There was desperation in their movement and hunger in their eyes as they started to haul the precious cargo ashore.

Marie and I emerged from deep within the bowels of the darkened hull, squinting in the intense light of the Libyan sun. No one seemed to be in control but our plan was cunning in its simplicity: find the most heavily-armed rebel with the best-looking vehicle and make a beeline for him. The rebel's name was Raeda Montasser, a fifty-five-year-old professional smuggler with kind, twinkling eyes.

Raeda seemed bemused by the frenzied American woman with an eyepatch who refused to leave him alone until she had secured a ride into town.

Introductions over, Marie kept nudging me and saying, 'Show him the letter, Paul. Show him the letter.'

The letter had been written for me by an advisor to the fledgling opposition government in the eastern rebel stronghold of Benghazi. I had been told to hand it to whoever I found in charge of rebel forces in Misrata. I had befriended the letter writer earlier in the year when I was working in Benghazi. I mistakenly gave him the impression that I actually wanted to go and fight in Misrata and I was nearly drafted into the rebel force. In fact, I had been trying to indicate, with hand signals, that I was a former soldier and had no problems going to the front. It wasn't until I was handed a bunch of forms to fill in and had my photograph taken that I realised what was happening. I then had a large amount of back-pedalling to do.

Having retrieved the crumpled letter from deep within my grubby pocket, I handed it over. Raeda took it in his chubby hands and began to read it, his face registering surprise as he absorbed the handwritten Arabic scrawl. He stopped, folded the letter neatly, handed it back and said casually, 'Get in the car and never show this letter to anyone else again, ever.'

Inside the car, Marie nudged me, shot me a quizzical glance and asked, 'What's in the letter?'

I replied, smiling, 'I haven't a clue, but it seems to work.' We hung on to that letter. We would show it to many, many people over the coming months.

Close behind the chaos at the port came the war. No sooner had we secured our lift than the shelling started. The telltale scream of GRADs filled the air as Gaddafi forces trained their artillery fire on the supply ship and the harbour.

Marie hated these weapons. The screeches and screams they made as they flew overhead were enough to end even the most battle-hardened veterans' conversations mid-flow. Rather naively, Marie believed that she would be able to escape one of these rockets. 'At least you can hear them coming and run for cover if one is about to hit you,' she once told me confidently, as we attempted to merge with the sandbank we were sheltering behind.

I replied casually, 'Actually, Marie, you won't hear the one that gets you.' She stared at me in disbelief. 'What? I've spent years convinced that I'll hear one coming and be able to dodge it, you bastard!' she half-joked.

Misrata wasn't a good place to be for someone who hated GRADs. As we clambered into Raeda's car, the missiles began to close in on us, impacting only five hundred metres away. The rebels and civilians unloading the supply ship could feel the compression waves from the explosions, forcing them to pick up the pace of their unpacking. The explosions also triggered a crazed and rapid exodus of vehicles. I wouldn't say the car screeched away from the harbour in panic, but a favourite saying from my dad's national service came to mind – PUPO (pack up and piss off). This we did with great speed and nimbleness.

The attack on the harbour, although a touch unnerving, convinced us that we had come to the right place. The siege had already reached its zenith, but the people of Misrata had begun to fight back. Signs of the intensifying conflict were everywhere. The bullets that carpeted the wide streets and winding alleys were testament to the running gun battles that were taking place inside the city; the blackened and jagged holes blown into the sides of homes, shops, schools and factory buildings were evidence of Gaddafi's brutal use of heavy artillery; the overflowing hospitals and cemeteries told their own story.

Driving with urgency through this bleak yet familiar scene of destruction, Marie and I knew this was our story. We were back in our comfort zone and it was time to start work.

'Raeda, can we go to the hospital?' Marie asked in excruciatingly bad Arabic.

He nodded and replied in perfect English, 'You can go anywhere.' I thought of the mysterious handwritten letter and pondered its contents.

We arrived at Hikma hospital, a private clinic that served as Misrata's central hospital (the original hospital had taken too many direct artillery hits, forcing Misrata's doctors to abandon it). In the hospital's car park, a large white tent served as a trauma unit. The team of doctors were dealing with an emergency and our old friend Mr Chaos was present: horns blasted, sirens wailed and emergency staff ran in all directions. As the sequence of events unfolded in front of me, little did I know that I would spend the next two months of my life watching the same scene, as if on a loop. It was an unrelenting story of devastation, personal tragedy and death, with a light sprinkling of comedy thrown in for sanity's sake.

Within minutes of arriving, we were whisked off to the office of Dr Mohammad Fortia. Fortia, a medical administrator, held a senior position in the hospital and was keen to get us settled into accommodation, even though we had just rolled in out of the blue. We drank tea. I smoked – smoked for two actually as Marie, who had technically given up, insisted that I blow smoke in her direction because she missed the smell so much. She even complained if I didn't smoke enough.

The situation in Misrata, Dr Fortia explained, was critical. The hospital was in range of the GRAD missiles that were causing most of the damage at the time. Until the rebels could push the GRAD units far enough out of range, nothing inside the rebel enclave would be safe. As Fortia described the unfolding humanitarian disaster inside the city, there was a sudden, loud bang on the door. In walked a figure I recognised. It was Andrea, a photographer and friend I had worked with in Libya for over a month. He looked devastated, as though he had withdrawn a hundred years into himself. His eyes were wet and red.

'What the fuck's happened, Andrea?' I asked, shocked at his appearance.

He stared straight back at me. 'Chris Hondros just had most of his brains blown out in a mortar attack, and Tim Hetherington has just died downstairs in the trauma tent. Bled to death. His femoral artery was cut by mortar shrapnel.'

The deaths of Tim and Chris sent shockwaves through the journalist pack and the Libyan rebels alike. To us westerners, it was a brutally sharp reminder of our own mortality. No one believes that they are bulletproof but most of us believe it will always happen to somebody else. It's never going to be me who gets hit.

Many organisations pulled their staff out of Misrata after the attack that killed Tim and Chris. Others left of their own volition. Chris Chivers and Bryan Denton, both on assignment for the *New York Times*, Marie and I, decided to stay on. Our logic was simple: even the wire services like Reuters and Associated Press had left, so if we were to leave now the siege of Misrata would once again go unreported. We were staying.

For both Marie and I, Misrata was a foundation course in the school of high-explosive supersonic death. After two months in the city, we could identify the cause of any explosion. It could be a GRAD or a 120mm tank shell, a mortar, Katyusha missile or a 155mm artillery field gun. If it came from the sky and went bang, chances were that we could identify it. Unknowingly, Marie had learned to identify the sound of the weapon that would bring about her own death

20 February 2012, Al Buwaydah, Syria

A sharp bang on the metal door in Commander Hassan's house shattered the silence and my recollections of Misrata vanished. Marie and I had both started to doze off but we woke now to find Wa'el and Commander Hassan looming over us.

'Marie, Paul, it's time to go,' said Wa'el. 'The guys are ready. We can go back to Baba Amr now.' My stomach felt like it was made of lead.

CHAPTER EIGHT

Bad omens

20 February 2012, Al Buwaydah, Syria

An icy wind cut through our clothing as we waited outside Commander Hassan's house on a beautifully clear but extremely cold February afternoon. We had said our goodbyes to J-P, who was heading back to Beirut, whittling our group down to three. Marie and I were standing outside the house smoking with Wa'el, Hassan and a few FSA soldiers when a whining sound filled the air, making us crane our necks to the sky.

'Teeny weeny airlines,' I said, searching the sky for the source of the mechanical whine as a small shudder ran down my spine.

'What?' said Marie, slightly puzzled.

'It's the drone, Marie.' I laughed.

'I hate those little bastards,' she replied, squinting in the sunlight as she struggled to catch a glimpse of the pilotless spy plane.

For the last three days a Syrian air force drone had hovered in the skies over Homs and the surrounding rural neighbourhoods, locating rebel targets whose location was then fed back to the government's ground forces. It was possible that two of these drones now patrolled the skies: the frequency of their circuits above us seemed to have increased over the weekend.

Our group continued its sky-watch as two cars turned off the dusty main road and into the wide alleyway on which Hassan's house stood. The vehicles accelerated down the alley towards us, screeching to a dusty halt close to where we stood. The drivers climbed out of the cars and immediately joined us in scouring the sky for the buzzing drone. The spy planes were making people very nervous about any kind of move.

Despite the drones and the journey that lay ahead, Wa'el had a smile on his face: he was returning to his friends in Baba Amr and he seemed happy enough at the prospect. One of the drivers tapped his watch and we began to say our goodbyes. Commander Hassan pulled me to his chest for a hug and a traditional Arab kiss to the cheeks. He looked me in the eye.

'Come back soon, Abu Falafel. When you return, we make you many falafels,' he said, his eyes sparkling with good humour.

I returned his gesture by puffing out my cheeks and patting my stomach. In the coming weeks I would dream of falafels.

Marie, dressed in a black jacket, jeans and hiking boots, struggled to squeeze into the car with all her body armour on underneath her jacket. I followed behind and Wa'el clambered in after me. An FSA guard took the front seat and the driver immediately gunned the throttle, making a tight U-turn in the street before heading for the main road.

I turned to Marie. She looked back at me with a serene smile and gave a gentle shrug of her shoulders, as if to say 'well, here goes nothing'. I smiled at her, said nothing and scanned the landscape as we drove. I still had an unpleasant feeling gnawing away at me. I couldn't pin it down. Something was wrong but I didn't quite know what.

We wove a tortuous route across open country and, as we neared Homs, the sun began to sink low over the horizon. It was reaching the golden hour. This is the time photographers love, when the weakening light of the sun creates the perfect conditions in which to shoot. The whole area was bathed in the sun's warm glow and the long shadows it cast intensified the beauty of the mountains around us. We marvelled at the light. I explained the golden hour to Wa'el and he listened in fascination. Given what we were about to attempt, I was genuinely impressed with his powers of detachment.

We continued on our cross-country route as the sun bade us its daily farewell. Slowly, with the silent and stealthy movement of a cat stalking its prey, we were robbed of vision. Night fell upon us and with the darkness came the fear. It wrapped its invisible tentacles silently around all of us in the vehicle. No one spoke. The night belonged to the hunter and the hunted. In the distance, tracer rounds streaked in huge arcs against the blue night sky. We could feel – not hear – the subsonic rumbles of heavy artillery and a feeling of unease rushed in. The siege of Baba Amr continued unabated. We had rested. It was now time to return.

Not a single light shone in any of the buildings as we snaked our way through the small villages in the FSA's vehicle. The occasional flash of a torch to signal the all clear was the only light that broke the blackness. Arriving in another village, we pulled up next to a large concrete house, dismounted and left the vehicles behind. We continued on foot, following the driver as we wove and stumbled our way through a winding maze of small stone houses, animal sheds and rocky ditches. Stopping at a modest house, where tiny shafts of light shone through the wood-slatted windows, we removed our shoes and were ushered inside.

We had been here before. Only six days ago we had left this same building and headed down into the three-kilometre-long storm drain that had delivered us, with aching backs and shortness of breath, into Baba Amr.

Marie, in her black commando chic, accepted a coffee from a bearded and battle-hardened rebel fighter. We sat cross-legged in front of the diesel-burning stove as a battery-powered LED light cast a ghostly gloom on the figures crouched around the heater. Smiling through the shimmering heat haze of the stove sat 'the Sheikh', a bearded and kindly figure who promised us safe passage into Baba Amr. Next to him, a dark-skinned rebel fighter toyed ceaselessly with his pistol, checking, unloading, reloading and then rechecking his weapon. Marie and I looked at each other nervously every time we heard the metallic clunk of a bullet slide into the breach. We had both had several bad experiences with rebels loosing off weapons by mistake. But, in the far corner of the room, lurked something far more sinister: fear.

The fear had been building in me all day, from the moment we decided to head back into Baba Amr. Initially, a small internal voice began verbally tapping me on the shoulder. At first, its message was indistinct and vague. But now it was loud and clear: 'What do you think you're up to? You're going back to Baba Amr? Really?'

Since arriving at the safe house, my mind had started to wander erratically. I cleaned my cameras, drank coffee and chain-smoked. I tried to hide my distraction from the others and I attempted to ignore the ominous voice that was drilling into my brain like a parasite devouring all other thought. The longer we sat in the room, the more withdrawn I became. For appearances' sake, I occasionally joined in the conversation, only for my mind to slowly recede into the near-schizophrenic argument now taking place inside my head. Just as the distant shelling shook the room, so my thoughts were shaking my inner being.

What was happening to me wasn't new; it was just rare. Now

the voice was back, in this cold oblong room, with its soldiers, coffee and cigarettes, and it was screaming, 'Do not get in that fucking tunnel. Do not go to Homs. Do not ignore me, you obstinate bastard.' I seriously needed to talk to Marie and Wa'el.

I took advantage of a break in the chatter to present my case. Marie and Wa'el were seated either side of me on the floor. I plucked up the courage to speak.

'Erm, chaps,' I muttered, a touch gingerly, 'I need a little word.'

They looked at me expectantly.

'Do either of you have a little voice inside you saying not to do this – go back into Baba Amr, that is?' I asked, my tone hopeful, my eyes slightly pleading.

Neither Marie nor Wa'el responded, so I continued, 'I've been doing this job for some time now and I have a little voice. I always obey it. If it says no, I don't do it. It's shouting very loudly not to do this trip.' My words were now more forceful.

Again there was silence. I pointed at my limbs and continued, 'I still have all my bits and I've never suffered a scratch in all the wars I've covered. If I go in now, it will be the first time I've ignored my instinct and it's got me very worried.'

Marie was first to respond. 'Based on what? What's your voice based on?' she asked, genuinely interested, her face serious.

I shrugged. 'Nothing tangible,' I replied, my tone one of quiet desperation as I felt the argument slipping away from me. 'I've done all the normal assessments. It's a high-risk job but we've done worse. You know I'll do just about anything, always have done.'

Marie nodded in agreement. 'So why now?' she asked sympathetically.

I felt lame and stupid, unable to explain what to her must have seemed like a supernatural epiphany. 'I really don't know. All I know is that this will be the first time I've ignored my own gut feeling. I feel something very bad is about to happen.'

Wa'el spoke next. 'Perhaps it's just a bad day. You know, too much time to think,' he said, offering me a way out.

'Nope,' I countered. 'This is real.' I fell silent.

Marie responded flatly with what sounded like regret. 'Well, I'm the correspondent and you are the photographer. I'm going in, alone if need be. You can go home if you want.' She looked resolute and I knew she meant it: she would never drop a story purely on a hunch.

'You know I can't let you go alone,' I whispered.

And that was it. I had voiced my fears, Marie had said her piece and I pushed my fears as far to the back of my mind as I could. We had a job to do and I needed a clear head to focus on the task in hand.

Marie poured another coffee. I lit another cigarette. The Sheikh smiled happily at the three of us. 'Time for tunnel,' he beamed. 'Now you go back to Baba Amr.'

We gathered in the bitter cold outside the house, our condensing breath visible in the pale moonlight. We struggled into our boots and made final checks to our kit. The pistol-toting rebel, along with two other rebels who would act as our guards, started off into the night. They moved quickly and with ease. Each twist and turn, wall and irrigation ditch seemed to be burnt into their mind's. For us, it was somewhat different. Marie struggled in the dark. This time Wa'el took her hand and led her through the obstacles while I hovered somewhere in the middle of the line, trying not to lose our guards while maintaining visual contact with Marie and Wa'el.

It was the same route we had taken on our previous run into Baba Amr but, like most journeys, it felt much quicker the second time round and it wasn't long until we were climbing the last wall before the tunnel entrance. As we landed on the other side, masked figures grabbed us and thrust us all face down into the sodden earth. They stooped to our level and pressed their fingers to their lips, urging us to remain silent. More sign language followed. This time they mimed a sniper taking aim before pointing towards the tunnel entrance. Silently, we nodded.

One of the masked men rose into a crouch before sprinting towards the entrance, stealthily hugging the treeline. We followed in turn. I went first, followed by Marie and then Wa'el, with an FSA guard bringing up the rear. Suddenly, the clatter of small arms fire shattered the silence. These weren't the distant echoes we had been hearing in Al Buwaydah; this was now close-quarter fighting, very near our position or, more disturbingly, near the tunnel's entrance.

Regrouping after two hundred metres, the three of us crouched together, panting from exertion and fear, our breath visible in the air as we gave each other the thumbs up. As we huddled at the corner of a brick wall, separated from the tunnel by a hundred metres of open ground, an FSA guard signalled for us to make a dash for the entrance. We nodded back at him in silence. I prepared to make the first run for it. My legs felt like lead and my breathing was deep and erratic as I readied myself, trying to focus on the imminent 100-metre sprint.

I set off, bent double and zigzagging over the exposed ground as I urged myself to run faster. I imagined the concealed sniper zeroing in on me, his cross hairs lining up on my lumbering body, his finger ever so gently squeezing on the two-pressure trigger. His breathing would be calm, unlike my own deep and desperate gasps. He would exhale and hold his breath, emptying his lungs before he took the shot. I was stumbling forward at full speed, my lungs burning as my leaden legs demanded more oxygen from my terrified system. Then suddenly rough hands grabbed at me and slammed my flailing body face down into deep mud. The rebels dragged me by my feet and threw me down the muddy tunnel entrance. 'Fuck you, sniper.' I laughed out loud as I picked myself up from the mud. 'Fuck you very much.'

Soaked to the bone and trembling with the adrenalin surge, I crawled through the concrete opening into the tunnel shaft and waited for the others to appear. I counted large numbers of walking wounded and even more seriously injured men, women and children who were being evacuated from Homs on stretchers. I knew this tunnel. The sheer hell of walking it with only a bag to carry had been misery enough, but to carry a human out on a stretcher required abnormal physical and mental strength. I could see the pain on the faces of the men who were carrying the wounded and dying through this unholy place.

Marie crash-landed into the mud next to me, followed closely by Wa'el and then our FSA guards. It was a great relief to see that they had all made it safely. One of the guards took the lead position and set off down the tunnel, followed by Marie, myself and Wa'el. The pistol-toting rebel took up the rear position covering our backs.

Splashing through the muddy puddles, Marie and Wa'el both remarked on the large number of casualties leaving the tunnel. It confirmed that government forces had stepped up their shelling campaign on the rebel enclave and conditions on the ground were deteriorating rapidly.

The conversation soon fizzled out as each of us dealt internally with the rigours of moving in such a confined space. And then the singing started. Not a choir this time, just a solitary voice that reverberated with a melancholic sadness through the narrow tunnel. It went on for five minutes or so until I heard Marie's voice over the gloomy lament.

'Who the fuck is that?' she shouted angrily from the blackness ahead of me.

'Wa'el,' I shouted back down the tunnel, 'Marie wants to know who the fuck is singing.'

'It's the FSA guard,' replied Wa'el.

'Marie, it's the FSA guard,' I relayed ahead to her.

'What the fuck's he singing about? It's horrible,' she yelled back.

I passed this message on to Wa'el, who listened for a few moments before replying. 'He's saying how we are all going to die, be martyrs and go to heaven,' shouted Wa'el.

Again I relayed Wa'el's message to Marie.

'Well tell him to shut the fuck up. It's depressing and he sounds like a fucking wasp,' was her final retort.

I shouted this message back to Wa'el who was by now laughing out loud at Marie's response and the surreal nature of our four-way subterranean conversation. Moments later, the awful singing stopped. The sounds of boots splashing through water and lungs gasping for breath echoed through the tunnel's fetid air. There were unfamiliar noises emanating from above: the deep rumble of tanks and explosions permeated the layers of earth covering the tunnel. The spooky sounds added another dimension to the claustrophobic ambience in the tunnel.

It was a continuous struggle to make room for the stream of wounded, bloodied and shocked civilians coming from the Baba Amr direction, we squeezed into small balls on the wet floor to allow them to edge past in the confines of the tunnel. It was clear evidence that the assault on Baba Amr had grown more violent and indiscriminate in its ferocity. The traumatised, ghostly stares of women carrying the bandaged and blood-soaked bodies of babies told their own story. The men, hollow-eyed, gaunt and bent double all carried an injury of one sort or another. The tunnel was their last resort, their last chance to escape the brutality, while the living and uninjured remained condemned to the purgatory of Baba Amr.

Suddenly, the rebel solo singer piped up again. His morose wailing from the rear of our group signalled the continuation of hostilities for Marie. The doom-laden rebel had decided it was time to add to the already macabre feeling in the tunnel. Marie was having none of it.

'Tell him to shut the fuck up,' she yelled. Her voice lacked any trace of humour.

Wa'el passed the message back and an angry exchange in Arabic echoed through the blackness of the tunnel. Shit, I thought, what we don't need now is for infighting to erupt within our small group. I could feel nerves fraying and I sensed a communal realisation that we had committed ourselves to something far beyond our expectations.

The heat was extreme. Sweat-soaked and wracked with cramp, we pushed on, chasing the dim glimmer of the lead rebel's torch. The tunnel was now my life and it was difficult to remember a time outside its rough, confining walls. This narrow concrete tomb, buried deep in the ground, was a hell from which the only escape was to another version of the same – Baba Amr.

And hell it was. We emerged gasping from the underground sarcophagus into a changed world. Explosion followed explosion, the earth shook and the sky flashed stroboscopic white, momentarily silhouetting a demonic, corrupted landscape. Our world had changed for ever. There could be no return from this place. We were about to enter Dante's sixth circle: 'You approach Satan's wretched city where you behold a wide plain surrounded by iron walls. Before you are fields full of distress and torment terrible. Burning tombs are littered about the landscape.'

We stood shoulder to shoulder and simply absorbed the scene before us.

'Holy shit,' muttered Marie.

I didn't respond. Marie had captured the moment. There was little else to say.

Wa'el broke our silent reverie by popping a cigarette into my mouth and declaring, with a smile, 'Guys, we need a coffee. Let's get into town.'

Wa'el proved to be the perfect antidote to the horror unfolding around us. If it weren't for his coffee and cigarette quip, I suspect we would all have been hotfooting it back through the tunnel to the relative peace of a 'regular battlefield'.

Luckily, unlike the last time we'd entered Homs, there was no waiting for trucks to be loaded and no bunch of singing rebels to scare the shit out of us. There was only an urgent desire to move. We jumped into the back of a pickup truck and our FSA guards, their weapons cocked and their minds on full alert, signalled the driver to move before the truck screeched off at full speed. Shouting above the noise of the engine, Wa'el had spoken to the local FSA commander who had agreed to take us directly to the media centre. Things had changed: nowhere was considered safe enough to stop en route.

It was a white-knuckle ride. The driver was relentless in his search to find more speed from the pickup. He didn't nurse it through the gearbox in any attempt at discretion but instead braked hard and accelerated out of bends with the dexterity of a rally driver. And rightly so: the amount of incoming fire we took was intense by comparison with our last trip. So much had changed in so short a space of time that I began to wonder whether this was the prelude to the much-feared ground invasion.

Marie seemed to think so. 'Paul, this is fucking nuts,' she shouted over the noise of the engine and nearby explosions.

'I fully concur,' I yelled back.

I could see her smile.

'Paul, you're so English.' She laughed, automatically ducking as incoming rounds whizzed past our vehicle.

We sped through the night, a cacophony of explosions and small arms fire adding to the sheer terror of the driver's throttle. A set of headlights in the distance drew closer. The FSA guards took up defensive positions and the driver pulled the pickup to the side of the road. The oncoming vehicle continued to approach, freezing us in its headlights. All we could do was hold our breath and wait. The other vehicle flashed its lamps and the FSA guards relaxed. Wa'el spoke quickly to the guards and reassured us that all was well. It was just another FSA patrol.

The pickup parked next to us and a brief conversation took place as Wa'el listened in carefully. The two vehicles then continued their journeys in opposite directions. Wa'el informed us that we would have to stop in Sultaniya – where J-P had lost his trousers on the previous trip – because the rebels needed our vehicle for a mission. We would sort out transport when we arrived.

This was depressing news. We had no desire to be stuck in the suburbs and time was against us. We understood the difficulty of working in Baba Amr and knew that every hour was critical. Marie pulled Wa'el closer to her and emphasised the importance of finding a vehicle as soon as we stopped in Sultaniya. There would be no tea drinking or laundry sessions this time, she told Wa'el.

In Sultaniya, we accepted the cups of tea offered by the FSA rebels as they sat watching us. A rictus of irritation contorted Marie's face. Wa'el looked as apologetic as he possibly could and I just took in the scene, laughing inside, desperate to hide any smile from Marie. It was an unavoidable situation: there quite simply wasn't a vehicle to be had, hence the ubiquitous tea and smiley rebels. Through bared teeth and a grimace, Marie politely asked

Wa'el to 'find a fucking car as quickly as fucking possible'. Wa'el never flinched. I detected his inner smile and he winked at me as he passed out of the room in search of a vehicle and driver.

It was a three-cup-of-tea wait before we finally got into an old silver Datsun, its cracked windscreen patched up with tape. The driver turned the key, the engine turned over and nothing happened. Again the key turned and again nothing happened. Silence all round. Marie caught my eye, said nothing and went back to staring straight ahead.

The ground rumbled, the sky flashed as detonations continued to rock the night and the engine started on the fourth attempt. I couldn't work out if this was a good thing or not. I wondered whether the car would ever start again if it stalled en route to Baba Amr. This was pointless speculation as we were now moving at speed. We all knew that this was the most dangerous part of the journey; we had to pass through Assad's military positions one last time.

The driver used a new technique. He pressed his foot to the ground and kept it there until it was absolutely necessary to slow down. It was my guess that government forces now had this road well and truly marked. The amount of ordnance fired in our direction was nothing short of spectacular, in a very grim kind of way. I adopted an eyes-closed approach: I didn't want to see what was going to hit us; I would much rather it was a surprise. Our driver had developed a variant of my own personal tactic: he crouched down behind the wheel with only his eyes peering over the top of the dashboard. He looked just like a pensioner behind the wheel of a Morris Minor.

We were now speeding through the narrow streets. At every junction we crossed, the ferocious and violent impacts of explosive bullets could be seen and heard just metres behind our vehicle. We bounced across craters, dodged fallen scabs of masonry and veered sharply around trees and telephone poles that had been blown out of the ground. It became increasingly unbelievable that there were an estimated 28,000 people still living in Baba Amr. I hadn't seen a single one.

Travelling at this speed through the ruins of the neighbourhood at night made it impossible to get our bearings, so it was with some surprise that we suddenly pulled up outside the media centre. Relief surged through my rigid body. I turned to Marie, who had her head back and eyes closed. I knew what was running through her mind: sheer and total relief. It had been a physically and mentally draining journey. I lit a cigarette and smiled.

Wa'el was chipper. 'Hey, guys, we're home!' He grinned as he exited the car and started taking our bags from us. Marie and I both stumbled out on to the street, stretching away the cramps as we looked at the media centre. It was still intact and, despite the ferocious assault, it really did feel like we were home.

A large mortar round at the end of the street blew away our sentimental musings and we made a dash for the relative safety of the three-storey building. We all knew the routine once inside: hop around inelegantly until you finally manage to unlace your clumpy boots. There, under the miserable pale green glow of an energy-saving light bulb, in the hallway of a doomed building, Marie Colvin removed her shoes for the last time.

We entered the familiar centre in silence. Nobody knew that we were heading back in and we hoped it was all still operational. Sliding back the glass door to the main room, we saw Abu Hanin first. He was standing up and swung his head automatically to the door when he heard movement. He froze momentarily, mouth half-open as if to speak.

'What the fuck, man! Abu Falafel, Marie,' he blurted out. 'What the fuck are you doing back?'

Marie beamed. 'Hey, a story is a story and this one ain't over yet,' she said. She was happy again. She was doing what she did best: she had returned to bear witness.

Abu Hanin turned to me. 'Abu Falafel, did you bring my tobacco and Nando's chicken?' he asked, his face alive with humour.

'Sorry, mate, the nearest Tesco was over a thousand miles away, and closed, and we ate the Nando's on the way in,' I replied, before belching and wiping my lips in mock satisfaction.

The familiar faces of the activists in the media centre were a pleasure to see. It was only days since we had said our goodbyes with the cloud of an imminent invasion looming over our heads. But here they were, still alive. Their numbers had halved and the room seemed unusually sparse. We stashed our bags next to the sliding glass door in case we needed to make a quick exit and took up our positions on the floor. Abu Hanin grabbed a blanket and sat down with us.

'Guys, this place has gone crazy in the last few days,' he began in his slightly Canadian-accented English. 'The shelling is getting worse, much worse. We lost two cars the other day to mortar fire. Now it's hard to move. We have to go on foot everywhere and the snipers know our routes. The doctors can't cope any more.'

We both listened. Abu Hanin's words confirmed what we had seen in the tunnel: the intensity of the siege had increased. Moving around was becoming increasingly difficult and the number of casualties was mounting daily.

'Can we get back to the field hospital?' Marie asked.

Abu Hanin looked puzzled. 'Why? You have seen it already. You don't need to go back there.'

Marie explained to Abu Hanin that we wanted to report on how people reached the field clinic, who was taking them there and how they were coping without vehicles for ambulances.

189

'It's very difficult,' he said. 'But we can try tomorrow. It will depend on the shelling, though. I can't make any promises.'

Marie had one last question. 'Do you still have my robe? I'm freezing,' she said, referring to the long, black Arabic robe she had worn last time. It was her Chechen queen robe.

Abu Hanin laughed. 'I will get it now, Marie.'

Marie, Wa'el and I settled back into the less than salubrious setting of the Baba Amr media centre. We took out our laptops, checked emails and nervously waited to see if Skype would work, which it did. I logged on to see if I had any messages. We had been without Internet during our time outside Homs, so it was a chance to catch up with the rest of the world.

Checking my Skype messages first, I noticed one from Miles Amoore. We had joined the first rebel unit to storm the Libyan capital the year before. His message was simple. 'Hey mate, great stuff you're getting out of Syria, am jealous, wish I was there,' he had written.

My reply was even simpler: 'No you fucking well don't.' This must have shocked Miles because he knew I wasn't one to exaggerate.

Amoore and I had been caught up in the vicious fighting in and around Tripoli as we covered the rebel advance on the capital. On our way in, watching rebels storm Gaddafi's palace, he had survived being shot in the helmet by a sniper. Despite openly confessing to drinking water and smoking 'girl's' cigarettes, he had carried on reporting.

2011, Bab al-Aziziya, Tripoli – excerpt from Amoore's report about the incident

The bullet clanged into my helmet, smacking the Kevlar into the left side of my skull. The force of the bullet threw me to the ground.

The shock of being floored by something I couldn't see confused me: it took a few seconds to realise I'd been hit in the head. I could hear a metallic ringing in my ears.

The image of a messy puddle of brain matter next to me flashed through my mind. These thoughts were quickly replaced with the realisation that I couldn't feel any pain, apart from a thumping headache that I'd had all day from having only one contact lens. My next thought was that I was still thinking. My brain was still working. That thought was quickly replaced with another: Perhaps this is what happens when you die.

I ran both my hands inside my helmet, checking for blood and praying I wouldn't find any. This was tricky because the chinstrap was so tight that I couldn't get my hands all the way inside.

It took a few more swipes to confirm that I wasn't bleeding from my skull and that my brains weren't in the sand: my hands were covered in black grit and dirt.

No blood. Good. The fear of dying, followed by the elation of being alive, made me forget where I was for a moment. Then I looked up to see a Libyan rebel gaping at me, frozen to the spot in shock.

Other rebels had fled when they saw the round hit me. I could see their feet racing away as I lay there.

I realised I needed to get up. Bullets were still flying overhead; splashes of dirt kicked up around me. I dragged myself up and ran towards cover, racing around the corner of a building, where I leant against a wall, trying to get my breath back.

I took my helmet off and checked my head again for blood. Nothing. Rebel fighters lined up against a wall on the opposite side of the alleyway looked on impassively.

It was my fault.

The Sunday Times photographer, Paul Conroy, and I had been crouching down behind a red gate on the side of a road leading towards Colonel Gadaffi's palace.

Rebel pick-up trucks drove up the road from our right, blasting deafening barrages of anti-aircraft fire from their mounted guns at Gadaffi's palace. The trucks were still taking small arms fire, sending rounds pinging down the road.

'I'll go first and you follow,' said Paul. I nodded. Paul timed his sprint to coincide with the next barrage of anti-aircraft fire, which he hoped would pin down the Gadaffi shooters long enough for him to race to the mosque. As he made cover, the rebel 4ft behind him had his arm blown off by a bullet.

I knew the gate was poor cover. I got up to make the sprint but a group of rebels dashed out ahead of me.

I didn't want to be the last man in the group, fearing that Gadaffi's snipers may have honed their aim by the time they saw me sprinting. So I watched a few rebel pick-up trucks race by and waited for the incoming rounds to die down. Another group of rebels joined me by the gate.

That's when the bullet knocked me to the floor. It must have pierced the gate to my left, slowing down the round just enough to prevent it from passing through the Kevlar and into my skull.

Paul didn't see me get hit: he was too busy treating the rebel whose arm had been blown off.

He found me smoking a cigarette and drinking water on the curb, talking to a rebel in a pink T-shirt who was trying to persuade me to go to an ambulance around the corner.

'What happened to you?' Paul asked.

'I got shot in the head,' I replied, grinning stupidly.

'Are you okay?' he asked.

'Yes,' I replied.

'Okay, well get up and stop whingeing,' he laughed.

Moments later, as we continued to advance alongside the rebels, a bullet snapped Paul's camera out of his hands. We'd both been lucky. As heavy fighting continued to rage around us, we bumped into a Reuters correspondent who quipped, 'What the hell are you two Sunday correspondents doing getting shot on a Tuesday?'

20 February 2012, media centre, Baba Amr, Syria

And that's how it was between Miles and me. He possessed a fantastic sense of humour and a genuine sense of the bizarre that would be tested to its limits in the weeks that lay ahead. We developed a strong bond, forged under the demanding pressure of street-to-street urban combat.

The bombardment outside the media centre was now easing slightly. It never stopped fully – the gunners would shell into the night – but a sense of relief set in as the heavy shelling gave way to more sporadic explosions.

I wrote emails to my family, replacing the words 'Baba Amr' with 'that place' to let them know where I was. It didn't feel right advertising we were back in town, and I hoped they would pick up on my slightly cryptic message. No one likes to cause unnecessary worry so on a Skype call to Bonnie, my partner, I tried to downplay the dangers and lied about our reasons for re-entering the neighbourhood. I told her that the only way out of Syria was via Baba Amr and that we had to lie low while the FSA worked out an evacuation plan. While we spoke, the staccato bursts of machine-gun fire and rumbles of shells bursting were transmitted back to Devon. Fear was evident in her face. My words of reassurance sounded trite and unconvincing. We said goodnight.

Settling in for the night, we commenced the familiar and laborious task of building our beds in our old room at the back of the media centre. It was arduous work. In full outdoor gear, we constructed our nests of thick, heavy blankets, clambering into them ungracefully before helping each other pull heavy layers of blankets on top.

Marie often professed a hatred of sleeping in rooms full of men due to a bad snoring incident on her escape from Chechnya. She had been forced to live and sleep in a cave with Chechen rebels and, according to her, the snoring reached epic sonic levels that no woman should ever have to endure. Marie snored like a Chechen rebel herself. Even with my headphones and music on I could still feel the rumble emanating from her nest.

As we tried to nod off to Marie's racket, Wa'el whispered to me, 'Paul, does Marie have a partner?'

I confirmed she did. 'Richard,' I said. 'Lovely guy.'

He waited for the snores to dip before whispering, 'He must love her very much.'

I lay awake for hours that night. I'm an insomniac by nature but the combination of Marie's outstanding audio performance and my growing feelings of unease at our predicament meant that sleep was even more hard to come by than usual.

It was never truly peaceful in Baba Amr. I wondered what battles were still being fought at such an ungodly hour. Were they unwinnable battles? Were they even real battles at all or was it just a psychological ploy, intended to make life unliveable for the inhabitants of this godforsaken piece of land?

I pondered the trauma being inflicted on the men, women and children who were being subjected to a bombardment that I, as a journalist and former soldier who had witnessed many wars, found psychologically distressing. My thoughts cascaded on, the explosions echoed across the dying city and Marie, the Chechen queen, rumbled on and on . . .

CHAPTER NINE

Brave renegade

21 February 2012, Baba Amr, Syria

During the early hours of Tuesday morning, Abu Hanin called everyone into the main room of the media centre. We all watched in hushed silence as the baby boy on the laptop's screen gasped and struggled hopelessly towards his final, dying breath.

The scene galvanised Marie, stabbing at the raw nerves that fuelled her need to bear witness. 'Paul, we have to get this out. This can't be allowed to slip by and disappear into the ether. They're murdering babies, for Christ's sake. We have to tell the world. It's why we're here,' she said, her furious gaze locked on me.

Beneath her anger simmered a steely defiance. In her previous dispatch from Baba Amr she had crafted a graphic, emotive image of life in the besieged neighbourhood. With Marie, however, there was always more. She would dig deeper and push further, refusing to be cowed by Bashar al-Assad's murderous regime.

'All right, Marie, I agree. But we have two problems,' I told her. 'Problem one: it's Tuesday morning, you don't need me to remind you of that. Can we really sit on this story until Sunday? Problem

195

two: nobody in the outside world actually knows we're back in Baba Amr. We should tell them.'

Marie and I had both failed to inform our respective editors – Sean Ryan, the foreign editor, and Ray Wells, the picture editor – of our planned return to Baba Amr. It was a unilateral decision we had taken in Al Buwaydah. Essentially, we had 'gone rogue'. Had we informed them of our intended return trip to Baba Amr, we knew permission would probably have been denied. Everyone at *The Sunday Times* assumed we were now covering the story from the comparative safety of Al Buwaydah.

In reality, Marie and I were crouched like frightened rabbits in a hole. The bombardment of Baba Amr had moved beyond comprehension as the ferocity and rate of shelling intensified by the hour. The screams of Katyusha rockets and artillery shells slicing through the air above us were now so close that they drowned out conversation. We huddled closer together in order to talk.

'I think I should let them know we're here,' she said.

'Probably for the best,' I replied.

Marie opened her laptop and began to type.

From: Marie Colvin
Date: Tue, Feb 21, 2012 at 10:30 AM
Subject: baba amr
To: Sean Ryan, Graham Paterson
Cc: Lucy Fisher

I am in Baba Amr, the shelling started at 6.30am. It is sickening that the Syrian regime is allowed to keep doing this. There was a shocking scene at the apartment clinic today. A baby boy lay on a head scarf, naked, his little tummy heaving as he tried to breathe. The doctors said 'We can do nothing for him'. He had been hit by shrapnel in his left side. They had to just let him die as his mother wept.

No electricity, no water, very very cold.

As discussed, I'd like to focus on the defence of the city to get a theme that is different from last week. But I feel strongly we have to include these stories of the suffering of civilians to get the point across, even if it does repeat last week a bit. I think again to focus on Baba Amr, 28,000 defenceless under shelling, all the FSA can do is repel the forays of the Syrian army with light weapons and try to get the wounded to treatment, or out to Lebanon if they are badly injured. The Syrian army is focusing on this neighbourhood, pounding it daily since February 4, this is the new Srebrenica. There were lots of investigations after Sreb fell about what the UN did wrong. But thousands of men and boys were still dead. Is that going to happen here?

Sunday Times is still the only Western reporter in Baba Amr as far as I can tell, probably in Homs although once in this besieged place it is difficult to tell what is going on in the rest of the city.

The Thuraya is not working here. It is email, or Skype. Please pass to Annabelle that Paul is here, and he got over a video last night.

Mx

Time stood still inside the media centre. We knew any attempt to move outside would be suicidal and even the most hardbitten activists expressed reservations about leaving the building. An onerous gloom had settled over all of us who sat huddled together for warmth in that cold, dank room. There was nothing anyone could do. Some attempted to sleep while others chatted on Skype to kill time and calm their nerves. The room had become our world.

Suddenly, we heard the echo of footsteps entering the house and a figure yanked open the glass door to our right. A young cameraman covered in concrete dust, panting and exhausted, stumbled into the room. He addressed the activists in a burst of fast, breathless Arabic. A low groaning sound spread through all of them as he recounted his story. Some activists put down their laptops, ending their Skype chats abruptly, while others simply cradled their heads in their hands. Whatever had transpired to cause the tremor running through the room had obviously been major.

Although desperate to ask Abu Hanin what had happened, both Marie and I had the wit to let them get through the moment. We would be told when they were ready to tell us. Possible scenarios raced through my mind. Shit, I thought, what if it's the land invasion? If this really is the start of it, then we're as good as dead.

Abu Hanin noticed the looks of concern on our faces and he came over to sit with us. His expression was blank. It seemed like all emotion had been leached from his soul by the events in Baba Amr. He told us that one of the first and bravest of their cameramen, Rami al-Sayed, had just been hit by shrapnel and had bled to death in the field hospital. It was a crushing loss to all and I felt the world slowly start to spin. When one of these guys dies you realise that no one is indestructible and that, if they can die, then so can you. The loss hit everyone extremely hard.

Rami al-Sayed's last tweet before he died had read:

Baba Amr is facing genocide right now. I do not want people to simply say our hearts are with you! We need actions. We need campaigns everywhere inside Syria and outside Syria. We need all people in front of all embassies all over the world.

In a few hours there will be no place called Baba Amr and I
expect this to be my last message. No one will forgive you for
just talking without any action!

I slumped back on to a cushion, lit a cigarette and stared vacantly
at the ceiling, the final lines of Rami's last tweet racing through my
brain. 'In a few hours there will be no place called Baba Amr and
I expect this to be my last message. No one will forgive you for just
talking without any action!'

'How bad do you think it's going to get, Paul?' asked Marie.
'Assad's dad murdered around thirty thousand when he destroyed
Hama in 1982. You reckon Bashar has the balls to do it again?'

'I think Rami got it bang on in his last tweet. It'll only get worse,'
I responded gloomily. 'Assad's ground troops won't come in until
every poor bastard in this place is dead or dying but yes, I reckon
they'll try. Those fuckers have no stop button.'

I lay back smoking and attempted to block the downward spiral
of events we were caught up in from my mind.

Marie's laptop pinged incoming email. It was a message from
the foreign editor, Sean Ryan. His first question was 'Are you safe?'
He told Marie that her stories were reaching a wider audience. Her
friend Jim Muir, a correspondent from the BBC, had given her a
name check on the *Today* programme that morning, quoting a line
from her story about the vet treating injured people at the hospital.
He also mentioned that Channel 4 had requested an interview with
her. But he quickly followed this with:

What we don't want to do is create an incentive for the Syrian
army to come looking for you because you're broadcasting
about their war crimes . . . if it's risky, I'll tell anyone inquiring

that it's not possible at the moment . . . please keep in close, regular email or hushmail contact about your movements and plans as fast as you can.

Sean x

'What do you reckon?' Marie asked tentatively, turning from the screen and looking me in the eye after she finished reading the email.

We both understood the risks of reporting live from Baba Amr. Marie had a big profile and we knew she could rattle cages in high places, potentially unleashing the wrath of the Syrian regime.

I considered it for a moment. 'I'm not sure it matters what we do any more, Marie. This place is fucked. It's raining death. Can we really make it any worse?' I asked. 'We'd better check with Abu Hanin and the boys though. We don't want to expose them to more risk. If they say it's okay, then let's do it.'

Abu Hanin translated our request to the other activists in the room, who all nodded their agreement. 'Yes, you should go ahead and broadcast. It's why you are here. You must tell your story,' he told us.

Marie's mood picked up immediately. Sitting here being shelled was mental torture. Marie needed to remain active to stay sane and so, with a new-found sense of purpose, she kicked into life. Anyone arriving from the outside was subjected to a Colvinesque grilling of the highest order. Puzzled activists and FSA soldiers who ventured into the media centre sat wide-eyed and obedient in front of her as she wrung them dry of information. By the end of their sessions, these young men truly understood the meaning of the word thorough. And so she continued, throwing every ounce of energy into watching videos brought back from the front line while cross-referencing names, times and incidents. Slowly, carefully and meticulously, she pieced together the jigsaw of the day's slaughter in Baba Amr.

While Marie worked, requests for interviews started to come in, one from Channel 4 in the UK, another from CNN's *Anderson Cooper 360* show and a request from BBC World. We agreed we should do all three interviews and I gave permission for my footage and images to be used by the BBC.

By now we had also started to freeze. The power had been down for most of the day and the only heating – a three-bar electric fire – remained resolutely cold. We were wearing every item of clothing in our possession but still the cold bit deeper into our bones with every minute that passed. The power situation was erratic. The electricity would suddenly come on for a few hours, triggering bedlam as everyone scurried to recharge his or her batteries before the next cut. Food was also becoming progressively more scarce. At one point I found Marie examining a plate. She had lifted it up to eye level and was busy prodding the scant remains of some food with a pencil. She continued to study it with great inquisitiveness before announcing, 'Damn, looks to me like someone's been eating tuna.'

Marie continued to collate her notes ahead of her first interview, with Jonathan Miller from Channel 4 News. The noise of activists talking on Skype was so loud that it forced Marie to move to the adjacent room. The room had a window on to the street, which worried me. I tucked her in a corner, away from the blast zone of any ordnance that might impact outside. There was also no lighting in the room, so she sat alone, hunched over her laptop, struggling with the intricacies of Skype in the dark. Marie, a self-confessed Luddite of the highest order, gave me the thumbs up. She was ready, apparently.

Two minutes later, I heard her plaintive pleas echo from the other room. 'Paul, no sound. Jesus Christ, Paul, they can't hear me. It's broken. Can I use yours?'

Chuckling to myself as I turned up the sound, using the not-so-invisible volume control, I plugged the headphones dangling from her ears into the laptop. Miraculously, she was set up for her first interview, live on Channel 4.

She was eloquent and impassioned, painting a picture of slaughter and despair in the besieged, crumbling neighbourhood in which we ourselves were now virtual prisoners. She told of the shattered bodies being dragged into the makeshift field clinic, of limbs hanging on by a fine thread and of lives hanging on by even less. She described how doctors were left helpless as they struggled to remove huge pieces of shrapnel from contorted bodies, terrified eyes pleading from stretchers as their lives slipped slowly away. She told of the dying: a baby gasping for breath and of doctors who could only weep as the children of Syria were massacred in front of them, the victims of a crude power struggle.

Her message was transmitted from a battered satellite dish on a broken, collapsing rooftop in Baba Amr to the homes of millions of warm Britons who were settling down to their evening meals a thousand lifetimes away.

Next up came the BBC World interview. Marie's narrative and the images I had shot earlier in the week portrayed the grotesque reality of the events taking place inside the neighbourhood. Marie spoke with passionate fury.

There's a small clinic. You can't really call it a clinic; it's an apartment that has been turned into a clinic. You have plasma bags hanging from coat hangers. There was just a constant stream of civilians.

I watched a little baby die today. Absolutely horrific. Just a two-year-old had been hit. They stripped it and found the shrapnel had gone into the left chest and the doctor just said 'I can't do anything' and his little tummy just kept heaving until he died. That is happening over and over and over.

No one here can understand how the international community can let this happen. Particularly when you have an example of Srebrenica – shelling of a city, lots of investigations by the United Nations after that massacre, lots of vows to never let it happen again. There are 28,000 people in Baba Amr in Homs where I am, besieged. They are here because they can't get out. The Syrians will not let them out and are shelling all the civilian areas.

Obviously there is Free Syrian Army here. They are very, very lightly armed. Kalashnikovs and I've seen a few RPGs [rocket-propelled grenades]. They're essentially playing a defensive role. In fact people are terrified they will leave. There are just shells, rockets and tank fire pouring into civilian areas of this city. It is just unrelenting.

Marie, the black-robed renegade, sat freezing, hunched over her laptop as she humanised the people of Baba Amr. Armed only with words, she transformed the anonymous victims of a far-flung conflict into people with faces and lives; people who demanded the world's attention.

Between the Channel 4 and BBC interviews she joined me in the main room. She wore a worried frown as she wrapped a blanket over her black robe and sat down next to me. The power had come back on and so we had all managed to watch her interview.

'How was it?' she asked, a trace of self-doubt in her voice.

'You nailed it, Marie. It's going to go big. Powerful stuff.'

'I hope so, I really do,' she said. 'I'm glad we got something out while we still can.'

I didn't pick her up on this last phrase – 'while we still can'. The two of us had reached an unspoken agreement. We were both aware of our situation and nothing more needed saying. Two hours passed. We sat. I smoked and she inhaled passively. If there was ever a proper time to break her resolution and start smoking again, it was now. She never did. In the wait before the CNN Anderson Cooper show, Marie emailed Sean at the foreign desk with an update.

From: Marie Colvin
Date: Tue, Feb 21, 2012
Subject: baba amr
To: Sean Ryan, Graham Paterson
Cc: Lucy Fisher

All well here. It is the worst day of shelling in the days I have been here. I counted 14 blasts in 30 seconds.

I did interviews for BBC Hub and for Channel 4. ITN is asking, not really sure of the etiquette, as it were. Is doing an interview for everyone just guaranteed to piss everyone off?

My plan for tomorrow, to get civilian casualties I will try to go to the only clinic and just spend the day there. It is simply too dangerous to move much. Two cars of the activists who tool around Baba Amr getting video both hit today, one destroyed.

Should we Skype, or do you just want emails. I am on mariecolvin1, it may be different from the one you have they seem to have cloned.

Mx

Marie was busy preparing for the final CNN interview when another mail came through. It read:

Ryan, Sean
21 Feb
to Marie

Let's speak now. I've asked to be added to your contacts on mariecolvin1. Can you Skype me please?

When Marie didn't respond we received another mail from Sean, who was by now extremely anxious about Marie's previous mail.

Ryan, Sean
21 Feb
to Marie, bcc: me

Hi Marie,

I'm alarmed to read what happened to the two cars today. There are a couple of questions we should be thinking hard about now. The first is whether it's safe to move at all. The second is whether the extra material about civilian casualties you'd get from a day at the clinic would be worth the risk, given the outstanding job you did of highlighting the impact on civilians last week. I'd very much like to talk to you about this. If for any reason we can't connect on Skype, let's discuss by exchanging emails.

Sean x

Marie had returned to the darkened room for her final interview, with CNN's Anderson Cooper. His show reached a wide audience.

She was about to tell the whole world about what we had witnessed in Baba Amr. By the time the evening was over, what was happening there would no longer be a secret. The so-called 'unverified' videos posted by activists on YouTube about the brutality of President Assad's assault on the neighbourhood, may have slipped past the world largely unnoticed, but things were about to change: the bloodshed was about to be verified by the western eyes of a highly trained, deeply revered and globally respected foreign correspondent. Verified, that is, in a very big way.

But not before a few last-minute technical glitches.

'Paul, it's broken. Fuck, help, the laptop's dead!' Marie exclaimed moments before she was due on air.

I rushed into the room to find her shaking her laptop above her head. She was cursing and swearing at the inanimate object, turning it upside down and scowling at it in the gloom. I pressed the power button and it came out of hibernation.

She laughed. 'You must think I'm a fucking idiot.'

I thought about it and looked theatrically around the room in which we stood. 'No, Marie. I think we're both fucking idiots.' I smiled.

Marie went on to deliver one of the most powerful interviews of her life. Her words were simple and strong and her piece was delivered with a suppressed anger that moved even the activists inside the media centre to silence. People the world over watched that interview. Her finely-tuned eloquence shredded the myth that Assad was conducting a military campaign. This was about the wanton destruction and murder of civilians on an industrial scale.

I sat, cigarette in mouth, watching CNN live in the main room of the media centre. Holy shit, I thought, this is going to ruffle a few feathers in high places.

Marie joined me on the cushions after it was over. She was visibly more relaxed. She had done as much as anyone could to get the word out. It was no longer possible for the world to sit passively by and feign ignorance.

'We've done it, Marie. We got it out and it's going to be huge. Well done,' I said.

'Well done you,' she smiled back, before yawning. 'I'm tired. I didn't sleep too well last night.'

'What?' I said, flabbergasted. 'Marie, you sounded like a fucking bulldozer. You put the Chechens to shame.'

'Really? Do I snore?' She was absolutely convinced she didn't.

'Hang on a moment.' I laughed. 'I'm going to call my first witness. Wa'el, come over here a second, mate . . .'

That evening, as the shelling slowly reduced in ferocity and tempo, we received a Skype call from Sean Ryan. Marie's first reaction was, 'Tell him I'm not in.'

'Not in? Where should I tell him you are, Marie – out shopping?' I laughed as I pressed the button to accept the incoming call.

Sean looked concerned; very concerned. He had read Marie's emails regarding the situation on the ground. He summed everything up succinctly. We'd had an exclusive story in *The Sunday Times* a few days ago and we'd just broadcast live to three networks. The world was now aware of the situation in Baba Amr. What more did we want, he asked, and what more could we add before the risks became too great? Sean wanted us to start making arrangements to leave the next day – Wednesday.

Marie wasn't quite convinced. She argued that we needed to get to the field hospital the next day so we had more colour for that week's issue. Yes, we had already been there but she insisted we went back to gather more material. She also played down the seriousness of the situation in Baba Amr, telling Sean that, even if a ground attack happened, we were more than capable of hiding in the rubble for a few days and lying low until we could escape. I think this did little to assuage Sean's misgivings. In fact, Marie's escape plan probably worried him even more.

Sean countered. He wasn't convinced of our need to stay. He would prefer that we left as soon as possible rather than hanging around for material we already had.

And so it bounced back and forth between the two of them. Neither gave ground. Marie was behaving like a rather slippery customer while Sean sought some form of confirmation from her that we would indeed leave. By the end, the only weapon left in Sean's armoury was to push the nuclear button and order her out. Even if she obeyed him, which was questionable, it would still mean leaving Wednesday night at the earliest as any movement in the daytime hours was a no go.

I felt uneasy after the Skype call. I had said little and left the discussion mostly to Marie and Sean. As a photographer, I felt a strong urge to keep shooting and I also understood Marie's sense of duty to the story. Yet I couldn't shake the deep look of concern on Sean's face from my mind. I knew he was right: the situation on the ground was rapidly deteriorating and it was plain that Assad's forces intended entering the neighbourhood with ground troops at the earliest opportunity. The tunnel through which we had entered was our only lifeline to the outside world: should it fall into the hands of Assad's men then our situation would be beyond salvage. I decided to email Sean an honest situation report.

From: Paul Conroy
To: Sean Ryan
21/02/2012
Subject: for what it's worth

Movement heavily restricted.

The one exit we do have out is vulnerable to attack at any moment. Once it has gone exit is impossible.

Hiding in burnt out building is a no go plan. Street to street clearance would flush us out. No reliable or confirmed exit route if this was to be the case.

I suspect that Marie's high profile due to this week's material in paper and TV interviews also compromises our safety. The Syrians have an efficient intelligence machine as we know.

In my opinion we are working to the law of diminishing returns regarding what we can achieve balanced with our safety. Marie has a brilliant nose for a story but lacks, in my opinion, a general strategic awareness when it comes to military operations and strategy.

I would appreciate it if this assessment was kept confidential and between us. It is just my reading of the situation here. As I'm sure you're aware Marie can be tricky to convince once she has the bit between her teeth but I think you need a more pragmatic reading of our situation.

Cheers,
Paul

An hour later, we received another email from Sean. He had done as I had hoped by weaving my concerns with his own.

to Marie, Paul, bcc: me

Hi Marie,

Good stuff on C4 News, which carried two segments of your interview with Jonathan Miller. The thrust of Miller's report was shelling intensifying as troops build up – but you know all that.

I want to reiterate what I said earlier so that you have this clearly in mind as you're weighing it all up before we speak in the morning. You're doing an important job brilliantly, no question. There are two questions for me.

The first is whether staying in Baba Amr would give you much more than you already have. You already have the rebels' view of how to defend their city and yet more harrowing detail of civilian casualties. If you stay on, are you likely to add any other important elements?

The second question is whether any extra elements would be worth the risk. From here, it looks as if the risks are growing – the shelling getting worse, the cars being blown up and worst of all, the troops who may be poised to enter. What would your position be if they came in by day and you couldn't leave? Or if your one escape route got blocked? You'd be in grave danger. Could your articles and interviews make you a target? I don't think we can rule that out.

We'll see how things stand in the morning, but barring any unforeseen improvement, I think you should consider leaving BA [Baba Amr] at the first opportunity, which would be Wednesday night. You'd come out with powerful material, you could add to it from a position of relative safety in the neighbouring district and you could weave in other developments such as the referendum and the international picture, eg this report tonight. WASHINGTON -- The United States says it will consider taking 'additional measures' to end the bloodshed in Syria if an international outcry and a strengthened sanctions regime do not convince the government of President Bashar al-Assad to stop its crackdown on the opposition.

I'm copying this to Paul so that we can all have a chat together in the morning.

Seanx

I had just read the mail when Marie sat wearily down next to me.

'Did you read it?' she asked in a monotone.

'Yes, and I'm sorry, Marie, but I agree with Sean. All I'm going to get tomorrow are more shots of the clinic and more blown-up people that will never be printed,' I said.

'We fucked up once and left and the invasion never happened. Do you want to do that again?' she asked, reminding me of our earlier escape.

'I know, Marie, but this is different. Things are coming to a head here. The FSA, as brave as they are, can't hold this place for much longer. Consider what we'll do if the tunnel is cut or they come in by day.'

'I could easily dress up in a burka,' she bounced back at me.

'Marie, I would look fucking ridiculous in a burka and really, what good will it do being in a burka? Think about it. They're fucking killing and raping women,' I said a little tetchily.

'Okay, Paul, you know we could survive in some bombed-out buildings. We should stash some water and food and have a bolthole prepared,' was her retort.

'Yes, we could do that, but what then? After a few days Baba Amr will be a garrison town. The soldiers will go house to house, there will be tanks and armoured cars on every corner and in we stroll in our burkas. With no communications, no power and not a chance of blagging our way through an Assad checkpoint, we are dead meat.' Take that, I thought.

Marie pondered this for a while. 'Hmm. Maybe you have a point,' she finally admitted.

Hallefuckinglujah, I thought in relief. She gets it, she finally gets it.

'Okay,' Marie countered, 'how about this for a plan. We get up real early, go to the field hospital, stay an hour or two, get some more colour for this week and organise it so we leave with the FSA tomorrow night?'

'It's a deal.' I laughed. She drove a tough bargain.

We had a plan, which is always better than sitting around waiting for events to overtake you. I sat back, lit a cigarette and felt a wave of relief trickle through my body. Now, when we made it out of Baba Amr, we could still follow the ground invasion, but this time from the correct end of a 240mm mortar.

The sound of the front door rattling in the media centre caused all our heads to turn. A face, familiar and smiling, beamed down at me from the entrance. It was Remi Ochlik, a good friend and fellow photographer who was a veteran of the war in Libya.

Three other mud-soaked and exhausted souls traipsed into the room with Remi: Javier Espinosa, a Spanish reporter I knew from Libya, and two French journalists, Edith Bouvier and William Daniels. Familiar faces increase one's sense of security, however false this sensation might be. I could see that the sight of Marie and I gave the four new arrivals confidence in their decision to enter the besieged neighbourhood. I could almost hear them thinking, Phew, we're not the only lunatics in town.

Remi grabbed a blanket and sat with me. He explained that the four of them had been holed up in a house outside Homs with the FSA, waiting to enter Baba Amr via the tunnel. It had been confusing, he mused. For a few days, as he twiddled his thumbs in the house, he heard many mentions of a mysterious character called Abu Falafel. He thought nothing of it until he was watching television one night when activist footage broadcast on Al Jazeera showed Marie and I in the field hospital. The rebels immediately started cheering and pointing at the screen, shouting 'Abu Falafel, it's Abu Falafel'. That's when it clicked. He immediately asked the FSA to bring their group into Baba Amr as soon as possible. And here they were.

I was frank about the current situation. I told Remi that it was nearly impossible to work due to the intensity of the bombardment and the lack of vehicles. We chatted and smoked for a while, catching up on what had happened since Libya. It was great to have company but, as we spoke, I grew increasingly concerned. Within minutes my fears turned into reality. Marie caught my eye and beckoned me over. With an impending sense of dread, I moved to where she had made her nest for the evening.

She looked at me with a mischievous twinkle in her eye. 'Hey, Paul, you still wanna go now the French are here?' she asked.

It was the killer blow. All the effort and work that Sean and myself had put into getting Marie clear of Baba Amr had just been blown out of the water. There was little hope of persuading her to leave now that other journalists were here. Marie immediately saw them as the opposition, as intruders on her story. Personally, my heart sank. I knew we were staying.

By then, Marie's mind had already switched back to the story she would write for Sunday's edition. 'Paul, we gotta get to the field clinic in the morning, before the French,' she said.

I laughed and reminded her that the cars had all been blown up. We would have to go to the clinic on foot. That meant a lot of

213

sniper-dodging: all the major junctions en route to the clinic appeared to have their own personal sniper who never seemed to sleep.

'Shit, I'd forgotten about the snipers. How about we go at five a.m. when it's very quiet?' she asked.

I shrugged wearily, pointing out that it was now past midnight and we should arrange the plan with Abu Hanin.

'You want to go when?' Abu Hanin replied in shock.

We explained our plan to get to the field hospital – before the snipers were up – and to stay as long as possible. Abu Hanin continued to look at us, baffled. But, having become accustomed to his guests' somewhat odd requests, he finally agreed to take us to the hospital on foot, at five in the morning.

'I will be ready,' he smiled. 'Five a.m. I do not sleep and will not need an alarm clock.' Marie eyed him dubiously but let it pass.

It was gone midnight when we said goodnight to the others in the main room. We had an early start ahead of us and we wanted to get as much sleep as possible. The new group of journalists had been with us for less than a few hours when we said our goodnights. They sat, freezing, writing emails and letting people know that they had arrived safely in Baba Amr. The words 'safely' and 'Baba Amr' had an extremely oxymoronic ring to them.

In our nests, we hunkered down for another night in the spare room. Marie set her phone for an early start.

'Paul,' she whispered, 'I think the shelling is making me deaf.'

'What?' I replied, shocked to hear this news. 'Let me look. That isn't good.'

I pulled out my small LED torch while she sat up and let me inspect her ear. What I saw shocked me. 'Wait a moment, Marie,' I said, reaching in my small bag for a box of matches. 'Stay very still. Do not move. I have to go into your ear.'

She fell silent as I gently probed her ear with the matchstick. I eventually hooked what I'd seen and slowly pulled it from her ear. I held it up next to her head.

'Okay, you can look now,' I said.

She squinted in the pale light. 'Jesus, what the fuck is that?' she gasped.

'Marie, that is the rubber earpiece from my headphones. It's been in there since you did the CNN broadcast.'

We tried to sleep but had little luck. The cause of Marie's temporary deafness was so ridiculous that one of us would erupt with laughter every five minutes, flinging the other into fits of unsuppressed, hysterical giggles. It took an age for sleep to come.

I will never know who drifted off to sleep first on that cold, black night in Baba Amr, but even now, when it's dark and sleep won't come, I still hear our laughter, our ridiculous and raucous laughter.

CHAPTER TEN

Farewell

22 February 2012, Baba Amr, Syria

'He's fucking asleep. Abu Hanin said he never sleeps but he's fucking well asleep!' hissed Marie as she stumbled about in the pitch-black room, her one good eye failing miserably to steer her in the right direction.

Oh shit, here we go, I thought, forcing my eyes open. 'Did you try waking him?' I yawned.

'I think he's fucking dead, Paul. He said he didn't sleep but he's still fucking asleep. Either that or he's dead.' Marie spat out the words and continued circling the room.

I sensed trouble brewing. Marie finally found her bed and burrowed herself into the mountain of blankets.

'Well,' she said after some consideration, 'I guess we're just gonna have to go later. But Assad's assholes will be awake by then.'

I laughed silently to myself. Marie could grumble when she wanted to. I had grown used to it when things didn't go to plan and learnt long ago to roll with it. I suggested we should wake Abu Hanin around seven o'clock and try for the field hospital then. She grudgingly agreed and, unbelievably, was snoring again within min-

216

utes. Wa'el groaned from his bed and we all slipped back into a deep sleep.

Predictably, after our earlier nocturnal activity, we overslept. It was cold and we reluctantly collected our belongings and prepared to head into the main room. Shivering as we tiptoed down the narrow, unlit corridor connecting the two rooms, I quite clearly remember Marie's words. 'Shit, the snipers will be awake now,' she said. Pausing briefly, she continued in a whisper, 'And so will the French,' referring to the four journalists who had arrived the previous night.

I had to suppress my laughter – the snipers and the French in one sentence. Only Marie.

We slid open the doors to the main room but in the gloom it was difficult to make anything out. It was impossible to tell who was still sleeping, who was awake and who was lying silently in the darkness, their eyes open, waiting for the shelling to start. All we could see were huddled mounds of people covered in blankets as we crept around the room trying not to disturb anyone.

Without warning the deep-throated scream of a rocket cut through the air. An explosion shook the building violently. Shit, I thought, that was close. Before the thought had time to sink in another scream, followed by another thunderous detonation, pummelled the media centre.

The explosions – no more than a hundred metres away – triggered frantic activity in the room. It was suddenly full of moving people. Some scrambled to untangle themselves from the maze of blankets and wiring, while others staggered around the room in sleepy confusion, looking for cameras and laptops. The darkness, coupled with the profusion of moving bodies, disoriented me.

Another explosion rocked the media centre. This one was closer and again the building rattled and shook as the compression blast hit the three-storey house. The activity in the room picked up. Twenty seconds later another rocket detonated, this time to the rear of the house. The effect was the same: the whole place trembled as debris and rubble landed on the roof like violent rain.

Shit, I thought as a sickening realisation stabbed at my brain. Shit! They're bracketing us. Bracketing is a military tactic used by artillery units to ensure that shells hit their intended target. An artillery gun fires shells at its target, then an observer spots where the rocket or shell impacts. This information is then relayed back to the artillery gunners who make adjustments and fire again. In this manner, artillery batteries can 'walk' rounds on to a target. This had been my job in the army. I had done it dozens of times and so I knew the pattern and timing. In this case, the only possible way that Assad's ground forces could bracket us was by using the drones circling above Homs as forward observers to report where the rounds were landing.

Holy fuck, I thought. These guys knew exactly what they were doing. This was not random fire. The next shell would be a direct hit on our building. I was about to stake my life on it.

A rocket impacted the rear of the building with a crunching, deafening explosion that seemed to uproot it. Immediately the room filled with smoke, concrete dust and the sickening smell of RDX explosives which the rockets used in the warhead. In the confusion a voice screamed in English, 'Get out, get out!' it was pure chaos, nobody knew what to do, some obeyed the order while others continued to try to get kit together.

I needed my camera, which was still in the back room. I ran through the thick pall of smoke as rubble continued to fall into what, moments earlier, had been our bedroom. The blast had completely destroyed the room. I rummaged among the ruins for my camera bag, grabbed it, turned and ran for the main room. Another huge explosion ripped open the side wall, blowing debris and shrapnel into the house. I could still hear the cries of 'Get out, get across the road!'

In the shadows I saw Remi, the French photographer, crouched on the floor. He had managed to get his body armour and helmet on but hadn't had enough time to put his T-shirt on underneath. He squatted low to the floor, darting glances to his left and right as he tried to make sense of the situation. He looked shocked. Remi had only been in Baba Amr for seven hours and he had arrived in the middle of the night when there was always a lull in the shelling. This was his first day under fire. Near to the double doors I glimpsed Marie pulling something from her bag. Her face was calm but her movements – unusually rapid and slightly frantic – suggested that she knew worse was about to come.

My mind raced. The continued screams of 'Get out, get out' rang in my head. My brain struggled to form a plan. Make a fucking decision, I told myself. I'll stay, I thought, I'll stay put. At least the media centre's concrete walls offered a degree of protection, whereas outside, on the tarmac road, with this level and proximity of shelling, death was almost guaranteed.

'Don't fucking go out!' I screamed into the gloom. 'Don't fucking leave, don't go out!' Another rocket smashed into the building. More acrid smoke and concrete dust filled the room.

I was standing directly opposite a wooden door that was never used. It was a weak point in the solid concrete wall that separated the main room from the stairwell and the exit on to the street. I saw William crouching to the right of the door. Wa'el, Edith and I were standing in a loose grouping in the centre of the room. I couldn't see Marie or Javier and there was no sign of Remi. I prayed they hadn't tried to run out of the building. Then I heard Abu Hanin shouting, 'Don't go out! Don't go out!'

That has to be it, I decided. Three direct strikes. There can't be any more. Three was enough. I need shots of this, I thought to myself. This is what the people of Baba Amr have suffered for months. I leant over to grab the camera I had dropped on to the cushions to my left during the previous blast.

A rocket impacted directly in front of the house and in that split second my world changed. Every single one of my senses became massively overloaded. It was like being hit by a tube train in a dark tunnel. My sight, my hearing and my touch all welded into a single, indistinguishable, malfunctioning sense as the explosion tore through the room. A spinning, red-hot shard of shrapnel ripped through my inner thigh, slashing the tendons and tearing out chunks of muscle. I felt a sudden, intense pressure in my leg as the piece of rocket scythed through my flesh and, unbeknown to me, another chunk of rocket cleaved into my abdomen. No pain, yet, only the high-pitched screaming in my ears, the acrid explosive gases and the concrete dust that filled the room, blinding me.

I knew I only had precious minutes to stem the flow of blood from my left thigh. Without thinking, I thrust my hand into the fist-sized entry wound. To my horror, it went straight through my leg and out the other side. I froze. Images of hospital food raced through my mind – cold slices of beef, leathery potatoes, custard, all cold and congealed. Not to worry, I thought. People could bring me food. I stood like an idiot with my hand through my leg until the reality of what was happening around me snapped me back into action.

I knew I had to find my artery to check it wasn't severed so I rummaged through the shredded muscle. I squeezed the pulsating vessel tightly in my right hand. It seemed intact. Again, I dug my hand inside my thigh, this time to check my femur wasn't broken. I withdrew it, relieved. Although the artery felt healthy, I had to tourniquet the wound immediately in case the shrapnel had nicked it and I bled to death on the cold concrete floor.

I yelled into the blackness of the room, 'I'm hit, I'm fucking hit.' There was no response. I thought I could hear Edith screaming behind me, but I could see little through the thick smoke and dust. Stumbling in the darkness, I found the remnants of a destroyed wall. Stabilising myself, I prepared to begin repairs to my leg. I tore at the keffiyeh around my neck and bound it as tightly as possible around my upper thigh. Despite my best efforts, blood still ran down my leg, soaking my tattered cargo trousers.

As well as spitting shrapnel into my leg, the explosion had also blasted the disused wooden door inwards, shattering Edith's thigh and Wa'el's arm as if they were matchwood. I hadn't seen either of them yet, but I could hear Edith's cries. That was all I could hear.

I had to find Marie, Remi and Javier. They must have made it out, I thought, so I stumbled and fell through the space where the main door to the hallway had once been. But after two or three metres my leg collapsed, leaving me breathless and gasping on the floor.

I checked it again. Blood was still flowing from the open wound. Blinking in the daylight, I caught sight of a yellow Ethernet cable that had been blasted from the house and now lay under a thick covering of dust. I grabbed the cable and fashioned another tourniquet, this time tightening it with a piece of wood so that I had my bleeding under control. Another shell impacted, maybe ten metres away, followed swiftly by yet another. Suddenly the street outside was under full attack as whining missiles sent screaming shards of steel and rubble in all directions. I stayed flat and tightened the tourniquet until the pain shot in lightning bolts through my body.

I heard voices. 'Abu Falafel, Abu Falafel.' Looking up, I saw Abu Hanin pop his head round the corner from inside the building. The explosions had destroyed the front section of the house and I was now essentially outside on the street. Abu Hanin tried to reach me so that he could drag me to safety. I waved him back as another shell landed close by. 'Wait,' I screamed, urging him to stay put. 'Wait until the shells stop.'

He stayed in position, watching me with horror as I lay helplessly in the rubble. I rolled over onto my front to make myself flatter and less of a target.

That's how I found Marie and Remi. There, in what had once been the entranceway to the house, lay the bodies of my two friends. Mercifully I could not see Marie's face. Her head and legs were covered in fallen rubble and I recognised her only by her blue jumper and belt. Of Remi, I saw only his back through the thick layers of dust and fallen masonry. They lay side by side, joined together in their silence. I couldn't be sure whether they had died trying to leave the house or trying to return after failing to cross the road to the apparent safety of another building. It didn't matter: the two lay dead before me, partially buried under the rubble of Baba Amr.

The wonderful, smiling Remi – together we had dodged bullets and bombs as we pushed our way through the cities and deserts of Libya. Marie, with whom I had shared a thousand adventures; Marie the sailor; Marie who had given a face and voice to millions of people whose lives had been torn apart by war; Marie the Martha Gellhorn of our generation who now lay motionless in the ruins of Baba Amr. I gently laid my hand on her chest and checked she was dead. Farewell, Chechen queen.

CHAPTER ELEVEN

Can I smoke?

22 February 2012, Baba Amr, Syria

I lay amid the rubble and dust next to the bodies of Marie and Remi. The immediate fear and chaos of the attack had passed but I felt neither grief nor sorrow. How could I possibly be devoid of any feeling, either physical or mental? I briefly wondered whether I might be dying, a thought I dismissed almost as soon as it entered my mind. Then it hit me. Huge waves of guilt surged through my body and the sheer intensity of the emotion made me freeze. My friends were dead yet I didn't feel anything. I wanted to cry but no tears came.

Death had been instant for Marie and Remi. The shell had impacted less than two metres in front of them. They would not have heard the explosion, nor would they have suffered, of that there was no doubt. In their determination to tell the world about the brutality being inflicted on the people of Syria, they had paid the ultimate price. Their names and memories would be added to the long list of the dead, murdered in a year of bloody uprising and ruthless suppression.

As I lay in the rubble, another withering salvo of mortars and rockets exploded with a characteristic, sickening crunch in the cratered street outside the media centre. Assad's forces clearly weren't finished with us yet. The controller of the circling drone had detected movement below and was now beaming back real-time imagery of the devastation that the artillery guns had wreaked on the building.

Squirming in the filth from the aftermath of the explosion, I desperately tried to burrow deeper into the rubble and fallen masonry for more cover. The shrapnel from the constant barrage of exploding mortar rounds was so close that it sent chunks of concrete from the partially demolished house tumbling down on top of me. How long could my luck hold, I wondered. Surely now it was just a matter of time before a shell with my name on it found me bleeding in the dirt.

From my position in what had once been the media centre's lobby, I felt myself being dragged backwards across the rubble. I turned to find Abu Bakhr running over to where I lay. He grabbed me by my jacket and began to drag me back into the house. Once inside, he and Abu Hanin manhandled me into the bathroom, which was the safest place in the house because the room had more concrete walls surrounding it than any other. I sat down, propped myself up against one of the walls and, with a trembling hand, managed to light a cigarette. The explosive gases and dust filtered out any light in the room so we sat together in the dark as detonations in the street outside continued to shake the remnants of the house.

I had been shot at dozens of times before and been close to many explosions, but now, for the first time ever, I felt like I was the target. This desperate, wounded group clinging to life in the darkness of a toilet had become the hunted.

I suddenly felt pain for the first time since the shrapnel entered my leg. It was a sharp, searing pain that ran from my foot to the back of my eyes. Fumbling in the blackness, I felt the calf of my left leg. Shit, I thought, as I realised that another large chunk of muscle was hanging off. I hadn't noticed the wound at first but I now knew that I had two holes in my leg. Whatever natural pain-killers my body had produced were gradually wearing off. Another piece of shrapnel – three inches of Russian-made Katyusha rocket – had penetrated my side and, unknown to me at the time, now rested precariously a few millimetres from my right kidney.

As I let the extent of my injuries sink in, I tried to ascertain who else was in the dark, stinking toilet. Edith Bouvier, the French journalist, was there. I could hear her groaning. Wa'el was also in the room with us. He asked me how I was. I grunted an okay and asked him about his injuries. He replied, rather nonchalantly, 'I have hurt my arm.' I couldn't see his face but I could hear the pain in his voice. He was downplaying his injury; he didn't want to worry me. William Daniels, the French photographer, announced that he was unhurt and informed us that the Spanish photographer Javier Espinosa had also escaped injury. But I couldn't see either man. Shrapnel had pierced one of the activists in his back, but he laughingly reassured us that he was fine.

In the gloom, Abu Hanin assessed the injured. He calmly assured us that we would make a dash for the field hospital as soon as the shelling stopped. How fucking ironic, I thought. We'll finally get to see the clinic again. For now, all any of us could do was to stay low and hope that no more shells hit the building. Ten minutes passed before the shelling decreased in ferocity, leaving only the deep moans of agony to hang in the air between us as broken bones and torn flesh slowly reconnected with our overloaded and numb nervous systems. The terrifying reality of our predicament was slowly beginning to sink in – two seriously wounded, immobile casualties would present the already overworked medical team at the clinic with a burden they didn't need.

The sudden roar of an engine, the screeching of brakes and the crunch of glass under wheels in the street outside heralded the arrival of help. I heard distant voices barking orders before an FSA fighter popped his head into our cramped, dark world. A rushed conversation took place between Abu Hanin and the rebel. As soon as the conversation finished, two activists picked me up from the floor, supporting me between their shoulders, and I hopped forward on my good leg, trailing my wounded leg uselessly as we wove our way through the remnants of the media centre. Cement dust and the fine black powder from the explosive chemicals coated everything in the room, which now bore little resemblance to the place that only twenty minutes earlier had echoed to the sound of Marie's laughter.

Stepping around the bodies of Marie and Remi at the foot of the stairwell, directly in the path to the outside world, I was helped to the parked saloon car. I nodded a brief and final farewell to my friends who lay, unmoving, in the rubble behind me. Once seated on the back seat, I took another look at the wound in my thigh. A steady stream of blood flowed on to the car's beige upholstery. I was losing blood at quite a rate and I knew I had to reach the clinic fast. Outside, the shelling was sporadic but still close by. The run to the clinic would be dangerous. With a drone still circling overhead, anything that moved on the ground below presented a potential target to the artillery guns positioned on the edge of the neighbourhood.

Taking in the scene of destruction around me, I pondered our chances of making it to the clinic. The attack on the media centre was unquestionably deliberate. The artillery gunners had done a good job: they were accurate and professional. The media centre looked like a huge cave that had been gouged into the front of the building. It was barely recognisable. I gave us a fifty-fifty chance of reaching the clinic without being hit again. As I weighed up the risks, movement came from the house to my right. William Daniels struggled through the detritus and swirling dust carrying Edith, her face a mask of agony as he manhandled her into the car. Every movement, however slight, ground the two ends of her snapped femur together, causing a pain I couldn't imagine.

The car accelerated into a tight U-turn, throwing up a shower of gravel, glass and dust as it powered its way to the first junction. Almost immediately, we drove into a stream of explosive bullets, kicking up puffs of fractured concrete, that followed the car as we made for the cover of a building a hundred metres away. More mortar rounds exploded ahead of us. The driver accelerated through the intersections of the roads where snipers again tried to pick off the moving vehicle. Edith grimaced silently. Every crater, every piece of rubble or swerve of the car caused grinding agony. She clenched her teeth and never made a sound.

We continued to dodge the incoming fire for the next five minutes as the car darted and wove through the narrow maze of backstreets towards the field hospital. The driver spun the car into a hard left turn, throwing us together on the back seat. A wall of black smoke and drifting dust greeted us as we turned on to the road, which was under artillery attack. We flinched as explosions caused debris from the surrounding buildings to clatter down on the roof of the vehicle. But the car continued to bounce and bump over scabrous chunks of concrete, twisted steel and broken glass as we approached the clinic at speed.

Everything became a blur as the driver slammed on his brakes outside the building. The car's doors were wrenched open before we had even had a chance to stop and a sea of arms dragged Edith and myself from the vehicle. The distance from the car to the clinic was only a matter of metres but the stench of high explosives, RDX and cordite that filled the street outside stung my throat and eyes. The clinic doors were thrown open and we were passed from one person to another before being bundled, finally, into the clinic. The sound of the car racing off to pick up another batch of victims was accompanied by the thunderous noise of more explosions; always more explosions.

On entering the clinic the old saying 'Out of the frying pan and into the fire' sprang, rather stupidly, to mind. The doctors who treated demonstrators and FSA fighters were a group of people the regime wanted to wipe out more than most and, as such, they were targeted relentlessly. We had just exchanged one target zone for another.

The screams of the clinic's wounded reverberated off the concrete walls and stone tiles. The volunteer staff frantically assessed victims as they arrived while overworked medics and nurses rushed from room to room, treating those who stood any chance of surviving. Others simply died where they lay. I lost sight of Edith as she was whisked off into another part of the building. I was helped into the same room, and placed on the same makeshift stretchers where I had photographed the dead and dying only days earlier. Shit, I thought, this is some déjà vu.

The concerned faces of the clinic's staff loomed over me as video cameras and mobile phones were thrust in my face. I laughed: I was receiving a definite taste of my own medicine here. For years I had done exactly the same to others. To complain now would seem a tad churlish.

Two familiar faces peered down at me. 'Hi, Paul', said Dr Mohamed, who I had filmed treating the wounded and dying.

Dr Ali smiled gently at me, the concern and shock at seeing me on his operating table, showed clearly on his weary face.

I felt embarrassed. The last thing these guys needed right now was for us to take up vital resources.

'Hey, Mohammed,' I replied. 'Sorry about this, mate.'

He looked at me with a great sadness in his eyes and said, 'Paul, Miss Marie is dead.'

I nodded silently. For a moment we held eye contact.

'Okay, let's fix you now,' he said, shaking the mood as a team of three people set to work on me.

First to go were my home-made tourniquets: the doctors sliced off my keffiyeh followed by the yellow Ethernet cable that I had tied tightly around my leg. Next, a pair of scissors cut away at the cloth of my blood-soaked trousers, giving me my first proper look at the wound in my leg.

'Holy fuck,' I said out loud, my eyes locking on to the bloody, fist-sized hole that gaped back at me. I could see the entrance wound clearly but, as well as the obvious hole, there was also a very large indent where the muscle had been blasted away to be pulped over the walls of the media centre. Not good, I thought as they turned me on to my side to examine the exit wound on my outer thigh.

What I saw next was a bit of a shock: a huge hole about eight inches long flapped open to reveal what appeared to be a large lump of hamburger meat. 'Oh, bollocks,' I muttered. It was much worse than I had imagined.

Dr Mohamed looked at me calmly. 'Paul, we will need to cut the damaged muscle off. It may hurt,' he said.

'Okay,' I nodded. 'Can I smoke?'

'Paul,' he replied, 'you can do whatever you want.'

A nurse placed a cigarette in my mouth before the medical team started working on the leg. Having produced a pair of scissors, they slowly began to cut off the muscle that was flopping out of my thigh. Trying desperately not to watch, I smoked and resolved to concentrate my mind on something slightly less morbid than the sound and feel of the scissors cutting through my muscle. I lit another cigarette.

Eventually, they finished cutting off the meaty bits before announcing that they now had to clean the wound. Okay, I thought, cleaning can't be as bad as what's just happened. It is curious, though, just how wrong you can be in such situations.

A large bottle of iodine was produced and I caught a glimpse of an implement, which bore a disturbing resemblance to a tooth-brush, being inserted into my leg. It was a necessary evil. Inside, my leg would be a collection of nasty items: probably some shrapnel, certainly material from my trousers, cement dust, old food from the media centre and possibly even dog shit from the road. It needed a good clean, as any infection would almost certainly result in a hacksaw amputation in a few days time. There was no anaesthetic. I lit my third cigarette.

The doctors worked quickly and methodically. The pain was now so intense that I had to convince myself it couldn't actually be pain I was experiencing and that therefore the operation wasn't as painful as it felt. Work that one out. I still can't, but it appeared to help at the time.

In addition to the lack of even the most basic medical supplies and the constant fear of a direct hit on the clinic, the doctors were presented with another problem as they cleaned my wound: every time they had almost finished, an explosion on the roof of a nearby building would send concrete dust drifting back down into the open hole in my leg. This was irritating and, as I clung desperately to my pain-killing cigarette, some bastard would land another shell close by, which would spur more cleaning and scrubbing.

We eventually reached patch-up-the-wound phase. Dr Mohamed informed me that normally with such a wound one hole would be left open to allow it to drain and prevent infection, while the other hole would be sealed. However, as I would need to escape at some point, he had decided to close both holes in the leg. Not too keen to watch this part either, I studiously studied the ceiling while they stapled up the wound.

As they worked on my leg, Javier Espinosa entered the room. He confirmed that Marie and Remi were dead and that he and Abu Hanin would take care of the bodies. I came crashing back to earth. In the chaos and pain, my mind had built a wall, allowing me to exist only in the immediate present but, with a simple reminder of the past, this wall now tumbled down around me. Marie and Remi – gone.

The grim and horrifying reality of the morning's events rose from the rubble of my fallen wall. My head was spinning. Explosions and gunfire merged with photographically real images of the morning in a kaleidoscopic attack on my senses. I had slotted together the final piece of a nightmarish jigsaw and the world had suddenly become a far darker place.

The doctors continued to work on my leg. They were now cleaning and repairing the wound on my calf, having stuffed the torn muscle back into place. While they worked, a pale-looking Edith was wheeled into the room and placed next to my stretcher. She asked how I was doing. Reaching out to each other, we held hands as the doctors finished their work and bandaged my leg wounds. Her hand was soft and cold but the human contact and the understanding born of a shared experience was deeply comforting. For a few moments I closed my eyes and wished for better times.

Edith's leg was heavily bandaged and rigged in a home-made traction system. Her injured leg was raised up and supported by a board and cushions at the end of her trolley. Five bags of serum were tied to her ankle in a bundle which hung over the bottom of the bed, to act as weights. The force created by the dangling weights pulled one end of the broken femur from the other, thus preventing them grinding together. Crude but extremely effective, the device highlighted not only the lack of any substantial medical supplies, but also the genius of the doctors who worked in these incredibly stressful situations. The nurse hooked me up to a litre of blood, which had been donated by one of the nurses in the clinic. She assured me, somewhat mischievously, that when I woke in the morning I would be a fluent Arabic speaker.

As we lay hand in hand on our stretchers, Edith and I reassured ourselves by telling each other that we would be okay. In the end, bearing in mind neither of us could walk, all we had to do was escape from Baba Amr through the tunnel, travel across Syria, smuggle ourselves across the frequently patrolled and heavily mined border, avoid the Hezbollah checkpoints in Lebanon and everything would be just fine.

From our stretchers, we observed the stream of dead and wounded who were dragged unceasingly through the clinic doors. Before leaving us to treat others, Dr Mohamed suggested we make a video, proving we were alive and explaining how the regime had targeted activists and foreign journalists in the morning's attack. Edith and I agreed it could be a double-edged sword: our families, friends and editors would be reassured but the regime would also be made aware of our survival.

Dr Mohamed and Dr Ali, who were both naturals when it came to filming, did a sterling job. They detailed the attack on the media centre, told of the deaths of Marie and Remi and then proceeded to give our names and precise medical accounts of our injuries. Within an hour the video had been posted on YouTube. It was all they could do before they had to return to the bloody business of treating the incoming casualties.

William Daniels came to see Edith and me. His unshaven face, his dark wavy hair still covered in concrete dust and his darting, haunted eyes made him appear older than his twenty-six years. He looked shocked and exhausted as he absorbed the severity of the situation. Wa'el's arm, he told us, was badly broken. He would be okay but he needed an operation to treat the wound properly. The same was true of Edith: her injury required an operation to reset the bones in her leg and the facilities for this simply did not exist in Baba Amr. There was a hospital only one kilometre away but to reach it Edith would need to surrender herself to Assad's forces. She politely declined the offer.

Dr Mohamed returned to our room within the hour. There wasn't enough space at the field clinic to keep patients after their initial treatment so he planned to move us to a safe house near by. It was an alarming prospect. In the few hours since we arrived in the clinic, I had become increasingly reassured by the presence of the doctors and nurses, so the thought of being moved elsewhere worried me. We insisted that we all stay together. Splitting us up was out of the question, we told the doctors. Edith and I understood that from now on we would need each other for moral support and comfort.

Preparations were made for us to be moved. Edith lay on a trolley with wheels while I lay on a stretcher. William and Javier joined us for the transfer to the safe house and we waited by the exit to the field hospital for a lull in the shelling. When it came, we moved fast and, heading in a straight line across the torn-up street, we quickly reached the other side, carried by medics and activists. Turning left, we hugged the line of buildings for shelter and continued for another fifty metres. We passed through a small doorway to our right and entered a narrow corridor leading to a small court-yard. Another corridor, cold and tiled, echoed to the sounds of boots and deep breathing from the rapidly tiring stretcher-bearers. I became completely disoriented inside the building, which felt more like a maze than a home. Eventually, having passed through an internal courtyard with a glass ceiling, we stopped outside a doorway. One of the stretcher-bearers opened the squeaking door and there it was: our new home.

The room was about 6 × 4 metres, pitch dark with a damp and unused smell to it. On entering, my heart skipped a beat: to my right, at the far end of the room, was the last thing I wanted to see – an enormous window almost the size of a whole wall. Holy shit, I thought, one shell close by and we're going to be sleeping in the world's largest liquidiser.

I was placed on a small mattress in the corner directly opposite the door, handed some pillows and then covered in a thick blanket. Edith was placed on a sofa in the far corner of the room. Her back was to the window wall and diagonally opposite me. Wa'el sat directly opposite me on the other side of the window from Edith. Her traction device was adjusted until she was comfortable. I sat, transfixed, staring at the window.

'William, Javier, do me a favour, chaps. Get as many mattresses, cushions, whatever you can and hide that fucking window as soon as possible, please. It's making me extremely nervous,' I said.

In the cold, dark room they constructed a window defence mech-anism out of anything and everything they could find. Salah, one of the medics assigned to us, lit the familiar diesel heater in the middle of the room and hung the saline drips, which both Edith and I were attached to, from nails in the wall. Then out of nowhere came a pot of steaming, sweet tea and a packet of biscuits. How frightfully English, I thought. Tea and biscuits – the cure for all ills.

'William,' I said, nodding towards the teapot, 'be mother.'

He laughed nervously, poured the tea and passed cups round. Every last one of us lit a cigarette. I remembered what Marie had once said: 'Trust me, I won't die from smoking.' I laughed at the memory and quietly absorbed the scene in the room. An oil lamp had been lit in the absence of any electricity and it now cast flickering shadows that danced on the walls and high ceiling. We sipped our tea, smoked and, for a few brief moments, found a tiny piece of sanity in a world gone mad.

It didn't last.

CHAPTER TWELVE

No way out

22 February 2012, Baba Amr, Syria

Day 1

Shafts of daylight penetrated the gaps between the mattresses and cushions piled high against the windows, resembling pale blue lasers as their beams cut through the cloud of cigarette smoke hanging in the fetid air. The pale glow of the oil lamp and tiny amount of natural light failed to penetrate the shadowy corners where we lay. The house, we had been assured, was one of the oldest and safest in Baba Amr. It was three stories tall, surrounded by other houses and built of basalt which, unlike standard concrete, wouldn't crumble under bombardment, or so we hoped.

For now, this cold and dark room was our world. I could barely make out Wa'el and Edith. Their pale faces stared back hauntingly from the shadows where they lay. I thought of the Edith who had entered the media centre less than twenty-four hours ago. Tall and proud with thick dark hair and striking good looks, a sparkling, charismatic smile and the gritty determination of a true war correspondent, Edith was imbued with an unmistakable presence. It was a stark, shocking contrast to behold the wounded yet resilient

Edith who now lay before me. But I was sure she had the grit to see this out to the bitter end. Edith was a natural survivor.

The all-encompassing gloom – an oppressive weight that seemed to pin us down – added to the paralysis we felt at being unable to walk this close to the front line, which was only five hundred metres away. Beyond that lightly defended line stood the might and fire-power of the Syrian government's 4th Division and 104th Republican Guard unit which, I was pretty sure, would dearly like to have a little chat with us. The Syrian army had successfully sealed off Baba Amr, surrounding it with troops and tanks.

It was impossible to predict how long the FSA rebels could hold back the emboldened government troops, whose violent forays into the neighbourhood were penetrating deeper and growing more aggressive by the day. The only thing we knew for certain was that the tunnel beneath Baba Amr provided us with our only chance of escape. If this route were to be cut off then we would be stranded. Simply put, there was no Plan B.

For Edith, however, there was no Plan A either. Memories of the agonising hikes through the tunnel were still vivid in my mind and, having seen the vicious effects of movement on Edith, the trip through the tunnel – if the chance ever came – would be a journey beyond the boundaries of pain. It simply couldn't be done.

The daily shelling of Baba Amr tailed off at around two o'clock, when government gunners halted their otherwise incessant barrage to grab a spot of lunch, making it the safest time to move. Our transfer from the field clinic to the house had coincided with this brief respite but, within minutes of the clock striking three, the artillery and rocket attacks resumed in earnest. The first shell of the opening salvo shook our world.

'*Merde*,' cursed Edith, instinctively reverting to her native French as the explosion died away.

'Shit is right,' I said out loud.

Hours after being blown up we were back in the firing line, only this time we couldn't even run away. We were trapped; all we could do was sit it out. The sky rained forth a relentless salvo of high explosives, sealed in a deadly case of hardened, fragmenting steel that would destroy, maim and kill anything it struck. The shelling was in no way episodic: it was a constant that we were forced to adjust to. If we were to escape, we needed to remain sane and we needed to resist despair.

Fuck it, I said to myself, lighting a cigarette. If we take a direct hit, that's it, we're dead. If we don't, then we live. Death will be fast and no amount of worrying can stop a 240mm mortar in its tracks, so in reality we have nothing to worry about.

I now had something to fall back on. That's not to say I wasn't scared every second I spent there – I was – but this handy home-spun philosophy meant that I didn't have to worry about being scared, freeing my mind to focus on more immediate matters, like how the hell we were going to evacuate Edith and the rest of us from Baba Amr.

The two volunteer medics who were assigned to tend to us – Salah and Maher – were both about eighteen-years-old. Maher was study-ing pharmacy, which in Baba Amr meant that he could be classed as a bona fide doctor, such was the lack of trained medical staff. The pair of them were wonderful and during that first day they tended to our every need with warm smiles and genuine care. They were also fearless. When a shell hit the house, they wouldn't so much as flinch. They just stood there laughing at us, once we'd stopped hiding underneath our blankets. These young boys had been here from day one. They had treated injuries and seen death on a scale no one should have to witness, yet they had kept their humanity intact and acted as shining beacons of hope in our twilight world.

Cheerfully they injected us with what they claimed was tramadol. It seemed to have little if any effect and I was always left wanting more. Nevertheless, it was reassuring to have the injections, if only for their psychological effect. They also pumped me with antibiotics via a valve fitted in my left arm. Infection was my real fear. I understood that if my leg became gangrenous then the only option would be to have it chopped off, making escape even more dangerous and problematic. What I didn't realise was that, every time I moved or twisted in my bed, the piece of shrapnel lodged in my abdomen was also moving. Just a scratch on the kidney from this sharp metal fragment could trigger an infection, which would lead to fever followed by death within a matter of days.

After the traumatic events of the day we all had time to think. Salah and Maher stoked the diesel burner and fed us cups of hot sweet tea. A contemplative silence fell between Edith, Wa'el and me. William and Javier had left with Abu Hanin to establish a link to the outside world, leaving the three of us to rest up. It was never truly silent in the room: the bombardment continued unabated, causing us to flinch with every impact. There was nowhere to hide, not even in your own mind. It was impossible to ignore the noise of the missile, mortar or shell that could easily be the last sound you would ever hear.

The shafts of light had now disappeared. It must be about eleven o'clock, I thought, checking my watch. Shit! It was only six thirty. I had been on two-week holidays that had passed faster than the last few hours. Time had begun to play a malign trick on us as, deprived of natural light, we existed in a sensory void. Lying in the glow of the oil lamp, all we had as a guide to events in the world outside were the explosive crunch of missiles, the gunfire and the earth-trembling vibrations. Time was standing stubbornly and painfully still.

Salah entered with a silver tray of food and a plastic bag of stale bread. There were olives, cheese triangles and a tin of tuna. Wa'el tried the food, I felt sick at the sight of it and Edith refused to even contemplate the idea of eating. The lads, Salah and Maher, made a few attempts at convincing us to eat, eventually giving up before tucking in themselves. We drank tea and smoked. The shelling was gradually diminishing in its ferocity and I imagined the gunners packing up and sitting down to meals not too unlike our own.

Javier and William returned to the room short of breath. They explained that in order to get around town they'd had to dodge the snipers. Javier, a craggy-faced Spaniard and a veteran of many wars, had so far remained calm throughout the ordeal. Despite our situation, he exuded an air of quiet confidence. He told us that they had visited a second, smaller media centre, which I didn't even know existed, and had made contact via Skype and email with some French government sources and their respective newspapers. Diplomatic efforts were apparently under way to secure our release and we were to sit tight and wait.

My, how I laughed. Sit tight and wait for diplomatic efforts! They were dealing with a regime led by a man who had been systematically murdering his own people for over a year. Only this morning his forces had murdered our colleagues. Good luck on the negotiating front, I thought. The cavalry were not going to charge in and rescue us. There would be no black ops or clandestine special forces team to pluck us from the rubble. We were well and truly on our own and only a fool would build up his hopes at this point.

The evening wore on and the shelling finally ceased, dissipating the tension in the air and allowing us, finally, to unwind. Javier and William made themselves beds, the heater raised the temperature and we prepared for our first night in the room. The silence, when it came, was a moment we valued and savoured. We could talk without being interrupted by constant shellfire. It gave us hope.

As a group, we tried to piece together the morning's events. How many shells had hit; what was the exact time of the strike; who had stood where and why? But mostly we spoke of Marie and Remi. We tried to figure out their last movements: why were they outside? We reached no conclusions; there were no real answers. We talked ourselves in circles for hours and eventually, one by one, we slipped off into the warm mercy of sleep.

23 February 2012, Baba Amr, Syria

Day 2

The first rays of dawn push back the dark. Shadows beat their morning retreat, taking hope with them. Eyes open. Silence still. Two hours of sweet peace broken only by a fool's shot. Check the clock and wait. Not long now. Two minutes . . . one minute . . . here we go. Thump. Thump. Thump. A distant, muffled timpani beat. Then silence. Count them in: three – two – one. Incoming. Screaming banshees. Eyes clenched tight as thunder and lightning tear down the dawn. If only. Falling – stone, glass, rubble, people. Still I'm alive. And that's how it goes. Thump. Thump. Thump.

'What the fuck,' I yelled, instantly awake but not sure where the dream ended and reality began. My heart was beating painfully in my chest and my eyes were unable to penetrate the absolute darkness of the room. The blast had been enormous, rocking the building and rattling the windows. 'Is everyone okay?' I asked.

There was a murmur of 'Okay' from all except Salah the medic, who slept through the whole event. It was six thirty in the morning. The start of each day's artillery barrage was something you could set a clock by. It was pure psychological warfare: the residents of Baba Amr had been forced to fear time itself.

Edith spoke in accented English from the darkened corner. 'Paul, what do you think that explosion was? It was bigger than anything we have heard so far.'

I pondered her question. I knew exactly what it was and for a few moments considered not giving her the truth. No, I thought, the more knowledge she has, the less she has to fear. If she learns the sound of what isn't going to kill her, then at least she will be spared the thought of death with every single, screaming projectile that heads our way. It will give us something to do in the long day ahead, I figured. Edith was about to become an artillery expert.

'Okay, since you asked, Edith, that was a 240mm mortar – the largest mortar in the world. It's about a metre and a half long, weighs 286 pounds and has a range of about six and a half miles. Oh, and it can also be fitted with a delayed fuse that allows it to penetrate a building before it explodes. If one hits us we won't know about it. Not a thing. Wait for the next one and you can tell how close it's going to be.'

'Oh,' replied Edith. 'Okay.'

We relapsed into silence. Everyone had heard what I had just said and we all listened for the next shell with a sense of anticipation. The burst of explosions around us continued. They were mostly rockets and 152mm field guns and mortars, each menacing in its own right but in a different league from the 240mm mortar. We didn't have to wait too long. In the far-off distance we heard three deep, muffled, bass-like thumps.

'Here they come,' I said. 'Now listen.'

There was a four-second delay before we heard the scream of the huge mortars. The sound was long and drawn out and the distance of the explosions from our house, by comparison with the explosion that had woken us up so violently, was far greater.

'You get it, Edith? You hear the thump of the launch, count the silence and when you hear a long scream you're going to be okay. The shorter the scream, the closer it will land. Try it on the next launch,' I told her.

Ten minutes passed before they fired the next salvo – three consecutive thumps, three screams and three explosions.

'They are far away,' said Edith. She sounded happy.

'You've got it,' I replied. 'They have six of them, I think.'

'How do you know that?' Edith asked, slightly puzzled.

'It takes about a minute to load each mortar into the launcher,' I replied. 'Yesterday they were firing six within a minute. I was counting them. They must have six otherwise they couldn't fire at that rate.'

Edith laughed. She seemed to be enjoying the distraction. The ability to ascertain where the big buggers were going to land seemed to offer her some comfort.

We fell back into silence, listening to the onslaught of the shells landing around us in our dark and timeless room. In the absence of coffee, I needed some water and so I tried to reach the spot where I remembered seeing the bottle last. I couldn't move. I tried again but discovered that I was stuck to the mattress.

'Please don't let me have shit my pants,' I muttered to myself as I reached for my small LED torch. That wouldn't be fair. Raising the blankets and peering underneath, a huge sigh of relief ran through my mind. 'Thank God,' I whispered. It was blood, so I hadn't shat myself. My leg had been bleeding through the night and the blood had formed a large puddle where I lay. It had started to congeal and the bandage had stuck to the mattress. Slowly prising my leg free, I raised my foot on to a cushion in order to keep the leg away from the saturated mattress. I then started to laugh. A strange thought had just entered my mind and I remembered my mum's words from childhood.

243

'Make sure you have clean underwear on in case you get run over and have to go to hospital,' she would say. 'You wouldn't want the nurses to see your dirty pants, now would you?'

I laughed out loud. My boxers were like cardboard. The blood had dried on them, so much so that I could almost crack them. Then I remembered that someone had filmed me wearing them at the media centre. By now, hundreds of thousands of people had probably seen them on YouTube. I made a mental apology to my poor mum, who had been right all these years. I giggled again as another crazy thought hit me – J-P would be wearing clean ones if he were stuck here. I made a mental note to myself: don't go crazy.

'What time is it, Paul?' asked Edith.

I looked at my watch and felt as if I was, truly, going crazy.

'It's eight thirty, Edith,' I replied, knowing the effect this news was going to have.

Edith moaned a long, sad sound from deep within. I understood her despair. I too was shocked and stunned. We had been awake for two hours, two long dark and painful hours, and once more the clock had ceased to tick. It was the most hopeless and demoralising feeling I had ever experienced but I knew we had to keep our balance. We had no idea how long we would be trapped here and the prospect of another twelve hours of heavy shelling could, if you allowed it, drive you insane.

The day ground wearily on. The oil lamp gave the illusion of permanent night and I took to studying the shafts of light that formed a tenuous link to the outside world. Salah and Maher tended to our dressings, bringing coffee, food and whatever painkillers they could find. More than anything else, the gift they offered, the offering we most treasured, was hope. They never faltered, never appeared down and always took time to reassure us that everything was okay.

William and Javier were preparing to make another dash to the media centre to check emails and see if there had been any progress with the efforts to find help. I asked them to pass messages to anyone they could and gave them a list of email addresses, but I held out little hope for any action on the diplomatic front. While they were gone, Edith and I continued with our gunnery lessons. For a few hours, we had been hearing different types of explosion. There was no warning with these explosions, just an almighty, wall-cracking boom.

'Tank shells, Edith,' I said after one perilously close impact. 'You don't have any warning with them. The shell reaches you before the sound and then the launch sound is lost when you hear the round explode. It's called direct fire, which means they can see the target, unlike mortars, which fire in a high parabolic curve that drops on your head. We should be quite safe from the tank shells because we're surrounded by other houses and they have to blast those away in order to get to us. I think we have a few days before that happens,' I droned on.

'So the tank shells are scary, but not as much of a threat as the heavy mortars,' Edith answered.

'Bang on, Edith,' I laughed. She would make a great gunner.

After a few long hours, which might as well have been days, William and Javier arrived back in the room. William was banging around the place and swearing in French. He looked furious and there was a slightly manic edge to his anger that worried me.

'Nothing has fucking happened,' he exclaimed. 'No fucking news about getting out.' He continued to pace around the room smoking.

'William, come here a second, mate. Sit down,' I said gently.

He sat down next to me, smoking and rubbing his forehead. His face looked older than his thirty-two years, his thick growth of stubble and exhausted eyes highlighting the stress he was under.

245

'Listen, mate,' I started, 'I know you're under pressure because you're not injured and you feel responsible for us. I get it. But you have to take control, William. Don't get too high when things seem okay because the more optimistic you get the further you have to fall when things fuck up. And, believe me, things will fuck up. Get yourself on a level. Don't go up and don't go down. That way you won't get any of the extremes. You want to find yourself a nice cruising altitude and stick to it.'

William seemed a little reassured. 'I'm sorry,' he said. 'This is all new to me. I was in Libya, in Benghazi, but it was nothing like this.' He shook his head sadly.

'Fuck it, William, you really don't have to be sorry. You're doing great. Just remember: try and find a level and stay on it. No ups, no downs, you just have to cruise. Now, can I have one of your nice cigarettes, please?'

Dr Mohamed called in for a visit that afternoon. He checked and dressed my wounds and pronounced, a touch optimistically I thought, that I was better. He also wanted us to make another video, explaining that we were not captives of the FSA. He urged us to make a plea to the outside world for help. I wasn't averse to doing the 'I'm not a hostage' bit, but I was a little uncomfortable with agreeing to the plea for help. As far as I was concerned, we were responsible for our current predicament and we ought really to get ourselves out of it. Nonetheless, we agreed to do the filming.

Edith went first and seemed to do a very good job. I didn't understand a single word but I imagined her speech would come across fantastically well on television. William went next. He was great too – full of Gallic passion – and he also had a huge explosion go off midway through his plea. Brilliant, I thought, that's a keeper.

I followed next, but the French outdid me with their performances. I succeeded in telling the camera who I was and what had happened to me, but when it came to the plea for help I think I let the side down. In fact, I was pathetic, saying something meek like, 'Any assistance from government agencies would be welcome.' That was it. If it were Eurovision I would have been awarded *nul points*.

That evening we had a visit from a chap called Abu Lailah, who was Wa'el's cousin. They had grown up together. Abu Lailah's entrance was an amazing boost for Wa'el, who was in acute pain from his wound. Seeing Wa'el's face light up when Abu Lailah walked into the room gave us all cause to smile. He wore a keffiyeh wrapped around his head and when he removed his long black coat he revealed a short-stock Kalashnikov and a LAW (light anti-tank weapon) slung over his shoulder.

'He's a Bedouin poet who speaks classical Arabic,' Wa'el announced proudly from his dark corner of the room.

'And he is an imbecile with the body of a man but the brain of a three-year-old. His body keeps growing, but his mind is like a pea,' retorted Abu Lailah, his face breaking into a huge smile. 'You see how tall he is sitting down? That is how big his mind is.'

I was laughing so much that my leg hurt. The man's towering charisma lifted the sombre mood in the room instantly.

'Abu Falafel,' he said, looking at me, 'do you know what a hippo-campus is?'

I shook my head, wondering what would come next.

He carried on staring into my eyes. 'Hippo-camp-sss,' he broke the word down into syllables. 'Sss, sss,' he repeated, making a twisting motion with his hand. 'Hippo-camp-sss. Sss for snake,' he finished, smiling wisely as he held my gaze.

'What the fuck are you talking about?' I choked, tears of laughter rolling from my eyes as he sat staring at me in the dancing glow of the lamp.

Straight-faced he replied, 'You don't speak classical Arabic? Then I will teach you. Let's start with the basic sounds.'

And so we went on for an hour or more. Between fits of manic laughter I managed to learn a sound: not a word, just a single Arabic sound that emanated from the back of my throat. Abu Lailah exuded a confidence that raised our spirits and brought much-needed humour into our bleak world.

'I must go and shoot at some tanks,' he finally announced. 'Do you need anything?'

'Cigarettes,' we all replied in unison.

He reached deep into his coat and threw us each a packet before shouldering his AK47 and LAW anti-tank missile and bidding us farewell.

'See you tomorrow, pea brain,' he said to Wa'el and left.

'What a guy,' I said.

Wa'el laughed. 'He's only just warming up.'

Slowly and painfully we reached the end of day two. We talked into the early hours of the morning, the tension draining from our damaged bodies. We drank tea, discussed the day that had passed and the possibilities of tomorrow. Nervous exhaustion caught up with us and so ended one of the longest days of my life.

24 February 2012, Baba Amr, Syria

Day 3

It was impossible to say for how long, or even if, I had slept. Not much though. My leg was bleeding again and the jolts of pain were shooting lightning bolts into my head. I had decided not to look at my watch for fear of an early onset of misery syndrome and so I was relying on the precious shafts of daylight to gauge the time. An occasional single shot echoed across the doomed neighbourhood. The explosions hadn't begun yet so I guessed it had to be before six thirty. I couldn't tell who else was awake but I could guarantee that the snoring came from either Salah or Maher. Those guys slept like pros, putting even Marie to shame.

And then it began. Three direct hits on our building sent tremors crashing through the room, blowing in a few of the windowpanes. Luckily, our window mattresses caught the glass, forcing it to fall harmlessly to the floor. Outside, the concrete and stone debris fell for about ten seconds.

'Paul, what the fuck were they?' asked Edith.

'Mortars,' I replied. 'Relatively small, probably 82mm. They have a range of about three to four kilometres.'

'So not the big bastards, then?'

'Nope. We wouldn't be having this chat now if they were,' I said, trying to sound comforting.

And so the day continued with its monotonous and terrifying routine. We knew we had at least another twelve to fourteen hours of shelling ahead, with only an hour around two o'clock for the lunchtime lull. Abu Hanin arrived at some point in the day. Now that I had given up on looking at my watch we lived by the rhythm of our surroundings.

Abu Hanin took William and Javier to see if they could get online and find out whether there had been any progress on the diplomatic front. I steadfastly refused to get excited in any way about such matters. If the cavalry were to come and rescue us, then great; if not, I would smoke and plot my own way out in case the worst happened and Assad's forces entered the neighbourhood on foot, launching house-to-house search operations to flush out the rebels.

My mind had already gone through so many possible escape plans that I was now on Plan F. Using the shafts of light, I had finally figured out which way was south. South meant Lebanon and

Lebanon was safety, of a sort. There was a high-energy chocolate bar in my bum bag and water was still available, so my provisions were sorted. I had also taken to stowing away the occasional ciga-rette in case the dreaded moment came and they finally ran out. My plan was pretty simple: travel only at night using a crutch that I would fashion from the bountiful supply of wreckage that littered the neighbourhood. I would hole up and sleep during daylight hours and then continue to move at night, heading south, always south. Reality only ever kicked in when I considered the others: I wasn't leaving Edith alone and I would not leave Marie's body in Baba Amr. Okay, on to Plan G. At least it kept my mind busy.

'Paul, Paul, are you awake?' whispered Edith urgently.

'Yes. Are you okay?' I replied.

'Yes, Paul . . . but I need to piss.'

'Oh, right, so do I. We haven't pissed since we got in here. We should ask Salah to get some piss pots.'

Salah went across to the hospital and returned with a piss pot for me and a female nurse with a bedpan for Edith. Wa'el, who was in agony, raised himself from his corner and left the room while the nurse prepared Edith for her first pee. Between fits of giggles and yelps of pain from Edith, the nurse manoeuvred the bedpan into position. Then began the long silence. I was trying to pee into the pot at the same time as Edith, but it wasn't happening: we both kept laughing and putting each other off. It's not easy to pee when shells are landing all around and you are in direct competition with someone only yards away. Eventually, after what seemed like for ever, Edith announced victory and sounded a lot happier for it.

'How was it?' she asked jokingly.

'I don't know. It won't happen,' I replied, a little frustrated.

We chortled away, the ridiculousness of the situation apparent to us both. It was a bright point in a day of little mirth. For the next hour or so I spent my time explaining to Edith how the artillery was guided on to its target; about the drone surveillance and how it relayed target coordinates back to a fire-control unit; how these were then passed down to a gun battery who adjusted its fire in order to hit the chosen targets. It demystified the process for her a little. In a situation devoid of information, any knowledge gave us a feeling of power over ignorance.

It must have been around two o'clock because Maher brought in some food for us. I noticed that the rations were getting smaller, the bread older and the visits slightly less frequent. The situation was in decline. A glance at the empty silver tray lying in the dark was all the evidence we needed. Maher kept us up to date on the hospital situation. Fifteen dead today, he announced, children and women, old men and young boys. For the first time, I saw something other than hope in his young, battle-hardened face.

He left us with the food and returned to the hospital. No longer did he or Salah stay just to keep us company: they were needed for more critical work back in the clinic. All the signs were ominous and the mood in our black hole darkened. Wa'el was suffering too. His shattered arm was causing him great pain and he was becoming more withdrawn.

'Wa'el. Please, mate, just leave. You know this place. These are your people. You can walk. Get in the tunnel and leave us here. There isn't anything you can do now. You need help,' I pleaded with him. 'There's no point in staying any more. Please go.'

Wa'el grinned through his pain. 'Not a chance. I got you here and I will stay until I get you out. Don't ask me to leave again. I will leave when you leave,' he said with finality.

'Thank you,' I replied, in awe of his bravery.

Time crawled doggedly and painfully on. As time itself had slowed, so too had my mental capacity. But a thought had begun to germinate in the hazy fog of my mind and, with trepidation, I looked at my watch and the hands read 15:30. I said nothing for ten minutes and then I spoke.

'Edith, Wa'el, are you awake?' I asked into the darkness. Both confirmed they were. 'How long has it been since you last heard an explosion?' I continued, hoping that I was correct and that I wasn't building up unnecessary optimism.

There was a very long pause before anyone responded.

'It's lunchtime, Paul,' replied Edith.

'No, that ended about half an hour ago. Listen carefully,' I urged them.

The room was silent but this time it was true silence, without explosions or small arms fire to break it. For the first time in longer than I could remember – weeks – it was truly quiet. We all said nothing, scared that if we spoke we would break the magic spell and hell would open up again. The tension among us was almost as bad as when the shelling was at its most intense. We had grown used to the routine of the explosions and, now that they had gone, the stillness had caught us off guard.

The sound of voices and running feet suddenly echoed through the house. Adrenalin flooded my system. That's it, I thought, they have broken through. Government soldiers have entered the neighbourhood. They won't shell their own men, which explains the lack of explosions. I had been a fool to think otherwise. Assad's men had obviously spent days softening up the target with barrage after barrage of artillery fire, and now came the dreaded house-to-house clearance. It was over. This is how it ends. I prepared myself for the inevitable. I wasn't going down without a fight. Fuck them, I thought, I'm not going out stuck to a mattress in a pool of my own stinking, dried blood. I pulled out the knife I had ready by my bed.

The door opened with a bang. Here we go, I thought, trying to stand. I failed miserably, ending up in a very awkward position, having to twist round to view the door. Fuck. It was William, Javier and Abu Hanin.

'Jesus Christ,' I said out loud. 'What the fuck's going on?'

The guys were breathing heavily and they struggled to catch their breath. My heart raced. I needed answers and quickly.

'There's a ceasefire,' said William. His face, peering out from the stubble and hair, was radiant with delight.

Abu Hanin spoke next. 'Paul, Hala Jaber from *The Sunday Times* is in Damascus. She and a team in Beirut have somehow brokered a ceasefire between the government and the rebels. They are going to send in the International Red Cross with diplomatic representatives. They will bring you out.'

'What?' I replied in shock. The news was like a smack in the face, so powerful were the words that tumbled from their lips. 'What the fuck are you talking about?' I said, trying desperately to make sense of the situation.

Abu Hanin repeated the information. 'You can all leave this evening with the Red Cross. Listen, there's no fighting outside and I have a message from Hala passed to us by the team in Beirut. She says to get in the ambulance when it comes.'

'Then please get Marie's body here. I'm not leaving without her,' I replied. 'Bring her and Remi here now so they are ready.'

'I will bring her when the ambulances come, but you must pack and be ready,' Abu Hanin said.

I ignored my own rule. Hope soared as I allowed myself to savour the idea of escape. I had no idea how the hell Hala had managed to pull strings to arrange a ceasefire but the lack of noise from outside was proof that she had. The atmosphere inside the room had changed the instant we received the news. Although physically still dark inside, the heavy burden of gloom seemed to have lifted.

In fact, it had lifted so much that I was now bursting to have that pee I had been promising myself all day. So, while everyone chatted excitedly about our imminent escape, I discreetly slipped my piss pot under the blankets, continued to chat and slowly relieved myself. The sensation was immense. I felt like a new man as I handed the piss pot to William, who stared at it for a moment before blanching when he realised what it was.

We continued to speculate about how the plan to evacuate us would be handled. Our best hope was for the Red Cross to take us straight to the Lebanese border and either hand us over to another ambulance or even take us on to Beirut. Either way, we were going home and it was now just a waiting game. As things calmed in the room, I began to come gently back to earth. Remember the rules, I told myself, don't count your chickens until they are fully basted, out of the oven and drowning in gravy. We chatted, drank tea and even ate some of the food on offer.

Edith was particularly pleased. During their communication with the outside world, Javier and William had received terrible news about Edith's wound from the doctors. Apparently, if the two bones rubbed together they would produce a fat-like substance that could be absorbed into her bloodstream. It could hit her heart and act in the same way as a blood clot, killing her almost instantly. Edith had lived with this fact for two days now. She rarely spoke of it, but it made it all the more unlikely that she would ever be able to make it out of Baba Amr via the tunnel.

Time continued to toy with our minds as the tension mounted along with our expectations. Soon, we would have the drugs we really needed to kill the pain. We would be in the secure comfort of an ambulance, travelling far away from the room in which time and purpose had ground to a halt. The shafts of light weakened and finally disappeared. We smoked more, our earlier efforts at rationing ourselves flying out of the window in the knowledge that we were leaving. It was then that we heard the sound of engines outside. They rumbled to a halt and we heard people cheering in the streets, welcoming the arrival of the ambulances, harbingers of our freedom.

William, Javier and Abu Hanin left the room and went to greet our liberators, leaving Edith, Wa'el and me to await evacuation. Try as I might, I could not stem the feeling of euphoria that was mounting inside me. Edith was grinning while Wa'el joined the others outside to see what was happening. Edith and I waited and then waited some more. After ten minutes the guys returned. Their body language told me something wasn't right.

'What?' I asked urgently. 'What's up?'

Abu Hanin explained the situation in a monotone. For a start, he told us, it wasn't the International Committee of the Red Cross (ICRC) who had arrived outside but the Syrian Red Crescent (SRC). The SRC had orders to pick up any civilian casualties from the field clinic and then to load us up. We would be taken to the hospital in Homs, located outside Baba Amr in government-controlled territory. From there, we would be transferred to ICRC ambulances.

William confirmed that he had spoken to a French ICRC representative over the Syrian Red Crescent's radio. She had confirmed that the ICRC ambulances were indeed waiting at the hospital but that the Syrian government had refused them permission to enter Baba Amr. She was in touch with government officials in Damascus, desperately trying to persuade them to let the ICRC ambulances through the checkpoint. There was also no diplomatic presence with the Syrian Red Crescent.

Abu Hanin spoke again. The Shabia, a notoriously violent paramilitary group who supported Assad, had used the ambulances of the SRC many times to enter rebel areas, even launching attacks from them. He also told us that the last time the SRC had evacuated people from Baba Amr many of the wounded who left in the ambulances had simply disappeared into thin air and were never seen again. There was a strong suspicion among Baba Amr residents that the SRC was being used as a tool of oppression by the regime.

We felt numb. We were now being forced to make a decision that might lead us into even deeper trouble than we were in already. Edith refused point blank to leave, saying, 'I'm not getting in a fucking regime ambulance.' I had a tendency to agree with her. Javier reckoned it would be okay and William hovered between the two.

'William,' I said, 'get back outside and on the radio to the ICRC rep. We need to stall for time to make a decision. Keep her talking. Explain the situation we're in and push her to keep talking to Damascus.'

From the small courtyard outside, the voices of men arguing among themselves reached us. They grew louder and more heated as the minutes passed. A few armed FSA fighters entered the room and spoke with Wa'el. He explained that the FSA thought it was a trap and that the members of the SRC were acting on the orders of President Assad. They advised us not to leave in the ambulances and added that they feared for our lives. Outside the room, tensions were rapidly rising. We couldn't tell who was shouting at who, but it sounded like a fight was about to break out. We had to take control. The situation was escalating and we needed some input.

Abu Hanin left the room and returned with a small, smiling man with glasses. He introduced himself as a senior delegate of the SRC mission and said he wanted to talk to us.

Wa'el and Abu Hanin translated for us, but by this stage the room had filled up with members of the SRC team as well as armed FSA fighters who all spoke at once, making it impossible to hear.

The room was electric. The thin line between argument and violence was creeping closer. We needed to take action. William, who had returned, was shouting at the SRC doctor in a pretty threatening manner. So much so that, before we even had any time to talk to him, the bespectacled doctor turned to walk out. I pleaded for him to stay, at the same time telling William to shut the fuck up and stop shouting at the guy.

'Abu Hanin, we really need to clear the room,' I said. 'It's just us five who need to talk to the doc. It's our shout on what happens next. Wa'el can translate if need be, so get everyone else out of the room and try to control the guys outside.'

Eventually, after much yelling and pushing, the room cleared, leaving us alone with the SRC doctor. We asked him to tell us what would happen if we left Baba Amr in his ambulances.

'I am a good man. I am a doctor and the people here know and trust me,' he began. 'We will give you over to the ICRC but first you must talk to the security services because you have no visas. They are the orders I have from my government.'

Silence fell over us. This vital piece of information changed everything.

'Can you confirm what you have just said, that before we get into the ICRC ambulances, we need to talk to the security guys?' I asked him.

'It's routine. You have no visa so they need to talk to you first,' he said.

We spoke among ourselves briefly and then asked him if we could have time to discuss it alone. He agreed, but told us that he would have to leave as soon as the last of the wounded from the field hospital had been loaded on to the ambulances. The pressure to make a decision was fierce. Having stagnated for days, time now passed by faster than any of us wanted. Edith and I argued against

257

entering the ambulances. Edith said she would only do it if we were guaranteed safe passage to Lebanon. She wouldn't, under any circumstance, go to Damascus. Javier rightly argued that avoiding a trip to Damascus would be impossible if we left in the SRC ambulances: the government would want their pound of PR and we would undoubtedly be paraded in front of cameras for the world to see that Assad was a magnanimous, kindly and misunderstood man. William was torn. The dramatic U-turn in events and the instant oscillation from high to low was messing him up. As with his emotions, he swung like a pendulum between the two options. I felt a deep sorrow for him.

We called the doctor back into the room to ask some more questions. I asked him if we could be taken directly to Beirut. His answer was an emphatic no. Again he confirmed that we would need to speak to the security people before anything happened. He then threw something else into the mix.

'My government has also asked that you make a video stating that you do not wish to leave Baba Amr, if that is indeed your final choice,' he told us.

We all refused point-blank to make any video on Assad's behalf. There were still just the five of us in the room when the doctor lowered his voice. Speaking in a furtive whisper while flicking glances at the door to ensure that there was no one outside the room who could hear him, he said, 'My friends, I understand your situation: when you are at sea and you are drowning you will clutch at any straw to save yourself. My advice to you is, do not get in my ambulance. Wait for the ICRC and ensure that you have diplomatic presence. I will be outside if you need me. Good luck.'

The silence after he left was deafening. The doctor had just risked his life by passing us information that could see him locked away. The bottom had fallen from our world. Only an hour ago we were to be set free but now the dream had vanished, causing us a bumpy reality check. We had broken the rules by allowing ourselves to smell a whiff of freedom. We faced an almighty low.

Two members of the FSA entered the room and sat down next to Wa'el. With them was an SRC medic in red overalls. Wa'el called me over and I dragged myself into his shadowy corner. The medic addressed Wa'el in a staccato burst of hushed Arabic. Wa'el's jaw dropped as his eyes registered shock at what the medic was saying. He turned to me and pulled me closer.

'Paul, this is a man the FSA trust. They have known him a long time and he passes on information to them regularly. He is a friend,' he whispered hurriedly. 'He has told me the real plan. It's not good. At the checkpoint at Baba Amr, they have a state television crew. The idea is to film us being put in Red Cross ambulances and then, when we drive out of Homs . . .' Wa'el paused a moment and then continued, 'we are to be executed. Our bodies are to be put on the road and the government would then announce that the FSA ambushed the ambulance and murdered us.'

I felt sick. My head spun and I could find no words. I just lit a cigarette and stared at the wall. I couldn't think, couldn't move. I was transfixed. 'Oh, shit,' I said finally under my breath as my skin rose in goose bumps. We're fucked, I thought. Any one of those SRC guys could have a GPS on them. All they had to do was press a button and the army would have a fix on our location. Our chances of escaping alive had just decreased enormously. The nightmare had entered an uncharted phase.

We sat in the room in silence. We had all run out of words. We fell back on trying to absorb the events of the evening individually. We heard the ambulances pull away, their engines disappearing into the night.

'Fucking hell,' said Edith eventually. 'It can't get any worse. It's a catastrophe.'

We nodded in agreement and yet there was still doubt. There was the tiny possibility that we had just made a huge mistake, a choice that could cost us our lives. But we clung to what we had been told: that in a few hours' time our bloodied bodies would have been scattered over a darkened street on the outskirts of Homs.

'Well, folks, you've got to admit it – we're lucky that we're alive. It's the best choice we could have made and we won't get any worse news than that,' I said, in a vague effort to rally the troops.

There was a knock at the door and, without waiting for an answer, in came a bearded AK47-wielding rebel. He spoke quickly to Wa'el and left immediately. We all turned to Wa'el. He stared straight back at us. I could see him struggling for the right words. He finally composed himself.

'Guys,' he said, 'the tunnel has been bombed and is unusable. There's no way out of Baba Amr.'

CHAPTER THIRTEEN

Escape from Homs

24 February 2012, Baba Amr, Syria

Day 3

It was to be another long night. The FSA rebel who broke the news of the attack on the tunnel had stolen any remnants of hope we still held about escaping. We sat in silence, gazing at the oil lamp. There were no words of comfort to share. Everything seemed completely hopeless. To add to the pall of misery that had descended over the room, the oil lamp, which had grown increasingly dim during the last few hours, petered out and died. Salah rose to refill it, shaking the container only to discover that it was empty. The lamp had gone but no one really cared, so crushing to morale was the news of the tunnel attack. Nevertheless, and perhaps because of the deteriorating mood, Salah set off to the field clinic in search of candles.

He returned half an hour later with the candles and more bad news. The fighting had killed more than twenty people that day. The hospital was now overrun with casualties. And, to add to the day's litany of death and disaster, a shell had destroyed our main source of water – a tank on the roof. From this point on we would have to ration our water. Salah lit one of the scavenged candles, shedding even less light on the room than the oil lamp it was replacing. The flickering glow was as weak as our spirits.

The only joyful moment of the evening came with the arrival of Abu Lailah. He brought gifts of sweets, a sort of hard-boiled candy, and American cigarettes. Adopting the same position as on his previous visit, he began by lovingly insulting Wa'el before telling us about the plan he had hatched. It was possible, he claimed, to get Edith out of Baba Amr in a car by dressing her up as a local and covering her face with a veil. Abu Lailah told us that he had been bribing the guards at a particular checkpoint in Baba Amr and he was confident he could get Edith out via this route. The plan offered a small glimmer of hope in an otherwise dark world. If anyone could pull off such a stunt, it was the indomitable Abu Lailah. The escape would be arranged for tomorrow, he told us, before adding that he could only take a woman – Javier, William, Wa'el and I would have to stay. This went down terribly with the increasingly demoralised William, who had to balance his own interests with the needs of Edith who was badly wounded. The rest of us felt that we had lost our real chance of escape once we learnt of the tunnel's destruction. To add to this gloomy outlook, the heating oil now ran out.

I spent a few hours with Abu Lailah working on my classical Arabic. We solved the problem of my tongue position, which was preventing me from pronouncing the sound 'hwhah' correctly, and my mood lightened a fraction. Eventually, though, I succumbed to the pain and nervous exhaustion and slipped off quietly into oblivion.

25 February 2012, Baba Amr, Syria

Day 4

My belief that the Syrian Red Crescent's visit had only succeeded in giving government forces a better idea of where we were proved depressingly correct: the regime's artillery gunners began their early-morning bombardment with a fierce assault on our building. This was the most ferocious attack yet on our location. We received direct hit after direct hit as chunks of plaster fell from the ceiling and covered us in fine layers of dust. Shrapnel, flying debris and compression blasts blew in more windows. I figured that today was possibly our last day alive: the building had taken a serious pummelling over the past three days and now the regime had our exact coordinates. It no longer mattered that the building was built from basalt. With the structure of the house already weakened, it would only take one hit from a 240mm mortar to finish the job.

We refrained from lighting the candle in the morning. No food arrived from the hospital. Neither Salah nor Maher stayed any longer than they needed, carrying out only the bare essentials before hurrying back to the field clinic where there was greater need for their skills. We lay in total darkness with our spirits at an all-time low.

Abu Hanin arrived during the afternoon lull in the shelling. He sensed the sombre mood in the room and made a solemn promise to get us out, even if it meant carrying us on his shoulders. The FSA were working day and night to clear the blocked tunnel, he told us. As soon as they had finished repairing it, we would make our escape. Abu Hanin also told me that Kate, my wife, had contacted him on Skype and that all my family passed on their love. I asked him to pass the same message back. I wrote a small note to Bonnie, my partner, telling her not to worry about the new kitchen sink; I would finish installing it when I escaped. I passed the note to Abu Hanin, who had one last thing to tell me.

'Paul, I have a message from your boss at *The Sunday Times*. He says get in the fucking tunnel and get the fuck out of here,' he said smiling.

'Erm, did you get the name of my boss?' I asked.

'Yes. It was Mr Miles. He is in Lebanon,' was his response.

I burst into laughter. Miles was the journalist I had worked with in Libya, the bloke who'd been shot in the helmet, and the knowledge that a familiar face was on the case boosted my morale instantly. The paper must have flown him in from Kabul to see what he could do to help from Lebanon. He had already been into Syria with me and he would understand the situation better than anyone else I could think of. I smiled, lit a smoke and my spirits rose. This was only the second direct message I had received from the outside. I had no idea of any other plans to get us out. I was getting in the tunnel when the time came.

Edith spent the afternoon waiting for Abu Lailah to arrive with a car to take her out of Baba Amr. She was to escape alone and so, if and when the rest of us got out, we arranged to regroup in the relative safety of Al Buwaydah. William had coped so far, but now, with escape imminent, he knew he couldn't go with Edith and was worried sick about her travelling alone. He was understandably agitated, pacing the room while trying to figure out a way to accompany her. He was as tightly coiled as a spring and needed to get out of this damned place.

But Abu Lailah failed to show up, dashing Edith's hopes as the frustration of waiting crushed her spirits and the bombardment of Baba Amr intensified outside the room. We could now hear street-to-street fighting for the first time, with the sound of running feet and small arms fire only hundreds of metres from our house. And then I heard it. The noise was faint at first but I was certain I knew what it was: the deep, guttural sound of an approaching tank. I didn't tell the others; it would only add to their worries. I could also hear the familiar sounds of rocket-propelled grenades (RPGs) – the only weapon in the FSA's arsenal that could repel tanks. The fighting was rapidly and inexorably closing in on us.

'Paul, I need a shit,' said Edith out of the blue, taking my mind off the tank for a moment.

'Not really my department,' I replied, groaning at her predicament. 'William, could you pop over to the clinic and get the nurse, Edith needs the bedpan again.'

Fifteen minutes later I lay facing the wall, whistling to make some noise while Edith got on with the job in hand. Finally the nurse left the room. There was a brief silence and then Edith spoke up.

'Paul, now that I have shit in front of you we really are best friends,' she said laughing. I chuckled out loud. Edith was the mistress of the one-liner.

The day drew to a close in the same way it had started: dark, cold and miserable, with no sense that we were any closer to making good our escape. We lit the candle for a few hours to lighten the mood. It worked, briefly.

Salah arrived with a two-litre bottle of water, placed it on the table and announced in a low voice that this was the last of the water. William reached for it and took a huge gulp until I gently reminded him that the water was for all of us and that it had to last.

To our horror we also discovered that we were down to our last three cigarettes. We shared them out between us – half each. It was a tragic blow to morale. We lay in silence for a few more hours until I decided that the rest of them had suffered enough. Struggling to reach one of the packets I had secretly stashed behind my mattress, I produced a box of Alhamra smokes – the worst cigarette I have ever tasted – and offered them around. Their faces lit up with glee at the sight of the packet.

The shelling faded, as did the talking, and one by one we drifted into what little peace sleep could offer. It was our fourth day in the room and there was no hint of an end in sight.

26 February 2012, Baba Amr, Syria

Day 5

I lay awake, waiting for the shelling to start and for the misery and torment it would bring with it. The first salvo saw four consecutive direct hits strike our building in quick succession. The house had done well to protect us so far, but now government forces knew our location. The concentration of incoming shells was slowly chipping away at our haven, piece by crumbling piece, and it wouldn't be too long before a lucky round penetrated a weakness in the building.

Abu Lailah visited us in the morning, reassuring Edith that his driver would take her through the checkpoint that day. He was currently out on an escape run but would be back by mid-afternoon to ferry her out. Her spirits rose as William's fell.

William and Javier left with one of the activists to recover whatever kit had survived the attack on the media centre. They returned with a bag of treasures. One of my cameras and my laptop had miraculously survived the attack undamaged. I also found a packet of chocolate biscuits that I had brought with me from Lebanon, providing us with a feast that served to keep morale a fraction higher than normal. Remi's camera was also among the bags, shredded and barely recognisable. I suggested they did not return it to his family or girlfriend; it would only conjure up bad images and was best left here in Baba Amr.

Fatigue had rapidly crept up on us. Not only had we grown physically tired as our bodies used up vital resources to repair the massive damage they had suffered, but we were also mentally exhausted. I had been in Syria for nearly two weeks now and had spent most of this time under heavy artillery bombardment. I shuddered to think what the people of Homs had been through: what we were experiencing was a mere snapshot of their suffering. For them, this was the daily reality of life under Assad's violent crackdown on what had begun as simple, peaceful protests against his regime.

The lunchtime lull came and went with no sign of Salah or Maher. We knew things were at breaking point in the field hospital. The tunnel's closure meant that none of the wounded had been evacuated for days now. Very few buildings remained intact, so there was little space to house the dramatically increasing numbers of wounded and seriously ill.

Edith's distress grew with every hour that passed. Her escape was supposed to take place in the afternoon, a deadline that came and went, draining her of hope. We couldn't understand what had gone wrong. Perhaps Abu Lailah's driver had been captured while returning to Baba Amr from his previous mission.

The clock ticked slowly on, the day turned to night and we started our dark slide into the black hole of depression. Wrapped in blankets for warmth, we had talked ourselves dry and so we resigned ourselves to the inevitable. Our luck had run out and there was precious little we could do about it.

We had all learnt to sleep through the relentless shelling. Sleep had become our only weapon against our most feared enemy – time. I was slowly drifting into its embrace when I heard the outside door bang open. The sound of people running and voices shouting snapped me to alert. I rummaged for my knife as adrenalin flooded my system.

The door swung open, revealing the figure of an FSA rebel. He began to shout at Wa'el in a rapid burst of Arabic. We were all awake now, waiting for the outburst to subside so Wa'el could translate the fighter's words. We feared the worst. The ground invasion must have commenced. Wa'el, his eyes wide, looked shocked. The fighter finished, turned and ran from the room.

Wa'el turned to face us. He looked dumbfounded, taking a deep breath as he prepared to speak. My heart beat crazily in my chest. Surely he was about to tell us that Assad's forces had penetrated the neighbourhood and that it would now be only a matter of time before they reached us.

'We must get ready to leave very soon. They have repaired the tunnel. We are going to break out tonight,' Wa'el said, as if not fully believing the words he had just spoken.

We fired rapid questions at poor Wa'el but he had no answers: all he knew was what the rebel had told him. We must be ready to leave as soon as possible. The apathy and exhaustion instantly evaporated and a new, dramatic sense of purpose struck the room with all the power of a lightning bolt. We had to get our priorities straight, and fast.

Edith would have to go down the tunnel. To do so, she would need to be strapped to a flat board to keep her and her leg immobilised. William immediately left in search of a suitable piece of wood, while Abu Hanin and Abu Lailah, who had returned on hearing the news helped to prepare us for the escape. I lacked trousers and shoes and I certainly wasn't going to flee Baba Amr in a blood-encrusted pair of boxer shorts. I considered tying plastic bags over a pair of flip-flops to improvise but Abu Lailah, sensing my dilemma, gave me his shoes in exchange for mine. Someone fetched me a pair of Adidas jogging pants that I wriggled into, an action that sent an excruciating shaft of pain through my leg. I hadn't left my bed once since arriving in the room. The thought of the impending trip through the dark tunnel and the route march that would inevitably follow was something I would have to deal with when the time came.

'Abu Hanin,' I called as he passed me. 'What about Marie and Remi? Where are they? Can we take them?'

He shook his head sadly. 'You will be gone very soon and they are in a safe place and we wash them every day. I promise you we will look after them. Please trust us,' he said, his voice tinged with a genuine sadness.

'I do, mate, completely. I know you'll do your best for them and thank you.'

I collected my belongings: a few packets of cigarettes, my knife, camera and laptop. I placed the camera and laptop into a bag that Edith gave me and put the knife and cigarettes into my pocket. I was ready. The room was now a scene of frantic activity as Dr Mohamed and Salah prepared Edith for the move. One of the medics strapped Wa'el's arm tightly to his body. I caught Maher, the medic, as he passed my bed.

'Do you have anything to inject me with?' I asked. 'Absolutely anything will do – I'm not so fussy.'

Maher laughed and promised he would try to find something before we left. Having hurt myself pulling on a pair of trousers, I was sure the trip was going to be pretty painful. Maher could shoot me up with water and it would make me happy. I sat up on my bed and lit what I hoped was my final cigarette in the room. Although excited, I was worried about how the rebels planned to get us to the tunnel. I couldn't walk and yet I could see no stretcher anywhere. Fuck it, I thought, I'll get out on a Zimmer frame if need be.

Over the noise of the others preparing for the journey, I heard the sound of engines gunning followed by voices outside. My heart rate rose a few beats as I began to worry that the rebels might suddenly call off the escape. I held my breath and waited.

An FSA soldier entered, briefly absorbed the scene in the room and then shouted to Wa'el for us to leave and head for the vehicles. Two people – I don't remember who exactly – picked me up and supported me between their shoulders. I placed my arms around their necks and took the first, tentative step of my escape from Homs. Slowly and painfully they led me towards the exit. The floor was strewn with glass and rubble that hadn't been there when we first arrived. I stumbled and hopped forwards until we reached the entrance to the house. I could feel the wind blowing on my face. The cool air felt fantastic and I filled my lungs with deep breaths as we passed through the doorway of the shrapnel-encrusted wall and hobbled in the dark on to the main street.

I stood still, blinking as I absorbed the sight in front of me. The reality of what was happening struck me hard and all I could do was stare, open-mouthed, at the scene unfolding around me. I had expected to see a single truck waiting to take us to the tunnel. Instead, there were six or seven vehicles, their engines running and their headlights on. The exhaust fumes from the vehicles were backlit by the beams of the headlights, casting an unearthly glow on the street. Silhouetted in this light, stretcher-bearers carried the injured from the field clinic. The walking wounded clutched saline drips, women struggled with screaming children and armed FSA rebels patrolled the street. This wasn't an escape: this was an all-out evacuation of Baba Amr's wounded and dying.

Looking beyond the vehicles, I was yet more astonished by what I saw. When I entered the building five days ago, there had been a street. Little now remained. Broken and uprooted trees lay on their sides where they had been blown out of the ground. The concrete, rubble and twisted mounds of debris were knee deep along much of the road. During the five days we spent inside the room, the Syrian forces had unleashed a blistering hurricane of destruction on the neighbourhood. Nothing remained unscathed.

I felt faint and asked my two carriers to prop me up against the wall of the building. They refused and carried me instead to a waiting pickup truck, where they placed me on the front seat. As soon as they left, a salvo of mortars exploded at the far end of the road, lighting the surrounding buildings in a horrifying white flash. Fuck this, I thought, pulling myself out of the cab and crawling to the relative safety of a doorway directly opposite. I took what cover I could as another barrage of mortars landed at the opposite end of the street. I tried to light a cigarette, my trembling hands making it almost impossible. Eventually I succeeded. I inhaled deeply and began to take in what was happening around me.

Clearly, a discreet escape had become impossible: Assad's forces were relentlessly pushing into the tiny enclave and it was now a question of evacuating as many casualties as possible before government troops overran the neighbourhood. It didn't matter that the rebels would have to coordinate the risky evacuation under the full glare of the regime's troops. The decision had been made for them. They had no choice.

We watched as the doctors, nurses and medics emptied the wounded from the hospital while I kept a worried eye out for the rest of the guys from the room. Eventually, I caught sight of Wa'el and called him over. He explained that we were waiting for the doctors to finish strapping up Edith and her leg.

'Are you ready to go home, Paul?' he asked.

'I sure am, mate,' I replied.

We smoked another cigarette as more mortars exploded close by. Neither of us flinched any more. Our bodies must have decided that to do so was pointless. There were shouts from the house as Edith was carried out on a stretcher, accompanied by Javier and William. She was loaded into one of the waiting vehicles. Fuck, I thought, no Zimmer frame for me, then. The driver jumped into our truck. Wa'el helped me on to the front seat before rebels hoisted him into the back of the pickup. The driver blew the horn and revved the engine before putting the truck in gear. Moving slowly over the wreckage of Baba Amr, we made the first tenuous movements in our last-ditch attempt to escape.

We had only travelled fifty yards or so when more mortars exploded behind the convoy, causing us to accelerate towards an intersection. I watched in horror as the wall of the corner building ahead of us erupted in a blistering hail of explosive bullets. The driver simply accelerated into the bend. The roar of the V8 engine and screech of the spinning wheels drowned out the noise of the next salvo. Explosions filled the night as we twisted and turned through dark alleys, driving straight into plumes of smoke from mortar rounds that had exploded in our path only seconds earlier. We pulled into a tiny alley and stopped. On the roadside I saw a line of stretchers containing more wounded people. They were quickly loaded on to our already overflowing vehicles before we accelerated off again at full speed.

We sped through the night, the zipping noise of bullets clearly audible over the roar of the engine. Our driver, cigarette in mouth, his eyes fixed directly ahead, said nothing. His only intent was to get us to the tunnel alive. More explosions rocked the truck. We were obviously visible to the government soldiers and Assad's gunners were determined to hit our convoy. I gripped the armrest and swore viciously as every pothole and turn shot searing bolts of agony through my leg and deep into the pain receptors of my brain.

We were approaching the front line and my body tensed in

apprehension. Foot as far down on the accelerator as possible, the driver begun to mutter '*Allahu Akbar, Allahu Akbar*' to himself. Another staccato burst of heavy machine-gun fire ripped through the air and the sickening sounds of RPG rounds screamed past our vehicles as we crossed the open area of countryside and orchards, past the still-burning oil pipeline and on towards the tunnel entrance.

The onslaught on the convoy was relentless. I couldn't understand how we had made it this far. The regime was fully aware of the escape attempt taking place under its nose and they were throwing everything at us. We turned under a bridge, then jolted and lurched up a small hill and on to a raised embankment where the unmistakable whine of high-velocity, single-shot sniper rounds zipped all around us. I was slowly beginning to drift in and out of consciousness, only to wake suddenly and painfully every time the truck struck a crater. I struggled to light a cigarette. The driver spotted the trouble I was having and lit one for me.

'*Shukran*,' I managed to say.

'*Afwan*,' he smiled back. (No worries)

The contact meant everything to me. I was hanging on to consciousness by a thread so thin that anything that distracted me from the onslaught outside the vehicle or the pain inside my body was welcome.

Still at full speed, our driver and the rest of the convoy cut the headlights, plunging the route ahead into near darkness. It was a sign we were approaching the tunnel. The FSA obviously still considered the location of the tunnel a secret. That won't last long, I thought grimly. Soon the ground would be crawling with infantry troops searching for our route out. Once the tunnel was discovered, the last link to the outside world would be cut, leaving those still trapped in Baba Amr to face the terror of Assad's soldiers, who would be desperate to unleash their revenge on a weak, defenceless population.

We ground to a screeching halt next to a darkened glass building. It looked like a single-storey office but one I didn't recognise from previous tunnel trips. The FSA soldiers quickly unloaded the wounded from the trucks. Wa'el opened the door for me and, with his functioning arm, helped me down from the pickup. Javier and Abu Bakhr, who had helped me from the rubble when we were attacked, propped me up on their shoulders before we joined the stream of wounded walking in single file towards the tunnel entrance.

I tripped and lunged forward, snagging my bandage on something, which caused it to peel off my leg and drag behind me in the thick mud. I sat down on the tailgate of a pickup and pulled down my trousers. The wound was now exposed but there was no time for fancy repairs. I wrapped the muddy bandage around the wound in a few short twists and, out of nowhere, someone passed me a reel of sticky tape with which I strapped the bandage back in place. I pulled up my trousers and continued down the path to what appeared to be a holding area. I had lost touch with everyone else at this point. Javier and Abu Bakhr had gone to help with Edith and I searched with rising panic for someone I knew. I found Wa'el.

'Wa'el, where the fuck are the others?' I asked, the tension apparent in my voice.

'Don't worry. They are okay. They will wait here while you go first. Edith will be safe. They want to get you out in the first group. Abu Bakhr will stay with you for the entire trip and make sure you are safe. Don't worry. It will be okay. Go with these guys now to the tunnel,' he smiled.

'Come with me, Wa'el,' I said.

'I will see you on the other side, Paul,' he said, then turned and went back towards the others.

'You'd better make it, Wa'el,' I said out loud as he disappeared into the darkness. 'You'd better fucking well make it.' It was the last time I saw him.

Without pause, Abu Bakhr and a rebel took me between their shoulders and helped me stumble towards the tunnel. We arrived at the small antechamber that led down into the belly of the tunnel. Inside, three exhausted, sweating FSA rebels worked by the dim glow of an LED lamp. Beckoning me inside, they prepared a rope with which to lower me down into the tunnel. Slipping the rope over my head and under my arms, they led me to the steel ladder embedded in the wall. I placed my good leg on the ladder and held on to the smooth, concrete edges of the hole. The two rebels took up my weight and then Abu Bakhr told me to let go.

The rope bit deep into my armpits and the weight of my dangling leg caused a rush of pain to surge through my head as I swung from the rope. Slowly and gently they eased me down through the shaft and into the tunnel entrance. A pair of waiting hands supported me by the waist and steadied me on my feet. The rebels down below unhooked the rope and I was led to sit down on an old upturned wheelbarrow. I felt exhausted. The pain was the only thing keeping me conscious, preventing the urge to curl up on the sodden wet floor and fall asleep. Someone put a lit cigarette in my mouth and I inhaled deeply.

More wounded were passed down the shaft until the entranceway was near full to capacity. The air was thick with tension. Those who could walk were sent, bent double, into the black hole to make the most important journey of their lives. For the immobile, time stood still. Around me, sitting in the filth and dim light, people clutched bottles of fluid connected to their broken bodies by tubes. Others lay in the dirt, moaning in pain, their legs and arms splinted, heads bandaged, some missing hands and feet.

As I looked at the wounded men, women and children, I heard the deep, guttural sound of the motorbike approaching. From experience I knew it seemed nearer than it really was so we had to wait a further fifteen minutes before it arrived. In the cramped and cluttered chamber, strewn with the bodies of the injured, the rebels manhandled the bike so it pointed once more into the tunnel, ready for its next mercy run.

'Abu Falafel, Abu Falafel, come on. Get on the bike,' Abu Bakhr yelled at me.

'No,' I said stubbornly. 'Please, some of these boys are dying. Put them through first.' I was embarrassed by the order of evacuation.

'Abu Falafel, get on the bike. You must leave now,' he said urgently, pulling me up to my feet before staring me in the eyes. 'We want you out alive to tell our story. Please, go.'

The rest of the wounded in the chamber waved me towards the bike. They were smiling. In this dark, stinking tunnel, their lives hanging by a thread, they still found time to smile. I smiled back weakly.

The driver jumped on the bike and revved the engine, which rather worryingly kept stalling. Helping hands placed me on the back of the bike. The driver leaned forwards with his chin on the headlight and someone pushed my head down so it rested just below his shoulders. A rebel tapped me on the shoulder and mimed for me to keep my head down so as not to bang it on the low tunnel roof. I gave him a thumbs up before the driver revved the bike and slowly nosed it into the black hole. I clung to the bike for dear life as we started out on what I sincerely hoped was my final trip through a tunnel I was now learning to love.

We moved slowly. The tunnel was curved, so the bike had a tendency to ride slightly up the side and then fall down the wall, only to ride up the other side. It was virtually impossible to keep it in a straight line. I had to grip with my legs to stay stable and the pain was no longer coming in fits and bursts but in a constant stream of raw signals that bombarded my brain. Yet I had to hang on and keep from passing out. Time became meaningless. I lived only for the next second. The noise, the smell and the fact that we were five metres underground on a motorbike escaping from a bunch of ruthless murderers was all very surreal and, had it not been for the pain, I am sure I could have dismissed the whole affair as a rather quirky dream. Sadly, this wasn't the case and, just when I thought I had seen it all, there was more to come.

The bike slowed to a halt. I looked ahead in the pale light of its headlamp. In all my years on the front line, of time spent in hospitals watching the wounded pass away, I had seen nothing as hopeless as the scene before me. A middle-aged man, bent double, exhausted and sweating, stood dazed in the light from the motorbike. In his arms he carried a young boy, aged about ten. The child's legs were shattered. The skin and muscle on his lower legs had been blown clean away, leaving only the skeleton exposed to the world. I felt faint. Here, in the stinking bowels of the earth, I finally felt I had seen too much.

I tried to climb off the bike to let the boy get on. It simply wasn't possible to drive past and live the rest of my life knowing I'd left them in that dark place. I struggled once more to get off but I was forced down by a set of hands behind me. Turning, I saw an armed rebel and Abu Bakhr, who had run down the tunnel behind the bike. They took the child from his father and placed him carefully behind me on the seat. I turned to look at the young boy, his large watery eyes only inches from mine. He was in deep shock. He gazed impassively back into my own tear-filled eyes.

The father thanked the rebels and, as we pulled off, he joined them in running behind us, keeping well within sight of his wounded, crippled child. There were no footrests or grips on the bike and so the young boy had to cling tightly to me to stay on. Unfortunately, he had grabbed my thigh in the exact spot where the shrapnel had exited and was digging his fingers deep into my wound. My vision blurred with the pain. I was finding it increasingly hard to make sense of anything.

As I started to drift off, the bike stopped and I looked up. Through the tears in my eyes I could see only one thing in the beam of the headlight – a solid wall of brown earth that had fallen into the tunnel when it had been hit by artillery fire. This wall of earth now barred our path to freedom. I bit my lip to keep conscious. My head was spinning and the boy continued to grip my wound. It was then that I saw the hole.

'No fucking way,' I shook my head. 'Please, not a fucking chance,' I said again as despair threatened to overwhelm me.

At the top of the mound of earth, I could see a small dark hole that the rebels had scraped through the earth blockage. It was perhaps twelve inches high and twice as wide, enough for a grown man to squeeze through. There was no way Edith could jam herself through the blockage strapped to a piece of wood. She would have to turn back if she got this far.

I was helped off the bike, supported by Abu Bakhr and the rebel. They took me to the edge of the slippery, muddy blockage and pointed to the hole. Pushing on my good leg and scrabbling with my hands, I found a feeble grip with my fingertips and pulled myself into position. I wedged my elbows firmly inside the entrance and pushed on my functioning leg until my head and torso were inside the muddy hole. I then reached forwards and grabbed a protruding piece of steel bar in order to pull myself through.

An enormous wave of claustrophobia hit me as I started to wriggle forward through pools of water that had collected in the scraped-out hollow. It was completely dark. I could see no lights ahead of me and had no idea how far I would have to drag myself. I tried raising my head. It hit the roof. My chin was in the mud and my shoulders were scraping the outer edges as I inched my way through. I yelped in agony. Something had penetrated the exit wound on my thigh, pinning me so I was unable to move in either direction.

The rising surge of panic I felt at this discovery threatened to crush me. Calm down, I told myself. Just think slowly and keep a lid on the panic. I lay face down in the mud, impaled on what I figured out was the steel bar that I had used to pull myself into the hole. I was so confined that I couldn't get my hand to my leg, so I tried wriggling my leg off the bar, which was deep inside my wound. Slowly, I squeezed my left leg closer to my right one and tried to pull myself forward. Nothing happened. I was still harpooned by the spike. Fuck it, I thought, and gave my leg an almighty yank forward. I felt something give and guessed it wasn't the steel bar. As the flow of blood warmed my thigh, I realised that I had ripped apart the staples holding the wound closed. However, I had also succeeded in freeing myself from the spike.

I continued forward into the black void. Inch by muddy inch I progressed, completely coated in thick mud. Just as I was beginning to wonder if I would ever make the end, I heard muffled voices ahead of me, spurring me onwards. Still blind but now with renewed optimism, I squirmed my way forward until I could clearly hear the voices. A light shone in my face, causing me to flinch, and a pair of arms reached in. They slowly dragged me out of the hole and into the relatively spacious confines of the storm drain.

Two rebels put me on a home-made stretcher and started off down the tunnel. I felt my left leg. The piece of steel bar had indeed ripped open the wound and it was now bleeding heavily. There was little to be done. We travelled for another ten minutes along the tunnel, the fighters grunting and gasping in the oxygen-depleted air, until eventually I sensed freshness and realised we must now be near the end. They placed the stretcher down in the mud about ten metres from the exit and I sucked deeply on the waves of air as the wind blew over me. I looked into the dark behind me. There was no sign of Abu Bakhr and, as I lay immobile on the ground, a steady stream of people passed by, stepping over me as they made for the exit.

A miserable wait ensued. I knew Assad's forces would find this tunnel soon enough and the desperation to be out of it rose in my belly. I was lying in a cold, rancid pool of water and I started to shiver. I tried stemming the flow of blood from my leg by applying pressure on it with my muddy hand, waiting silently for my turn to clamber out.

My stretcher-bearers returned and pointed the way forward. In order to exit the tunnel I had to crawl through the smashed concrete hole of the storm drain, which was now flooded by inches of water. I had no choice but to drag myself through it. I felt the water flooding into my wound as I did so. A pair of hands dragged me out of the concrete tunnel into the muddy hole that lead to the outside world and fresh air. I gasped in pain. My leg felt like it was about to explode. Nonetheless, the air tasted sweet and I filled my lungs with rasping gulps.

Around me six fully armed rebels crouched silently in the mud at the bottom of the entrance shaft; they were there to get people in and out of the tunnel as quietly and efficiently as possible. Abu Bakhr stooped and came over to talk with me.

'Paul,' he whispered, 'they are going to slide you out of the hole. When you reach the top you must crawl to the corner where you waited the last time you came in. You understand? Do not make any noise. The Syrian army are in the next field. They are searching for the tunnel now.'

I nodded. Shit, I thought, that's a long crawl. I had run across the patch of land before but the prospect of slithering on my belly over such a great distance was daunting.

'You must go now. Wait at the corner and people will come for you,' Abu Bakhr told me.

Immediately, three pairs of hands grabbed me by the waist and good leg, lifted me to the top of the hole and gave me a final shove over the edge. I scrabbled about, found a handhold, pulled myself up to the surface and lay face down, panting into the sodden earth in exhaustion and pain. I remembered the Syrian army in the next field, which spurred me on, and I began my crawl across the wide-open space, devoid of moonlight and tree cover.

I used my elbows to move forward. They sank into the wet, muddy ground, giving me good leverage to pull on, but the pace was still painfully slow. I could manage only six inches with each pull forward. Sweat mingled with mud, stung my eyes and, with each and every movement forward, I felt the energy sap from my body. I avoided looking ahead: I didn't want to know how far I had left to travel and, in my fevered head, I started to empathise with snails. If this is all life has to offer a snail, then it's no wonder they eat all the good stuff. I vowed never to pour salt on one again. My ridiculous fixation with snails killed time as I crawled through the mud, and when I next looked up I saw two dark, crouched figures waiting silently at the corner of a wall. I had made it to safety. I laughed with elation as the men broke from the shadows to pull me to cover.

There was no great ceremony. The rebels simply picked me off the ground, supported me between them and set off at speed. I knew the route well but I was less sure about how they intended to make it with a wounded man. We moved through a walled area with trees either side that gave us cover from snipers. We paused momentarily. One of the rebels indicated for me to climb on his back. As soon as his friend had lifted me up, I knew it was the wrong move. The rebel grabbed my thigh and the palm of his hand penetrated the wound in my leg. But it was too late: we were already on the move. I tried gritting my teeth, to no avail. The pain was too intense to deal with and so I banged on his shoulder to put me down. He took this as a signal to go faster and accelerated to running speed. Shit, I thought, I can't do this. I banged once more on his shoulder, only for him to speed up even faster. Half-laughing and half-crying, I appealed for help from his friend, who eventually understood the meaning of my gestures and signalled my carrier to put me down before we resumed the more orthodox carrying procedure.

The night air still echoed to the sounds of war yet somehow it all seemed so distant now. I paid it little heed but it was there; the noose was slowly tightening on Baba Amr. The staccato rattle of AK47 fire was close. We may have been out of Baba Amr but we certainly weren't out of trouble.

The rebels carrying me picked up the pace. The gunfire was close enough to spur them on. Arriving at a ten-foot wall, they halted and gave a little whistle. Moments later, two fighters appeared on top of the wall to pull me up. I was lifted by the waist and passed into their waiting hands before they dragged me up the wall. I was unceremoniously dangled over the other side and dropped to the ground as gently as possible. I reached down to feel my leg, which seemed to have lost even more of the staples holding it together.

Once more, hands lifted me to my feet and we continued, hugging a line of trees that led to another wall I knew well. More bursts of machine-gun fire erupted, this time closer, and we picked up the pace again. I was struggling to hop, so my bearers had to drag me through the mud. I was exhausted and losing too much blood. Making sense of what was happening around me was increasingly difficult and I began to lose all sense of time. We pushed on through ditches and over rough boulder-strewn farmland. We climbed up more walls. Everything hurt now. It didn't matter what was happening: the pain was constant but I knew it had to end.

We had travelled about two miles like this when, through the sweat and mud that had dried on my face, I recognised a building up ahead. Holy shit, we've made it, I thought. But we carried on past the house. My spirits sank. We should have stopped there, I kept saying to myself. Why aren't we fucking stopping? I was losing my temper along with all hope that we would ever reach a destination. Please stop, I thought. Please.

I was now semi-conscious. Carry me to Lebanon if you want, I thought. At least I'm not the one doing the lifting. Eventually, something broke through my rambling and inane thoughts. In the distance, not too far away, I heard an engine. It might well be Assad's mob, but it could just as easily be help. I flopped my head forwards indifferently. I didn't care who they were any more. Lucky bastards, whoever they are. At least they have a car. Next time I'm bringing my own Land Rover. I'm not doing this shit again without one. Probably doesn't need an MOT out here and fuck road tax. They don't even have proper roads. These random thoughts tumbled through my mind.

Suddenly I was blinded by a searing white light that forced me to clench my eyes shut. I must have passed out, or died, I thought, but my money was on the former as I could still feel the searing pain in my leg.

'Ha ha, it's Abu Falafel,' I heard a voice say in English.

I opened my eyes, convinced that I was alive: that nickname couldn't possibly have followed me beyond the grave. It was Abu Hassan, whose house Marie and I had stayed in while we waited in Al Buwaydah to enter Homs. He lit a cigarette and put it in my mouth.

'Come,' he said, smiling gently, 'you need a falafel.'

I was carried to the back of a white box van with a sliding roll-up door. In the back I found a heap of bodies; people smiled at me as helpful hands reached out to pull me in. I instantly recognised one of the activists who had been injured in the attack on the media centre. All I could do was nod and smile back. The other injured guys made me a cushion out of sacks so that I could rest my head.

Within minutes the door closed and the van shifted into gear. We pulled off along the deeply rutted dirt road. A dim bulb illuminated the back of the van, giving me the opportunity to film some footage of my fellow wounded and to record a small piece to camera. Their injuries ranged from broken legs and gunshot wounds to multiple shrapnel blasts. Common to all of us was the sense of relief we felt – we had made it this far, alive.

We drove for an hour, perhaps more, the groans of the wounded providing an unnerving soundtrack to the journey as we bumped and slid our way across the unseen countryside of rural Homs. I drifted in and out of consciousness, waking when we hit a particularly deep hole in the road, only to pass out again moments later. My body had now reached its full capacity for pain and exhaustion and it fought to close down. I knew I had to fight back and stay awake but it was a battle I was losing.

The van turned on to a tarmac road and within minutes rolled to a gentle halt. The sound of voices and running feet greeted us and the roller door slid open. We were met by a small sea of anxious faces, some of whom jumped into the vehicle. I had been the last one into the van so I was first out. I was disorientated by the sudden appearance of so many people and struggled to work out my location. I was manhandled out and although it felt like familiar territory I couldn't put a name to it. I was certain I had been here before. Two medics in surgical scrubs carried me into a brightly lit room. For five days I hadn't seen daylight and my eyes now stung in the glare of the bulbs that lit up the room.

I was placed on a mattress in the corner, from where I took in my surroundings. The usual diesel heater threw out a tremendous heat. Cushions lay against all the walls and the wooden shelves and bookcases were piled with bandages and bottles of medicine. Also present were six other casualties with various injuries. They nodded and smiled at me reassuringly, as if to tell me that I was finally safe. They passed me a smoke and one poured a cup of sweet tea, holding the cup to my lips so I could sip it. The hot liquid tasted like nectar and the cigarette, I swear, was the best I had ever smoked. I closed my eyes, not out of exhaustion but out of a desire to savour this moment. I never wanted to move again.

As I lay on the mattress with my eyes closed and the warmth returning to my body, I heard the door open. And then someone called my name. 'Abu Falafel, what are you doing here?' said a gentle, quiet voice.

I opened my eyes and sat bolt upright. It couldn't be, I thought to myself in the brief moments before I saw the beaming face tower above me. It was Dr Hakim. I had met him on my first trip into Syria in January. He was the doctor who ran a field clinic from a tiny tent in Al Qusayr. We had stayed at his house and it was he who had got Miles Amoore and me out of Syria when Assad's forces were hunting us. I counted him as a true, much-loved friend and now he stood before me. I stared at him, smiling like an idiot, and he laughed back at my gormlessness.

'I was coming to get you from Baba Amr,' he said. 'I'm glad you've saved me the trouble, though. It sounds very shit where you were and I hate tunnels. Your government asked me to go in to try and get you out. I said no to them but I came to get you anyway because you are my friend. I take it you want to go home now?'

I laughed and Hakim bent down to kiss me and then stared into my eyes. 'Paul, why do you want to leave our beautiful country? Are you crazy?' His eyes twinkled and he smiled a huge, wonderful smile. 'Now all we have to do is fix you up and get you out of Syria.'

Shit, I thought, I'd forgotten all about that bit.

CHAPTER FOURTEEN

Codename: Liverpool

27 February 2012, Al Buwaydah, Syria

Dr Hakim's first priority was to clean and patch my wound. The journey out of Baba Amr had taken its toll and my leg looked disgusting and felt even worse. An hour later, after more painful cleaning and a little sewing as a result of the damage done in the tunnel, Dr Hakim put me on a drip to replenish some of the fluid I had lost. With a shot of antibiotics, some food and an industrial dose of coffee and cigarettes, I felt ready to take on the world.

I asked Hakim if I could send a text on his satellite phone. I had to let Miles Amoore in Lebanon know I was out of Baba Amr. Although I was wary of sending out too much information, it was important to let Miles know that I would head for the border once I'd rested. Writing texts on a satphone is a fiddly business so it took me twenty minutes to write one to Miles. I hoped he was sharp enough to decipher the coded message. After I'd punched the message into the phone, Hakim went outside to send it for me. It read:

Mate, have started moving the hard way. Have met up with our friend from tent although not in that place yet. Am hurting like hell. Let Bon Kate and Dad know. Keep men in suits busy, need enemy to think still in and not look outside for us. Heading to place where you had lovely fatty meal. Probably tomorrow. Thanks for all mate. Off to whine to anyone who will listen. Love px

That should confuse any bugger listening in, I thought, hoping it didn't confuse Miles too much as well. All I had to do now was sit tight and wait for Edith, Wa'el and the others to arrive.

I felt a strange form of guilt at being the only one out so far. The escape didn't feel complete without the others. I wanted to celebrate with them. But the tunnel and the blockage halfway down it kept niggling at me. I worried that Edith, with a broken leg and strapped to a wooden trolley, would never make it through such a tiny hole. Three tense hours passed with no news of any of them. The fear that something dreadful had happened began to mount in the field clinic. Everyone knew that they ought to have been out by now. We should at least have heard something.

The sound of vehicles crunching to a halt outside the clinic made the medics spring to their feet and rush for the front door. Thank fuck, I thought. What had taken them so long? The sense of relief was enormous. I waited for them to come through the door wearing huge smiles. Now we could celebrate.

The door burst open and two medics stumbled through the doorway carrying a blood-soaked, muddy rebel. He had been shot through the face, the bullet exiting through his temple. He was barely clinging to life. Behind him followed a stream of casualties. One of the civilian casualties had been shot in the gut – one of the most agonising places to be hit – and was writhing on the floor, his face contorted in agony as he lay there, screaming and clutching his gaping stomach wound with his hands. Within a few minutes the room was full of seriously wounded fighters and civilians. It couldn't have been worse: the floor of the clinic was awash with blood. Hakim, the vet we had met when we first arrived in Al Buwaydah and all available medics struggled to stabilise the wounded. I watched in horror, but at the back of my mind ran one thought – where the fuck are the others?

As he worked, Dr Hakim told me what had happened. 'Paul, twenty minutes after you got out of the tunnel the army found it and attacked. They threw in grenades and fired AK47s down the tunnel. Javier was shot, Wa'el has been captured by the army, Edith and William had to turn back to Baba Amr,' he said and continued to pull the bullet from the groin of a fully conscious rebel.

'Hakim, have you seen a little boy, about ten-years-old, whose legs are partially blown off?' I asked.

Hakim thought for a moment and then shook his head. My world imploded. After all we had been through – the shelling, the tragic deaths of Marie and Remi, the despair of Baba Amr, the crazy ride to the tunnel – it seemed like everything had been in vain.

I was in little doubt that the Syrian security services would torture and execute Wa'el. William and Edith would have to return to Baba Amr. Even if they made it back, I wasn't sure how they would cope with the psychological torment. And somewhere out there Javier lay wounded. I felt sick. The bravery of the activists and the FSA's Farouk brigade, who had battled to defend Homs and had sacrificed so much to get us this far, had ended in death and disaster. I owed these brave men my life and yet now I sat watching the result of their courage in a room awash with blood. I closed my eyes in an effort to block out the hell opening up before me.

Hakim stabilised the wounded and then came and sat with me. He spoke softly and gently, clasping my hand in his as he spoke.

'Paul, I have to send you away from here,' he began. 'It's not safe any more and your leg is very bad – worse than you may think. We have to get you to Lebanon as soon as possible and you know what that involves, don't you? The situation has changed while you were in Baba Amr. It's now all-out war and the journey to the border isn't as easy as it was.'

I nodded silently. I needed no reminder of the arduous trip that lay ahead.

'Soon a car will arrive. I want you to go with the FSA. They will get you to Lebanon. You can trust them. I will wait here for news of your friends,' he said sadly.

'Hakim, thanks, mate. You've been a good friend to me and I won't forget what you have done, you know that,' I told him. 'Please, say hi to Abu Sallah and the boys and tell them I will visit when I'm fixed up.'

He smiled back at me.

Twenty minutes passed before another car arrived outside. It was four o'clock in the morning and I was exhausted, but it was time to move. Hakim and the vet lifted me up and helped me to the waiting car. The driver and a guard in the front seats welcomed me as Hakim placed me on the back seat. Hakim and the vet leaned in and hugged me goodbye, triggering a wave of sadness. I hoped to God they lived through this filthy war but I couldn't help fearing the worst: in this Syria there were no guarantees. I watched my friends as they disappeared into the darkness, waving at the car until we were out of sight. The guard turned to face me, smiled and said, 'Abu Falafel,' before offering me a cigarette, which I accepted with a weak smile.

We drove for an hour, slowly winding our way through meadows and woodlands, up muddy tracks and across ploughed farmland. As we drove, a slow realisation grew like a cancer in my mind. I was still deep within enemy territory, and about to cross a major battlefield. I had watched Remi and Marie being killed and I had lost contact with the very people who had helped me survive the last five days. Fuck, I thought in horror, I'm feeling sorry for myself. To fend off the gloom, I imagined the faces of the Assad regime's high command as they stood on trial in the dock of the International Criminal Court at The Hague. I soon felt more like my old self.

Arriving outside an old farmhouse, the driver honked his horn and immediately three FSA rebels appeared from the doorway, helped me from the pickup and carried me across the stony ground into the building. The interior of the house was of the standard design – cushions all around the edges of the room, the diesel stove piping hot air into the room and the television on full blast flashing scenes of familiar destruction.

The three rebels, dressed in combat fatigues, made a bed for me on one of the cushions, removed my sodden jacket and trousers and then covered me in a blanket. None of them spoke any English and so we communicated in pidgin Arabic and sign language. They offered me coffee as well as a bowl of oranges and a cup of honey, which I ate like a starving child.

Suddenly all three men started shouting. I flinched at the noise, fearing an attack, only to realise they were pointing at the television. 'Abu Falafel, Abu Falafel,' they shouted until I looked at the screen and saw my own face staring back at me. They laughed and smiled among themselves, occasionally looking over at me with huge grins. They had Abu Falafel on their cushions and they seemed mighty happy about it. It was nearing dawn and I took the opportunity to sleep. Exhausted mentally and physically, with the heat of the fire and a belly full of oranges and sweet honey, I passed into dreamless oblivion.

One of the rebels woke me at about ten the next morning. He had a steaming cup of coffee in one hand and a packet of Marlboro in the other. A full English breakfast, I thought. After a few coffees and smokes I gradually drifted back into the world. I felt my leg. It hurt to the touch and I tried moving it carefully but all I felt was an excruciating pain. I pondered my next move. I could be here for days but then again they might want me out as soon as possible. I was probably being hunted and my presence would attract more trouble.

It wasn't long before I had an answer. I heard a motorbike pull up outside and loud greetings reached me in the room where I lay. Two of the men from the previous evening entered the room and helped me dress. They smiled and made the signs for a motorbike. I smiled back but inside my heart sank. Shit, another motorbike ride. Exactly what I don't need right now. But who was I to argue? I sat in great pain on the back of a Yamaha 250cc, a young cheerful rebel at the controls as the men who had nursed me stood smiling and waving their goodbyes.

Initially, the ride was pretty comfortable. And then we left the tarmac road. Swearing profusely through gritted teeth, I told myself it would all be over as long as I hung on tightly. And so we progressed, twisting and turning along lanes and over fields, around farms and through woodland on a journey that, were it not for the awful pain, would have made a great off-road adventure. And then someone had to go and spoil it for everyone.

We were crossing a field, hugging the hedgerow for cover, when someone let rip with a volley of heavy machine-gun fire that caused small explosions of dirt to erupt in the mud around the bike. I looked in the direction of the gunfire and, on a ridge about three hundred metres away, spotted a Syrian army patrol. I was absolutely livid: until that moment it had been the first time in weeks that I had gone through a day without being shot at or shelled. More shots kicked the dirt up around us but this time I retaliated. Twisting around on the bike to face the patrol, I violently waved two fingers in the direction of the Syrian soldiers while screaming at the top of my lungs.

'Up yours, you sick fucking bastards,' I yelled manically, thrusting two fingers at them.

As a stress-buster it beat yoga and I settled back on the bike, content that I had done my bit for the war effort. The army responded by firing mortars at us. They were poorly aimed and managed only to scare the shit out of a few grazing goats. From my pillion position I heard the driver laughing.

'Abu Falafel, you are crazy,' he said.

'I certainly hope so,' I replied.

We continued happily on the bike, the occasional shell screaming over our heads. I could feel fresh, warm blood seeping from the wound in my leg and I was soon praying for the bike ride to end. Ten minutes later I got my wish as we wound through the streets of a medium-sized dusty town, which reverberated to the sound of distant artillery. Sod it, I thought. Unless a shell lands within ten metres of me I'm not going to bother worrying. After Baba Amr, these explosions seemed a long way off.

We entered a dark, smoke-filled room. Around the edges sat ten FSA fighters in various forms of battledress, cleaning weapons and smoking as they laughed among themselves. The young boy introduced me to the group as Abu Falafel, eliciting laughter and broad smiles from the men. I was given a cushion and pumped full of super-strong Arab coffee, Fanta and enough cigarettes to keep a lab-smoking beagle happy. Only one guy spoke English. He explained that the fighting on the border was too fierce for us to make the crossing yet and that we should wait for a while. I nodded.

As I sat down on the cushions to rest, a tall character entered the room from the adjoining kitchen. He carried a short stock Kalashnikov and wore a combat jacket, white baggy trousers, a keffiyeh around his neck and a long, greying beard. He looked directly at me, caught my gaze, smiled, and then ran his finger across his throat. He smiled again and left. Fuck me, I thought, it's Osama Bin Laden. Ten minutes passed before Osama entered the room again, performed the same throat-cutting routine and then left.

I turned to my English-speaking friend. 'Who the hell is that?' I asked.

My friend looked worried. 'He was the Sheikh's bodyguard in Tora Bora for seven years.'

'You mean Sheikh Osama?' I asked.

My friend nodded and changed the subject.

Half an hour later, Bin Laden's bodyguard passed through the room and repeated his finger-across-the-neck routine. I asked my friend to ask him if I was supposed to be scared of him. My translator, somewhat nervously, did as I asked. Bin Laden's bodyguard stopped pacing the room and stared straight through me. Oh shit, I thought. Wrong question.

He walked over to me, stooped down to my seated position and looked me squarely in the eyes. 'I love you,' he said, planting a big kiss on my lips before bursting into laughter. He then said something to the translator in Arabic.

'Erm, he wants to know if you can get him a visa for England. He is wanted by Interpol and he has trouble travelling nowadays,' my English-speaking friend told me.

'Tell him I'll work on it,' I said, hoping I wouldn't have to exchange email addresses with the guy.

The Sheikh's bodyguard laughed and walked off.

The atmosphere in the room was pretty mellow and everyone

appeared relaxed, all except one man who sat in the corner earnestly studying a piece of paper. The chap next to him was busy berating the poor man, jabbing his fingers at the piece of paper over and over again. I asked the English-speaker what the matter was. He replied, 'He is your driver. He is learning the way to take you to Lebanon.' Shit, I thought as confidence ebbed from my body. Why can't I have one of these really tough-looking bastards?

The evening turned slowly to night and I was told it was time to leave. Packing up my scant possessions, I was helped to my feet. The driver and another young guy led me to a pickup truck and bundled me into the back seat. We drove off but the car began to screech and groan unhealthily. The young driver tried with all his might to steer but only just missed hitting a lamppost. After two hundred metres the truck broke down completely and we performed the walk and hobble of shame back to the house, where we picked up another car. The replacement vehicle worked a lot better and off we set, with no headlights, into the night.

As we drove, the sound of heavy shelling drew closer until, after an hour or so, we passed straight through the middle of the bombardment. The odd shell landed a few hundred metres from the pickup, shaking the ground but causing no damage. I could tell they weren't meant for us. In the distance stood the town of Al Qusayr, which we had passed on the way into Homs. I was sure that the town and its inhabitants were the target, not us. What we were seeing were drop-short rounds and we would have to be really unlucky to be hit by one.

The journey was the usual mix of back roads and fields. We never stayed on the same route for more than a few minutes at a time, driving in silence as neither the driver nor guard spoke English. I drifted to sleep on the back seat, waking only when a large bump sent pain bolting through my leg. For two hours, we wove through the night before halting at a brightly lit house. The driver honked his horn and out came a young boy with his father. The driver waved me farewell and father and son helped me into the house.

This house was different from all the others. It was lavishly decorated with thick, expensive carpets, kitsch dabs of gilt on the walls and a huge widescreen television hooked up to a large stereo system. It was obvious that the house belonged to smugglers. That meant we were close to the border now. I was treated like a guest of honour. Huge plates of food were laid before me with coffee, freshly squeezed orange juice and a packet of Marlboro reds to wash it all down. I lapped up everything on offer. The room slowly filled with visitors, eager for a glimpse of the bedraggled, wounded foreigner.

In walked a large, round-faced character who was introduced as the doctor. He was pleasant enough and we chatted about Homs and events on the ground there. Eventually, he asked if I would mind staying the night while they found a video camera so that they could film me saying something jolly nice to camera about the heroes who had rescued me. Now, if my leg hadn't been half hanging off, if the camera had been ready and if I hadn't been quite so desperate to escape Syria, I may well have agreed. However, I was badly wounded, felt awful and had no desire to sit and chat all evening about what had just happened. I politely refused the offer of a bed and turned down their movie request.

The atmosphere grew darker and an argument broke out among them. The doctor told me I had to stay the night. It was too dangerous to cross now, he told me, I must wait until the morning. There was only one thing for it. I pulled down my trousers, undid the bandage and showed them my leg. They all gasped before talking heatedly among themselves once more.

Ten minutes later I heard the sound of a motorbike pulling up outside. The doctor, who was smiling again, told me it was time to leave. They could take me to the border that evening after all. I breathed a deep sigh of relief. The atmosphere here had been different from that in all the other FSA safe houses. I smelt money not passion in this house, and I had grown increasingly uncomfortable during my hours there.

Waving a polite goodbye, I mounted another motorbike, glad to leave even if it was on the back of a bike. Travelling across open fields, I knew I was very close to the border now. I could just make out the distant lights of a town in Lebanon and I imagined that this would be the final leg of my journey. But I was dropped off again at what looked like an old school building and told I would be taken into Lebanon from here.

I was helped inside and given a seat in an old administration office. Coffee was served and we watched the news in Arabic. The men here were more caring and I felt comfortable. Old men continually offered me their seats, tut-tutting when I refused. They kept me well supplied with drinks and smokes and eventually, after an hour, I fell asleep in the superheated room.

I woke with a start. A kind-faced old man was gently tugging at my jacket and pointing outside to a teenage boy who sat revving a motorbike. The old man smiled a toothy grin and said 'Lebanon' quite clearly, while pointing at the bike. I sprang into life and, for the first time in nearly a week, I allowed myself a moment of real optimism. I can do this, I can really do this, I told myself.

Two wizened old men assisted me out of the house and on to the bike. One proffered a walking stick, which I gladly accepted.

'Ma'a salama, Abu Falafel,' said one of the old men as they waved me off on the bike.

'Ma'a salama, Syria,' I joked in response, before slipping off into the night once more.

The border crossing was in a wide-open area of farmland punctuated with small orchards that offered little cover. All the time I clung on for dear life. I knew the border was heavily patrolled and that the journey wouldn't be an easy one. I was right: within minutes I could hear bullets zipping past our heads. The border troops couldn't see us but the bike was clearly audible across the open terrain and the soldiers here would shoot at shadows, which they did. At one point, an RPG round screamed past ten metres to our rear, close enough to make us shrink lower on the bike. Bollocks, I thought. To make it this far only to be taken out by a stray round would be a crime. Another bullet passed so close I felt the wind on my cheek. I marvelled at the driver's courage. We were passing directly through Assad's lines and he would have to make the journey back once he had dropped me off.

We entered an area with high hills and dense tree cover, and to our relief the shooting finally subsided. Turning on to a tarmac road, the reduced bumps caused the pain in my leg to lessen a little. The driver turned to check on me and I gave him the thumbs up. Minutes later he drove into the courtyard of a building that had all its lights blazing and nimbly pulled the bike to a halt. Exiting from a doorway to our left came a sleepy-looking rebel, a cup of coffee in one hand and an AK47 in the other. He took one look at me and burst into a smile.

'*Salam al-aykum*, Abu Falafel,' he welcomed me.

'*Al-aykum salam*,' I replied, propping myself up with my donated walking sick.

I was shown into a toasty room where three men dressed in combat gear lay sprawled out on the floor, Kalashnikovs close at hand, watching cartoons on the television. I stood, taking in the scene before asking in Arabic, 'Am I in Syria or Lebanon?'

The cartoon-watching rebels laughed at me and responded in unison. 'Lebanon,' they said.

My head spun. I felt a surge of elation course through my body. I've made it, I've fucking well made it, I said to myself in disbelief, searching for the nearest seat on which to slump. I fumbled for a cigarette and lit up. A coffee was produced and I savoured every sip of the beautiful cup of instant Nescafé. It was time to let Miles know that I had finally escaped from Syria. I rooted around for my Blackberry and turned it on. To my surprise, it still had power and full signal. I found Miles' number and dialled. He answered.

'Miles, it's Paul. I'm out, mate. I've done it!' I said happily.

'What are you doing calling me on this number?' he replied, rather curtly.

'Erm, because it's your number,' I ventured.

'Listen, only use text and whatever you do, don't talk in English. Pretend to be an Arab from now on,' he said urgently and then hung up.

Jesus, what a weirdo, I thought. Pretend to be an Arab? That made me laugh. About the only words I could say in Arabic were 'hello', 'goodbye', 'thank you' and 'can I breastfeed in here?', a question Miles and I had learnt in order to see what response it elicited from hardened rebels. Plus, I had just come from a country where it seemed everybody knew me. I was Abu Falafel, the English photographer. In fact, I think Miles and the team in Beirut may have been more than a little paranoid. Here's an example of how our text messages went back and forth from then on.

Miles: Ambulance with you in 10. Doc with you in 20 mins. You have to pretend to be an Arab. So don't speak and don't make phone calls

Paul: Roger

Paul: Question. Arab speaking for the doctor too?

Miles: Yes. Point at wounds.

An hour later no ambulance had arrived so I decided to travel to Beirut with the help of the local FSA. I had got myself this far and was fed up waiting for medical help. I wanted to be clear of the border, so I contacted Miles again.

Paul: Nothing yet. Can forgo ambulance if needed and get to town on my own.
Town where you are, where the beer and whisky flow? [This last was the code I tried for Beirut.]

Miles: If they can take you to whisky and women now, then do that. Let me know

Paul: Ok mate. It's getting sorted now.

Miles: Roger, get the driver to call this number 00961772941, once you are in the car and moving. This will fix everything. Confirm receipt.

Paul: Roger received. On the move.

Barring the coded doubletalk on text, arranging transport was all jolly easy. I simply asked the rebels for a lift to Baalbek, a town on the way to Beirut. They smiled, nodded, made a call and produced another coffee. Within twenty minutes I heard the familiar sound of a motorbike outside. I wondered briefly why I had to get on another motorbike now that we were inside Lebanon. I checked the dressing on my wound, swallowed a mouthful of paracetamol the locals had given me and prepared for what I hoped was my final motorbike ride of the journey. I hobbled over to the bike with my walking stick, mounted up and waved another goodbye to the rebels.

The bike driver nodded, gave me the thumbs up and we headed towards the mountains once more. The pain returned instantly, pulsing through my leg as the nerves linked directly to the pain receptors in my brain. I started to feel sick with the ache but I was reluctant to vomit on a moving bike. After ten minutes the driver stopped, pointed at a small town with glowing lights, spat on the ground and said with disgust, 'Hezbollah,' referring to Lebanon's pro-Assad political group and its military wing. He kicked the bike back into gear and continued moving.

We had been travelling along goat paths or muddy roads but now, out of the corner of my eye, I saw a field of boulders to our right. Fuck, I thought, so boulders are an actual crop and this is where they grow them. I'm glad we're not driving across that field, I said to myself. As if sensing my thoughts, the driver immediately turned right and so began the hardest and most painful part of my whole escape. It wasn't possible to avoid the boulders and each one we hit sent a lightning bolt of pain through me. After fifteen minutes my body was ready to surrender.

Finally, we turned out of the boulder field and on to a paved road. After five minutes of smooth riding we pulled up next to a rather shiny Toyota Land Cruiser. Pretty fancy, I thought to myself. The FSA must be doing well for themselves in Lebanon. Three men climbed out of the vehicle. They were each immaculately dressed in camel hair overcoats and suits, complete with shirts and ties.

'Please, get in the car. We must move now,' said the man I'd identified as the leader.

I obeyed without question. These men didn't seem like FSA rebels. I had no idea who they were, but what the hell; they had a nice car.

Once seated inside, we pulled off immediately. The powerful engine purred softly as we accelerated and seemed to intensify the silence in the vehicle. Not a word was spoken. I asked if I could smoke. A window lowered but still no one said anything. I glanced around the vehicle and noticed the weapons clutched by the men in smart suits. They weren't the Soviet Kalashnikovs so common to these parts of the world. Nope, these guys had the best: they looked like Heckler & Koch MP5 machine guns with laser sights. Then I noticed that each of the men wore coiled plastic tubes fitted to earpieces. Shit, I thought, they must be Lebanese intelligence officers. I began to worry. In front of us, out of nowhere, appeared an identical Land Cruiser that now led the way. In the rear-view mirror another set of headlights joined us. This is turning out to be some taxi ride, I thought as our convoy sped down the road.

After half an hour all three vehicles pulled over to the side of the road. Waiting there were another three identical vehicles. Six in total now, as well as guys in black combat gear, radio headsets and black scorpion body armour all carrying sophisticated state-of-the-art weapons. I was put in the middle vehicle and we continued our trip. Occasionally the vehicles changed positions, slowing down or speeding up as they overtook each other so that I was never in the same place in the convoy for too long. I felt like Gaddafi or Tony Blair must have felt as the cars swapped over to prevent anyone assassinating me. It was all rather flattering.

I texted Miles again:

Mate, I'm on the move and seem to have some pretty powerful new friends.

I then spoke to the main man in the front of my vehicle. 'Could you call this number and tell them where you are taking me?' I asked, passing him my phone.

He had a brief conversation with the man who answered before hanging up and passing me back my mobile. 'It's okay,' he said. 'Everything is organised.'

Chatty sod, I thought. 'Excuse me,' I said, as politely as I could, 'you seem to be doing me a pretty big favour here. Can I ask who you are?'

There was a long pause while he considered his answer. 'We are your friends,' he said. And that was it.

I stared out of the car window. Suddenly, a Lebanese army roadblock loomed up ahead. I could see the soldiers at the checkpoint pulling every car over and searching them, probably looking for wounded FSA rebels fleeing to Lebanon. We were flagged over by a young-looking conscript. We halted alongside the soldier. My driver wound down his window and said a few words in Arabic. The soldier blanched, stood to attention and waved us through. Whoever my new friends were, I liked them.

Tiring of the novelty and endless chatter of my well-connected friends, I passed out, exhausted, in the back of the Land Cruiser. I must have been asleep a fair while because when they woke me I realised I had dribbled all over the leather upholstery. I discreetly mopped up after myself. The driver told me to exit the vehicle and I was immediately transferred to the back of an S-Class Mercedes. I was relieved to see the standards hadn't dropped. By the time I looked up again from the back seat, the mystery convoy had already vanished. We were now in Beirut and I realised I must be close to my destination. We had hardly travelled anywhere before the driver pulled into a car park outside a hotel and informed me that I would now meet my friends.

A man and a woman came out of the hotel and walked directly to my car. They opened the door and introduced themselves. The girl's name was Monica, the guy's Wissam. I politely said hello. I had never seen either of these people before. Monica, sensing my confusion, laughed.

'Paul,' she said, 'I am Monica, Javier's wife. I have been helping Miles.'

'Oh shit, I'm so sorry. I didn't make the connection,' I spluttered.

'Watch that door. Miles will be out in a few moments,' she smiled.

And so I did. I sat and waited. Even now the bastard was late. I laughed to myself. He emerged, blinking into the night air while scanning the car park for our vehicle. He saw us and walked over. I climbed out and leant on my crutch. Miles smiled and just said, 'Hello, mate.' We hugged in the middle of the car park. Emotion filled us both. I had never been so happy to see anyone in all my life. I was embarrassed too: in the middle of such a public space, there I was hugging a ginger.

'Let's get in the fucking car, mate,' I whispered into his ear.

We transferred to Monica's car and headed to her apartment. I was completely lost for words. Seeing Miles had really brought home to me the fact that I was now safe. The relief manifested itself in a rather strange way – stupidity.

'Miles, let's get cleaned up and head to Danny's bar and go for a drink,' I said, referring to one of the city's favoured haunts.

Miles blinked and looked at me as if I'd lost my mind.

'Mate, half of Damascus is looking for you right now. Most of them trying to kill you,' he added for good measure. 'We are not going to a bar. We need to get a doctor to you tonight.'

'If you call a doctor tonight I won't be your friend any more. I need a bottle of whisky and some painkillers. I saw a vet the other day, everything is okay,' I replied, as if that were the most normal thing in the world to say.

'I have a bottle of Jameson's I bought at the airport for you,' replied a slightly bemused Miles.

'And I have lots of Valium,' Monica chipped in.

'Cool,' I said. 'Let the party commence.'

We arrived at Monica's apartment and, with a little help from my friends, I was taken upstairs and deposited on the most comfortable sofa I had ever enjoyed sinking into. Whisky glasses were produced and Miles handed me the bottle. I opened it slowly, breathing in the aroma. Surely I was dead in a stinking room in Baba Amr and this was the afterlife: whisky and Valium. I was grinning like a buffoon as I poured the drinks. I passed round the rather large shots and we all clinked glasses. The room echoed to the sound of cheers and laughter. I raised the glass to my lips but paused momentarily. I pictured Marie and Remi lying in the dust. I thought of Edith and William, of Javier and Wa'el. None of them were here to taste the drink with me. 'To you all,' I whispered, quickly downing my drink.

Monica announced that she had to go to bed. She had children and the morning would be an early start. Her partner, Javier, was still missing, feared shot. Passing me a box of Valium, along with a thick, soft quilt and pillows, she hugged me and said goodnight. My heart bled for her. It must have been incredibly difficult to see me free while Javier remained trapped inside Syria.

Over more whisky and a handful of Valium I debriefed Miles on the whole story, from the attack on the house that killed Marie to the moment we met in the car park. He sat, open-mouthed, until I reached the end. 'Fuck, mate,' was his general response to most of the things I told him.

'So what's been going on here?' I asked.

'I don't know where to start,' he said.

'Try the beginning,' I replied.

Miles was clearly exhausted. Since arriving in Beirut he had survived on less than three hours sleep a night. So too had the rest of the team who assisted with my escape: Ray Wells, the head of *The Sunday Times* picture desk, Monica, Wissam Tarif, the head of campaign group Avaaz's Syrian operation, and another Avaaz member, Alex Renton. Together with the Lebanese fixer, Leena, who had arranged for Marie and me to enter Syria with the smugglers, the team had worked tirelessly to secure my escape.

They had set up a secret operation centre in the Lebanese capital, a room they swept for electronic bugs every day to prevent Syria's intelligence services from listening in. They were extremely anxious to keep the Syrian government in the dark about our possible escape routes, afraid that the government would deploy more ground soldiers to the border to block our evacuation should they get wind of it. From this room, the Beirut team made contact and met anyone they thought could help end the crisis: rebels inside Baba Amr, British and French ambassadors, defence attachés, Red Cross delegates.

I had been right to assume that no one was coming to get us out. From the very start, it was made clear to the team in Beirut that a British special forces rescue operation was out of the question. The Russian navy anchored off Syria's west coast could easily pick up an enemy helicopter flying over Syrian airspace. Even if the helicopter did evade Russian naval detection, it would almost certainly be shot down by Syria's air-defence batteries, which were apparently manned by former Russian military contractors who knew what they were doing. Sending in Lebanese special forces, intelligence agents or militia, who could at least walk across the land border and blend in with the locals, was impossible: their discovery or capture could ignite the already volatile tensions in the region as a result of the war in Syria. The Americans and the British couldn't even send up drones to assess possible escape routes for us: again, the team were told that Syria's air defences would prevent the spy craft flying low enough to spot anything useful. However, the Brits did tell the team that they could help us once we reached Lebanese territory.

On the other side of the Syrian border, in the Syrian capital Damascus, another team made up of senior *Sunday Times* correspondent, Hala Jaber, and the paper's Egypt correspondent, Sara Hashash, banged on the door of every Syrian government official they knew. Hala and Sara finally persuaded the Syrian government to agree to a ceasefire, a mighty feat. The team in Beirut then had to persuade the rebels in Baba Amr to agree to the same, which they did. Every day, as the deadline for the ceasefire approached, a highly fraught and complex four-way telephone conversation took place. Hala would telephone the mayor of Homs who then telephoned the Syrian army commander near Baba Amr; messages were passed back via the mayor to Hala who relayed these via Sara to Miles, who passed them on to the rest of the team in Beirut. They forwarded the message to rebels in Baba Amr via satellite phone and the rebels' replies were then sent back along the same long line.

During this process they were given a hand-drawn map marking the location of Marie and Remi's corpses. The rebels had initially stored the two bodies inside a cheese factory, in refrigerators that were powered by a generator. As the siege dragged on, fuel for the generator had run out and the rebels were forced to bury the bodies. They had marked the location on the map with a cross.

For four days both teams watched in frustration as the ceasefire agreement they had worked so hard to hammer out broke down. Miles said neither team could understand why I had refused to enter the Syrian Red Crescent ambulances. He only figured it out a few days later, when he was told that many of the wounded civilians picked up by the same ambulances had been taken to a hospital under armed military guard. This, coupled with strong intelligence the team received about the start of the much feared ground assault on the rebel enclave, led them to believe that the only way for us to escape was via the tunnel, hence Miles' urgent message delivered by Abu Hanin while I was still in the room in Baba Amr.

As Syrian intelligence was trying to hack into the Beirut team's computers and almost certainly listening to their telephone conversations, it was decided that Hala and Sara in Damascus should be left in the dark about the plan to escape via the tunnel. The team in Beirut thought it would provide better cover for us if the two of them continued to negotiate a ceasefire in Damascus, thus tricking the government into believing we were still trapped inside the city.

The team in Beirut knew the moment I left Baba Amr and they began to track my movements anxiously. They endured several nerve-wracking hours as they waited to hear whether I'd made it through the tunnel. Miles described the joy and relief of everyone in the room when I finally resurfaced in the relative safety of Al Buwaydah, and then again when they received my text telling them I'd made it to the border. But it was a relief tempered by the news that Javier had been shot and was now lost and that Edith and William had never even made it into the tunnel. Monica, who had remained implacably calm throughout the ordeal until then, was devastated.

It became more important than ever to keep my whereabouts and the news of my escape a secret, lest the Syrian government discover the escape route and send reinforcements to capture the others who had yet to make it out alive. Miles and the others still had work to do.

'Jesus Christ, mate. I think I got the better end of the stick,' I said, absorbing what Miles had told me.

We emptied the bottle and I swallowed another handful of Valium. 'Mate, I think I'll try to get some rest. I'm a bit done in,' I said.

Miles played mum, covering me in a feather duvet and tucking me up for the night. 'Good to see you, mate,' he said, smiling somewhat drunkenly.

'Not half as good as seeing you.' I smiled through a whisky-and Valium-induced haze.

The warm duvet, whisky and drugs pulled me slowly into a soothing world, free of pain and death. I was, as my brother, Neil, used to put it, going night-time hang gliding, and within minutes I had launched into the black void of nothingness.

29 February 2012, Beirut, Lebanon

I awoke with a start, shocked to see Miles' face inches from my own. For a few fleeting moments I considered what was worse: being woken by 80mm mortar explosions or Miles. I didn't have a clue where I was or how I had got there and I blamed it all on the Valium.

'Mate, the British ambassador called me earlier. He's here now and wants to see you,' Miles told me as I struggled to take stock of where I was.

'Oh shit. Can't you just tell him I'm okay?' I replied groggily.

'No, mate. He wants to physically see you, to make sure you're really out,' Miles explained.

'Okay, bring him in and I'll pretend to be asleep. He can look at me and all will be well. Good by you?' I said.

Miles agreed and left the room while I feigned sleep. He arrived a few minutes later with Tom Fletcher, the British ambassador to Lebanon, and an official from the embassy. Miles pulled back the blanket so the ambassador could see my face. 'It's definitely him,' I heard Miles explain. 'He's in good mental health but his leg's a bit of a mess.'

I sniggered under the blanket at the words 'good mental health'. A bit rich coming from a war correspondent, I thought. They left me alone to go for a cup of tea in the kitchen, where I heard Miles trying to impress on them the importance of keeping my fate a secret.

After half an hour earwigging on their conversation, I decided I liked the sound of the ambassador, who didn't come across as the regular Foreign Office type.

'Miles, ooh Miles,' I shouted feebly to the kitchen, feigning pain. 'Can you help me, please?'

He entered the room and saw me laughing. 'Let him in, mate. He sounds like a good guy,' I said.

A minute or two later, they all came back into the room and I sat up on the couch. Tom reached over, shook hands and introduced himself. My instinct proved correct. The ambassador turned out to be a great guy. We chatted for half an hour, and the more we spoke, the more I grew to like and trust him. He was straightforward, down to earth and had a cracking sense of humour. He asked me what my plans were and whether I would like to stay at his place, the ambassador's residence. It was more secure there, he said, and I would be well protected from certain factions in Beirut who wouldn't be too happy to learn that I'd made it out of Syria alive.

'Okay,' I said, 'on one condition: I must be able to smoke.'

I watched as the senior consular official Tom had brought with him nearly fainted. 'There is no smoking in any official British premises in the world,' she told me.

Tom laughed. 'Paul, you can smoke, mate. Don't worry about that,' he said.

'Then, sir, we have a deal,' I said in response.

I dressed myself and made ready to move. A couple of reassuringly tough-looking guys from the ambassador's close protection unit arrived in the flat carrying reassuringly tough-looking weapons.

'Liverpool is ready to move,' one called into his radio.

Excellent – I have a codename, I thought as the close protection team surrounded me and bundled me into the apartment lift. As we left the lift, I saw a little old man cleaning the lobby. One of the close protection guys lifted him quite literally off the ground, opened a cupboard full of broomsticks and popped him inside, closing the door on him while I passed. They placed me in the back of a black Land Rover and we immediately pulled off into the Beirut streets, blue lights and sirens flashing as we wove through the traffic. Half an hour later we arrived at the ambassador's residence in a pretty suburb outside the centre of the city. The guards opened the gates and we disappeared inside, pulling to a halt near the main entrance. I was greeted by the ambassador's wife, Louise, and his mother, Debbie, before I hopped inside the residence on my crutch.

'Nice gaff,' I said to Tom, who smiled.

Tom and Louise gave me a residential tour before we headed upstairs where I was shown into my suite. 'Baroness Amos stayed here last week,' the ambassador told me. 'It has a balcony for smoking but actually you can smoke in bed if you want.'

The more I spoke to Tom, the more I liked him.

That day I made my telephone calls to England to tell my loved ones I was free. It was an emotional time and I had to reiterate to everyone that under no circumstances were they to announce publicly that I was free. William, Edith, Javier and Wa'el were still inside and any news that leaked out could be harmful to their chances of escape.

For the next two days, Tom and his wonderful family treated me like royalty. Louise and Debbie, both of them angels, did everything possible to make my landing as soft and trauma-free as possible. The lovely Louise scrubbed my feet with a bar of soap, a brave undertaking considering the state of them. She was one of the kindest people I have ever met and I was truly humbled by her generosity of spirit. They helped me to the balcony to smoke and brought me an endless supply of coffee and biscuits. The residence's cook made me delicious meals to order and that evening Tom told me that the previous ambassador had left behind a stunning collection of malt whisky. He said it would be very rude if we didn't at least sample some of them. The whisky flowed like sweet nectar. To say I was spoilt rotten would be an understatement. I owe the Fletcher family a lot, far more than I can ever repay, although Tom promised he would take me up on my offer of a sailing trip when I put my boat back in the water.

Ray Wells, the paper's picture editor, was ever present and by God the man had been through hell over the past week. He had expended every ounce of his energy to help coordinate my release, working like a man possessed. The pressure he had been under was enormous and I could only imagine what he and Miles had gone through. When the chips were down, both of them had rallied to the call and I will forever be in their debt for the efforts they made on my behalf. *The Sunday Times* never ceased in its attempts to secure my release. The paper's editor, John Witherow, and its foreign editor, Sean Ryan, who had both lost a loved and treasured friend in Marie, ensured that no stone was left unturned in their attempt to secure my release from Baba Amr. Annabelle Whitestone on the picture desk had kept in touch with all my family and friends, often hampered by the fact that the passage of information between Beirut and London was deliberately kept to a minimum because of the security risks.

30 February 2012, Beirut, Lebanon

On the second day of freedom, I learnt that disaster had struck. Only hours after I was placed in the back of the ambassador's car, news of my safe passage into Lebanon was leaked to the press. Miles and the team in Beirut were devastated. They had tried so hard to keep the information under wraps until the others were all out safely. Soon the airwaves were full of the news. I felt awful. All of us in that room in Baba Amr had made a solemn vow that we would remain silent about our escape until every one of us was safely out. We understood the dangers of going public while the others were still trapped inside.

While lying in bed watching the drama unfold, I saw an interview on the BBC by a slickly dressed and even slicker tongued Riken Pattel, who represented an activist group called Avaaz. The cheeky bastard claimed that Avaaz had coordinated and carried out my escape from Syria. All I knew of Avaaz was that they had charged Remi and Edith the extortionate sum of $3,000 for the privilege of getting them in to report from Baba Amr. Pattel then went on to say that between thirteen and twenty-three activists had died in the rescue of Paul Conroy.

What Pattel didn't tell the world was that it was the Farouk brigade of the Free Syrian Army alongside local Baba Amr activists who had organised and carried out my escape. The figure of twenty-three dead was also spurious: Pattel had simply added up all the people killed over a couple of days and attributed them to my name. Since then, Avaaz have admitted privately that they got the numbers wrong and that no Avaaz people on the ground were involved in my escape. But they have still never publicly retracted their claims and, to this day, I still take great pleasure in imagining Pattel limping about the place with a crutch embedded firmly up his backside.

Between them, Ray and Tom had organised a doctor to come and check out my leg. I suspected infection had set in and I needed more antibiotics. We couldn't go to a hospital as intercepted radio chatter had indicated that the Syrians were still actively looking for me in Beirut. A 'friendly' doctor was brought to the residence to see me and, after a full examination, he confirmed that my leg was indeed infected. I had two choices: stay in Beirut and be operated on, with all the problems that brought, including a lengthy stay in Beirut, or return immediately to the UK for treatment.

Tom informed me that he couldn't completely guarantee my safety if I remained in Lebanon. Although my room was surrounded by a full close protection unit, the building was not bombproof. It was easy to make the decision: I would return to the UK that evening. A button was pressed and the plan was put into action.

Louise and Debbie both fussed over me, making me feel loved and special, while Ray and Tom made the preparations for the trip home. A Lebanese customs official came to the residence and I cleared customs from my bed. Tom donated a tracksuit for me to travel home in. I told him that I was from Liverpool and that a tracksuit made me feel uneasy. Tom laughed at my snobbery and persuaded one of the close protection guys to donate some more appropriate wear. It all happened very quickly, perhaps too quickly. I felt awful about leaving because William, Edith and Javier were still unaccounted for and I desperately wanted to find out what had happened to Wa'el. I also knew that Marie's death would be big news back home. I wasn't sure I was ready to face it all yet but I had made my choice so I would stick by it.

In the residential compound three black Land Rovers waited with their engines running. I said my heartfelt goodbyes and thank yous to Tom and his wonderful family. Ray assisted me into one of the Land Rovers, with its full complement of bodyguards. The gates swung open on to the crowded Beirut streets. I waved to the ambassador's family and staff and we moved off.

The close protection team took no chances, their sirens blaring and blue lights flashing as we wound our way at speed through the chaotic Beirut traffic, bullying cars out of the way. We arrived at the airport via a back exit and drove at full speed on to the runway to a waiting medical jet, a tiny plane designed to carry a single patient. As we stopped, members of the close protection unit jumped from the vehicles and formed a defensive ring around the jet. Tom accompanied me to the stairs and I was introduced to the British military attaché.

'I believe you used to be a gunner, sir?' he asked.

I nodded. He then threw me a salute and said, 'Welcome aboard, sir.'

I turned and mounted the stairs to the jet. Once aboard, a particularly pretty nurse introduced herself, as did the doctor, who wasn't as pretty. The taxiway cleared as the plane manoeuvred for take-off. I looked back over Beirut. Memories of Marie flooded my brain and a small tear rolled gently down my cheek. Goodbye, Chechen Queen.

We eased effortlessly into the sky and, once fully airborne, the doctor unstrapped himself from his seat and came to sit next to me. He looked me seriously in the eye. 'Paul,' he said, 'we want to

315

make things as comfortable as possible for you, do you understand?' I nodded. 'So we have two options for you regarding pain relief. Option one: paracetamol and ibuprofen.' He paused for a moment. 'Option two: morphine and whisky.'

I struggled to free myself from the straps of the stretcher and, once released, I held out my arm. 'Fill me up, doc.'

EPILOGUE

Edith Bouvier and William Daniels were forced back into Baba Amr after the tunnel was attacked. With the assistance of Abu Lailah they were smuggled out of Baba Amr and, after a perilous journey, eventually escaped into Lebanon. Edith made a full recovery and is now back working in conflict zones, as is William Daniels.

Javier Espinosa, contrary to all rumours, had not been shot. He managed to escape from the tunnel, fled into the surrounding orchards and made contact with the FSA, eventually crossing the border safely into Lebanon.

Wa'el, our beloved translator, hadn't been captured and eventually made his way into Lebanon where his broken arm was treated. I have since spoken to him on Skype and he is still smiling.

Marie Colvin and Remi Ochlik's bodies were eventually handed over by the Syrian authorities and repatriated to their families. A Syrian autopsy report stated that Marie was killed by an improvised explosive device planted by terrorists.

I was hospitalised for four months and the wonderful Doctor Parri 'OO7Foxy' Mohana, one of the country's top reconstructive surgeons, performed approximately fourteen operations on my leg, successfully 'gluing' me back together. Anna Williams, my physiotherapist, and the wonderful staff of London Bridge Hospital are still reeling from the trauma of having me as a patient. I wish them all a speedy recovery.

I remained in London for the rest of 2012 recuperating from my injuries. Bonnie Hardy sentenced herself to a year commuting from Devon to London on the esteemed British rail system to nurse me.

Kate Conroy, despite all the pressures on her, managed to look after my beautiful children, Max, Kim and Otto while I recovered in hospital from my injuries.

On 12 December 2012, Professor Neil Greenberg, my psychiatrist and Defence Professor of Medical health declared me, 'When physically able, fit to return to high threat work: Ideally this would be on a gradual rather than cliff edge process.'

My personal life remains one of the most dangerous places on earth for a journalist to operate in.

Dr Mohamed Al-Mohamed was injured by shrapnel in the shelling of a field clinic he was running. He suffered leg and arm injuries but his situation is stable.

At the time of writing, President Bashar al Assad remains in power in Syria. His army continues to wreak havoc, mayhem and murder on his own people. The pictures of massacred men, women and children have now become routine images on our screens. In the two years since the beginning of the carnage, no nation has offered protection to the people of Syria.

INDEX